THE TRAVELS OF BENJAMIN ZUSKIN

Judaic Traditions in Literature, Music, and Art
Harold Bloom and Ken Frieden, *Series Editors*

Other titles from Judaic Traditions in Literature, Music, and Art

Early Yiddish Epic
Jerold C. Frakes, ed. and trans.

*Finding the Jewish Shakespeare: The Life
and Legacy of Jacob Gordin*
Beth Kaplan

*From Our Springtime: Literary Memoirs
and Portraits of Yiddish New York*
Reuben Iceland; Gerald Marcus, trans.

My Friendship with Martin Buber
Maurice Friedman

Place and Ideology in Contemporary Hebrew Literature
Karen Grumberg

*Rhetoric and Nation: The Formation of Hebrew
National Culture, 1880–1990*
Shai P. Ginsburg

Who Will Die Last: Stories of Life in Israel
David Ehrlich

Yiddish Poetry and the Tuberculosis Sanatorium, 1900–1970
Ernest B. Gilman

THE TRAVELS OF BENJAMIN ZUSKIN

Ala Zuskin Perelman

Translated from the Hebrew by Sharon Blass

Foreword by Mordechai Altshuler

Syracuse University Press

Originally published in Hebrew as *Mass'ot Binyamin Zuskin*
(Jerusalem: Carmel Publishing House, 2006).

All photographs in author's collection. Photographer unknown unless stated otherwise.

∞ The paper used in this publication meets the minimum requirements
of the American National Standard for Information Sciences—Permanence of Paper
for Printed Library Materials, ANSI Z39.48-1992.

For a listing of books published and distributed by Syracuse University Press,
visit www.SyracuseUniversityPress.syr.edu.

ISBN: 978-0-8156-1050-2 (cloth)   978-0-8156-5324-0 (e-book)

Library of Congress Cataloging-in-Publication Data

Zuskina-Perel'man, Alla, author.
[Mas'ot Binyamin Zuskin. English]
The travels of Benjamin Zuskin / Ala Zuskin Perelman ; translated from the Hebrew
by Sharon Blass ; foreword by Mordechai Altshuler. — First edition.
pages cm — (Judaic traditions in literature, music, and art)
Includes bibliographical references and index.
ISBN 978-0-8156-1050-2 (cloth : alk. paper) — ISBN 978-0-8156-5324-0 (e-book)
1. Zuskin, Benjamin, 1899– 2. Jewish actors—Soviet Union—Biography.
3. Actors—Soviet Union—Biography. I. Blass, Sharon, translator. II. Title.
PN2728.Z87P881513 2015
792.02'809—dc23
[B]   2014045716

TO MY BELOVED ONES:

Yuri
Alexander and Tamar
Yonatan
Uri
Shahar
Benjamin and Ana
Daniel
Lola

Ala Zuskin Perelman was born in Moscow to Benjamin Zuskin and Eda Berkovskaya, both actors in the Moscow State Jewish Theater. After Benjamin Zuskin was executed upon false charges, Ala and her mother were exiled to the Siberian part of Kazakhstan, 1953–1954.

Back in Moscow, Zuskin Perelman graduated with an MSc in engineering studies (1961), and also qualified as a translator and information expert with an MA (1962). She worked in these fields and raised a family. In 1975, she immigrated to Israel with her husband Yuri Perelman and two sons.

For two decades, Zuskin Perelman ran the Information Center at the Standards Institution of Israel. This included, in addition to ongoing in-house responsibilities, activities in various international projects.

At the same time she volunteered, and continues to volunteer, for projects commemorating Benjamin Zuskin and his milieu: speeches, lectures, interviews, and publications in different media, 1975–2013.

Zuskin Perelman also volunteered as a consultant, offering assistance to organizations, forums, and audiences as follows:

- The Diaspora Museum in Tel Aviv—during preparation of the exhibition on the Moscow State Jewish Theater, 1979; creation of *Zuskin's Collection*, 1980, and its completion, 2004–2005;
- The Cinemathèque in Jerusalem, 1999—organization of an evening in memory of Zuskin's 100th anniversary;
- Israeli filmmakers—assisted during the work on a documentary film about Zuskin, 2000;
- The New York Jewish Museum—supported the curatorial team with photographs, written documents, and personal knowledge in preparation for the exhibition *Chagall and the Artists of the Russian Jewish Theater*, 2001–2008, and in lecturing during the opening week, 2008;
- The Hebrew University (Jerusalem) and also Tel Aviv, Haifa, and Bar Ilan Universities in Israel, and different forums—provided data and lecturing, 1979–2011;
- Theater arts scholars and the public in Israel, Russia, the U.S., Italy, Holland, and Germany—in person or by correspondence.

The last fifteen years were dedicated to this book, *The Travels of Benjamin Zuskin*: from collecting information all around the world, through writing in Russian (published in 2002) and rewriting in Hebrew (published in 2006), up to numerous launches and public discussions.

What an awful and tragic fate! Can it be that all of this will be forgotten?

—EDA BERKOVSKAYA

Contents

Illustrations

Foreword

Zuskin in My Mind's Eye

There are people who are the foundation for the existence of the Moscow State Jewish Theater. One such person was Solomon Mikhoels, whom I imagine everyone has heard of. And there is another such person, Benjamin Zuskin, and only a few have heard of him. And it is not a coincidence. First, Mikhoels was a man who was abundantly self-confident. Second, Zuskin was an actor divinely gifted. After almost every production, he was not convinced that he had given all that he could have. There were directors, and not only Jewish directors, who attested to that. For example, one of them related how after the production of *King Lear*, Zuskin, who had played the Fool superbly, said to him, I am not going to appear on stage anymore because my acting today was not all that I would have wanted it to be.

That is Zuskin.

He was not always sure of himself, hesitant, as far as I was able to learn about him. He was an actor of extraordinary talent, who joined the theater at the age of twenty-two, who had hardly studied acting but had absorbed the way of life of the Jews which was full of pain but also full of humor, wisdom—a slightly amused attitude through the pain.

And for a "little man" who had a bit of this and of that Zuskin gave expression in his roles, or at least in some of them.

He is the Jewish Sancho Panza in *The Travels of Benjamin the Third*, he is the Fool in *King Lear*, he is the Badkhen in *Freylekhs*, which was staged in the theater in 1945. After the enormous tragedy, when there was a stark sense that the Jewish people had ceased to exist, the theater put on *Freylekhs. Freylekhs* is a Jewish wedding. What is a wedding in Jewish tradition? The continuity of life, the continuity of family, the birth of a people. New growth. The theater staged the Jewish experience with folk dances, folk songs, the whole way of life of the people. The character that led this production was the Badkhen.

This man whom I have tried to portray in a few words—it is upon him that a grave and serious role falls, perhaps the most difficult of his life.

On January 13, 1948, I don't know what they announced—accident, not an accident, I don't really know—Mikhoels was murdered.

In the theater, confusion reigned. The actors were wandering about the theater, not knowing what to do. There was no leader, no one to show the way. In those crucial moments for the fate of the theater, Zuskin felt that it was his responsibility to take up the burden. The theater's situation was grim: there was a sense of despair. There was whispering in the administration and among the actors: What would be? The rumors that Mikhoels was murdered were known. However, this was whispered only in secret. At the same time, the theater was cut off from state funding. They said the theater had to survive on its own revenues. But the theater could not survive that way.

Doctor Rapoport, one of the detainees in the *Doctor's Plot*, wrote: at the institute where he worked, there were rumors that he had a subscription to the Jewish theater. He did not have a subscription to the theater. The theater did not interest him, but that was enough to arouse suspicion that there was something wrong with him.

That is to say, on the one hand the theater was cut off from the state budget, and on the other, the atmosphere was such that anyone who bought a subscription to the theater was considered a suspect.

And in those very difficult days when the theater still managed to hang on, days that are not always given attention, Benjamin Zuskin shouldered the burden. This was perhaps *the* role of his life. With clenched jaw, he held out and guaranteed the continued activity of the theater for almost a whole year. His hesitations, doubts, all of the pain and the torment he did not let the actors see, and of course, he did not share them with his staff so as not to demoralize them. But this burden broke the man.

He stopped sleeping at night, and he was eventually hospitalized at one of the medical clinics. There he was anesthetized in the hope that a sleep of a few days, or a few days and nights, would benefit him. From this clinic he was taken by the secret police on a stretcher, as he lay sleeping. Could we ever imagine the feeling of the man when he was removed from the clinic where he was being treated in his sleep only to wake up in torture chambers?

This is Zuskin.[1]

Mordechai Altshuler

Preface

What remains of an actor?

Vapor, the mist of memory, photographs, old films, or words that were said and written—do they hold the secret of his art? Can the ungraspable be grasped?

An actor lives on the stage. Does he disappear when the curtain falls? "What I prize in a doughnut," writes Osip Mandelstam, "is the hole. You can gobble up the doughnut but the hole will still be here. Real work is Brussels lace, the main thing in it is what holds the pattern up: air."[1] The air that held the pattern woven by my father, the actor Benjamin Zuskin, "one of the most dazzling talents in world theater in the first half of the twentieth century,"[2] was suffused with Jewishness.

They sucked out this air completely, they turned the lace into ash, and the actor himself, they executed.

This book will tell the story of Zuskin, of the air he breathed and of the pattern he wove.

The chapters of the book are titled "Acts" as in a play, both because my father was an actor and because the events in his life, external and internal alike, unfolded like a classical drama, until the final scene. Such a scene, I think, could never have been conceived in the mind of any playwright. The chapters are divided into sub-chapters, each referring to a certain period of time in my father's life, and the name of the sub-chapter refers to the role that my father played, either in life or on the stage.

At the end of the story that I tell of my father, his own words as well as various letters are brought to complete my account.

When writing about my father, I regret having been born too late, because I was prevented from witnessing a substantial portion of the things that I wish to describe.

And I wish to describe many things.

I wish to describe his life history, for example.

In this narrative, I attempt to blend my own memories with those of other people, but I feel that I cannot present my story in any logical order because logic has no place here. In my mind, the shadow of my father's fate hovers above every event of his life, and of mine. Therefore the narrative occasionally goes back or forward in time.

I wish to describe his creative work.

How wonderful it would have been if I had been able to go to the box office, buy a ticket to my father's theater, and together with the readers of this book, sit in the auditorium and watch my father acting. But of course that is not realistic. To "watch" Zuskin's acting by studying his notes—that too is not realistic.

STATEMENT

Moscow, February 25, 1950

I, Polkovnik Tsvetaev, senior Investigator in the Investigative Unit for Especially Important Cases in the USSR Ministry of State Security have destroyed by burning the following papers and letters that belonged to the detainee Benjamin Zuskin which were confiscated during the search of his apartment . . .

Handwritten notes by Zuskin on theater art—55 pages . . .

Notebooks in Zuskin's handwriting—24 . . .

Ledgers in Zuskin's handwriting with listing of stage roles and notes in Yiddish—8 . . .

Various letters in Russian and Yiddish—184, on 208 pages . . .

Notes in Yiddish on stage roles—470 pages.[3]

And so, everything was burned.

Is that truly so? "I have invented for myself a kind of ruler for notes," my father writes in his article, "Curriculum Vitae," "and in my textual analysis of the role I mark on it pauses or emphases . . . When I return to

working on my role, I read these annotations like a musician reads musical notes."[4] This reminds me of the cantillations in the Torah that show,
among other things, the intonations of the words. The signs that my father
invented were destroyed together with his ledgers (8), notebooks (15), and
notes (470 pages). But the intonations remained. To hear them, I use all
manner of witnesses.

My story is not a collection of memories but rather an attempt to produce a portrait of my father as he appears in my mind's eye, the portrait of
a man in whom one saw a combination of hard work and dizzying success,
a tireless quest for artistic expression and brilliant inventiveness, profound
thought coupled with conspicuous achievement, a lack of self-assurance
with accolades earned, an aspiration to perfection with a tragic end.

As to whether I have achieved my goal, let the reader be the judge.

Acknowledgments

I am very grateful to all those who supported my work on this book.

To Professor Mordechai Altshuler whose unique attitude to Zuskin and Zuskin's life work was reflected most inspiringly in the address that he delivered about him on the evening marking the 100th birthday of Benjamin Zuskin, and that became the foreword to this book; and before all this—for his deep faith in my ability, and my duty, to write such a book.

To Aviva Dor, (the late) Rina Shlayin, and the entire production staff—for creating the documentary film on Zuskin that gave further momentum to my decision to write a book.

To art historian Hillel Kazovsky, who after reading the first, unfinished draft of my book urged me to continue.

I am expressing my full acknowledgment to Israel Carmel for his having published my book in Hebrew and for generously providing me with permission to have it published in English.

I am expressing my gratitude to Tirtsa Yoel Wiener for her wonderful work in editing the Hebrew version, which served as the basis for this translation into English.

And I am extremely grateful to Sharon Blass for her excellent translation into English that was combined with her deeply felt connection and empathy for the people and events described in this book.

To Professor Olga Gershenson for being unstinting in her support and advice to me on my way to the English-language edition.

To Professor Joshua Rubenstein for his intense interest in the fate of my father and those who were executed with him, for editing and providing an introduction and comments to the book about their trial, and for being unflaggingly encouraging and sympathetic to the idea of having my book appear in English.

And of course, to Dr. Ken Frieden, the Editor-in-Chief of *The Judaic Tradition in Literature, Art and Music* series of Syracuse University Press, who generously proposed to publish the English edition of the book, to Jennika Baines, Chief Acquisitions Editor, and Kelly Balenske, Editorial Assistant at this publishing house, as well as to the entire production staff, and to the wonderful copy editor Hila Ratzabi—for their devoted, meticulous, patient, and faithful handling of the manuscript that I see as an expression of consideration and caring for the memory of my father.

I owe a full acknowledgment to Yale University Press, publisher of the book edited by Joshua Rubenstein and Vladimir Naumov, *Stalin's Secret Pogrom: The Postwar Inquisition of the Jewish Anti-Fascist Committee* (2001) for the permission to reproduce from the above book an illustration and numerous excerpts.

To Liuba Yuniverg, director, Israel Goor Theater Archives and Museum, Jerusalem for generously permitting me to use the archives.

To Benny Mer and Michael Handelzalts, authors of the impressive reviews about my book in Hebrew, and to *Ha'aretz*, for the permission to quote excerpts from these reviews.

I would like to thank many fine people who have given of their knowledge, time, and good will to support my work on this book:

Prof. Antonio Attisani, Prof. Gennady Estraikh, Mikhail Greenberg, (the late) Levia Hofshteyn, Prof. Vladislav Ivanov, Gennady Kostyrchenko, Ethel Kovenskaya, Mark Levinson, (the late) Nina Mikhoels, Prof. Avrom Novershtern, (the late) Shalom Rozenfeld, (the late) Israel Rubinchik, Natalia Shurman, Prof. Jeffrey Veidlinger, (the late) Natalia Vovsi-Mikhoels, George Zilberblatt and many others—for demonstrating great interest in my father's personality, his art, and his fate; for encouraging me and giving me information and testimony, both written and verbal.

My beloved ones:

My (late) sister Dr. Tamara Platt for sharing with me her memories.

The Perelman Family: my sons Alexander and Benjamin, my daughters-in-law Tamar and Ana—for always being willing to help me with whatever they could.

And finally to my husband Yuri Perelman for being patient and involved in my work on a daily basis; who read the manuscript very meticulously many times over; with whom I discussed the concept of the book and its various aspects; who was generous with his comments and uncompromising with his attitude toward everything related to writing the book and bringing it to the publishers, to the point where this book became an integral part of his life—and whose help to me was, and still is, immeasurable.

PART ONE

1

Prologue

Whirlwind.

A dancing crowd moves unwaveringly from the depths of the stage toward me. It is led by Reb Yekl. He is Badkhen,[1] the spirit of happiness, and a small part of him is the spirit of sadness. This is Benjamin Zuskin; this is my father.

The day, July 23, 1945, two and half months after Nazi Germany was defeated in World War II, the Moscow State Jewish Theater presents the debut performance of *Freylekhs* (merry dance tune, mostly used to express a wedding joy).

Zuskin sweeps the dancing throng along after him; Zuskin flies. This is not a slip of the tongue: he soars into the air, like the flying figures of Chagall.

I watched the play *Freylekhs* countless times, because they put it on again and again until the theater itself ceased to exist. And by then I had managed to grow up. That is why it is so easy for me to imagine myself a spectator in the audience, a wondrous legend unfolding before me.

A wedding tune is being played. The tune is growing louder, steadily becoming stronger. It sounds familiar, something that we have not heard for a while and seem to have forgotten, although we have always felt it in our hearts.

Reb Yekl flies and the crowd follows him, dancing and swaying to the music, becoming lighter, swifter, more enthused.

Reb Yekl stops and the crowd freezes in place. Reb Yekl leans on the post of the painted stage-set door. Nothing in this play is meaningless. "Behind the doors also and the posts have you set up your memory" (Isa.

3

47:8). Memory is in fact what this wondrous play is about. The voice of Reb Yekl is filled with pain, warmth, and anguish as he turns to the audience and delivers a speech in memory of past suffering, in memory of the souls of relatives and dear ones who are no longer.

And immediately the poignant story is replaced by the story of the forthcoming wedding. Reb Yekl's words flow from him and he doesn't forget to fly.

After that he bursts forth in a folk song, "There once was Elimelekh/ And music he played freylekh [joyously]." And how that song is sung by Zuskin! How he actually lives that character! Elimelekh, of the song, plays his violin or flute and the vocal intonations by Zuskin, his movements, his gestures toward the orchestra—all of these blend with the sounds of the violin or the flute in the orchestra.

As the wedding tune plays in the background, the wedding participants, cups in hand, fill the stage. And this whole spectacle takes place against a magnificent stage set and is accompanied by remarkable music.

Looking down over all of this with mild scorn and fervor, leading, clothing it in spirituality is Reb Yekl.

Zuskin/Yekl leaps and soars, sings and dances, chuckles and laughs. He is the spirit of joy, and he is also the spirit of sorrow who carries on his back the sack of grief. Light of movement and lively as mercury, he knows how to glorify and heighten the expression of the eternal spirit of the Jewish people.

For a quarter of a century now Zuskin has been on stage. In his role as Reb Yekl, he encompasses everything that is of value to him: unbounded theatricality with limitless profundity of thought. Here he is alive once more.

He lives the life of a lyric-tragicomic actor.

Toward the end of the play, he is still weightless and shows no signs of imprecision of speech, movement, song. Mazel tov! Zuskin/Yekl exults with infectious exuberance:

> After the grief there will be joy still
> Celebrate weddings our people yet will![2]

The curtain falls. The audience applauds Zuskin, receiving him with acclamation and cheers. He returns to the stage, bows respectfully to the audience and leaves, tired, drained of the tension that had gripped him only a short moment before. In his dressing room, he sits in his armchair, and before he removes his makeup, he studies himself in the mirror. Perhaps Zuskin, too, like the hero of "Poem without a Hero" by Anna Akhmatova, does not identify himself in the creature who stares back at him, and perhaps it seems to him, as it did to that hero, that in the depths of the mirror

Is approaching the Twentieth Century
Not the calendar's, the real one.[3]

Zuskin was born in 1899 and his age paralleled that of the twentieth century as noted on the calendar, but the "real twentieth century" would lie in ambush for him when it reached its halfway mark.

CERTIFICATE

The sentence of the Military Collegium of the Supreme Court of the USSR of July 18, 1952, regarding Benjamin Zuskin, born in 1899 in the town of Panievezhys, Lithuany, and condemned to the severest measure of punishment, execution, was carried out on August, 12, 1952.[4]

For Zuskin, the "real twentieth century" begun actually four and a half years before this unimaginable, intolerable verdict was handed down. It began the night between the 12th and 13th of January in 1948, the night of the murder of Solomon Mikhoels, whose connections with Benjamin Zuskin could not be disentangled.

Zuskin is plagued by insomnia. The doctors hospitalize him in order to cure him with anesthesia; and in their naiveté, they believe that they can cure what appears to them as an illness.

He lies in the hospital bed, wrapped in starched white sheets, and for the first time in many long months, a happy smile lights up his face. This blessed sleep lasts four days out of the ten the doctors prescribed for him.

The fourth night arrives, the night between the 23rd and 24th of December 1948.

JUNE 11–12, 1952
TRIAL
TESTIMONY BY BENJAMIN ZUSKIN

CHAIRMAN OF THE MILITARY COLLEGIUM (PRESIDING OFFICER OF THE TRIAL): When were you arrested?

ZUSKIN. On December 24, 1948.

CHAIRMAN: And that same day you gave the testimony that we are talking about now. In that testimony you confessed to being a nationalist.

ZUSKIN. Because I was brought to the interrogation in a complete stupor wearing a hospital gown. I was arrested in the hospital . . . while I was asleep, and it was only . . . when I woke up that I saw that I was in a cell and learned that I had been arrested . . . They said to me that I was a "state criminal."[5]

DECEMBER 24, 1948
PRELIMINARY INVESTIGATION
INTERROGATION OF BENJAMIN ZUSKIN

ZUSKIN. My arrest is the result of a coincidence.

INVESTIGATOR. It was no coincidence—there were facts about your hostile activity.[6]

JUNE 11–12, 1952
TRIAL
TESTIMONY BY BENJAMIN ZUSKIN

CHAIRMAN: I have your testimony . . . here in front of me.

ZUSKIN. I repudiate all the testimony and am now telling the truth . . . You should judge me not by the interrogation records, but by my deeds . . .[7]

CHAIRMAN: Get to the point . . .

ZUSKIN. I am an actor.[8]

      I'd like to describe . . . things that are not found in the forty-two volumes of the Investigation File.[9]

CHAIRMAN: In brief. You were born where?

ZUSKIN. In Ponievezh.[10]

2

Act One
(1899–1920)

Nyomke

On April 28, 1899, in the city of Ponievezh in Lithuania, a son was born to the family of the tailor Leybe Zuskin and his wife Chaya—Binyomin or Nyomke in Yiddish, Benjamin in English, my father.

He was the third son in the family, coming after Abraham, six years old, and Yitshak, three years old. Later, three girls were born—Sarah (Sonia), Menukha, and Frieda. Their livelihood was not plentiful, but this did not prevent the family members from being devoted to each other, good-natured, and outstandingly hospitable. Nyomke grew up in an atmosphere of warmth, compassion, and love.

My father could have presented himself the way Antoine de-Saint Exupéry did: "Where am I from? From my childhood."[1] For him childhood was not just an indicator of the beginning of life or a collection of touching memories. Zuskin's childhood was his ego, and it is spun into his life and the story that the pages of my book tell.

It seems to me that I know my father's childhood as though I had experienced it myself. When we were together, my father used to ask me, "What story shall I tell you?" And I would reply, "Tell something from 'ME'!" ("ME" being MEmories of childhood, my father's). This was a joking byword that we shared between us, only my father and me.

Now I understand how those ME stories were a work of art. Whatever my father absorbed in his childhood lived in him permanently and was incorporated into the ME stories. And not only into them but also—and

8

primarily—into his artistic creation. I was not lucky enough to see my father in many roles, but fate granted me the ME stories as a compensation.

Neither was I fortunate enough to know in reality the people surrounding my father as a boy, but to this very day they take shape before my eyes out of the mist; they are clothed in flesh and blood. I see and hear them, and they speak, they move, they eat and drink, sing, weep, and laugh.

I see a silhouette darting among them, dark as in the black and white films, the silhouette of a small sensitive boy who wants to be everywhere, to see and know and absorb everything and everyone. The silhouette grows before my eyes, it mounts the stage, becomes colorful, its movements become brisk. Gradually it grows blurry, ceases to move, reverts to being a small boy. The silhouette is replaced by that of a man who turns his back to me, his shoulders slumped. A flash of light blinds me; I hear a shot ring out. Fire devours everything. And out of this, scattering the ashes with his feet, the little boy races toward me.

What joy! Father is not busy; he is lying on his dark-green upholstered sofa, his feet on the armrest, and so I am allowed to ask: "Daddy, tell something from ME!"

And he would begin a story.

Leybe, my father's father, was a special person. In his youth he dreamed of being a doctor. But his life took a different turn. Leybe's father forced Leybe to leave school and become a tailor—to continue the dynasty of tailors, lest it come to an end.

In Nyomke's early youth, his grandparents still lived in his father's house, and his grandfather worked in some kind of sewing workshop there. The connection with the elderly tailor was the first station on a path that led to Zuskin the actor.

The child saw that the adults were wary around Grandfather even though they were respectful. Although elderly and frail, Grandfather was still able to hurl fire and brimstone at anyone who behaved improperly as he saw it.

However, Nyomke noticed something else. Those crushing statements made by his grandfather were a game! Sometimes he would even pronounce them in rhyme, like a seasoned comedian. At those moments he loved to trill a broad scale of notes from a deep bass to a high, reedy tenor. And to be sure, he knew how to do it. His voice could be warm and jovial, especially when he was engaged in his beloved sewing and he sang his songs. One of them Nyomke was to remember all of his life and even to sing it to me, and I do remember it, as well:

> Tell me, my eye: of what do you have more—
> Of twinkles for a joy, or tears for a sorrow?

The song is accompanied by the refrain, Tridle-lidle-le-li-li, and by an old man's and Nyomke's gestures as in a Russian folk dance. Nyomke's mother Chaya, toiling near the oven, notices the child repeating all of his grandfather's tricks and complains to her husband, "Look Leybe, your father is infecting the baby with his clowning."

Clowning for its own sake? But no, here is a peerless tradition: a sense for music, the facial expression that seems to speak, imitating intonations, a talent for mimicry, and the understanding that sadness is mixed with joy, and joy with sadness.

Leybe was not cured of his attraction to medicine. When he became advanced in years, and bearing the burden of supporting a family with many children, almost every evening after a day of taxing work, he would sit down and read medical texts. He learned Latin unassisted in order to understand the medical terminology. In the local pharmacy they respected his prescriptions because they knew him and relied on his vast knowledge.

In Ponievezh, as in every small town, everyone knew everyone. In the eyes of the Jews, Russians and Lithuanians, Leybe was a respected and decent man always ready to lend a hand and offer advice at all times. They came to him even from the nearby villages and towns to seek his advice. Relatives and strangers alike came to him.

When they decided in Ponievezh to establish the Charity Society on behalf of the needy sick Jews, Leybe was among its founders.

Nyomke admired his father with all his might. He adopted his father's readiness to participate in the suffering of others and a sincere interest in each and every person. These characteristics would accompany Nyomke the child, Benjamin the youth, and later would be revealed in Zuskin the actor. Years later Mikhoels would refer to Zuskin with these words: "Every human being was for him like a flower for a bee; it has a unique drop of honey in it. The artist will soak up this drop and then incorporate it in his honeycomb, in Zuskin's beehive."[2] Meanwhile Nyomke darted between the legs of the adults and collected "honey-bearing pollen" from everyone around his parents' house, and they were many and colorful.

Nyomke began to attend the *heder*[3] at the age of five. He knew his teacher Reb Genokh from his parents' home as a desired and honored guest there. According to my father's ME stories, Reb Genokh had a rare gift for acting. When he discovered that Nyomke also had an inclination toward acting, a boy of five and an old man of seventy started to entertain an audience of adults. This old man played a colossal role in Nyomke's life and, to a large extent, led to Benjamin Zuskin the actor. Reb Genokh could not know, of course, while dubbing the kid Nyomke the Jester, that the roles of jesters that would fill his pupil's life as an actor would include the role of the Fool in a Shakespearean play.

I never met Reb Genokh, but my father knew how to fascinate me as he clothed himself in this character. I could imagine, for example, the elderly teacher taking off his threadbare coat after having a drink, jumping into the center of the parlor, and like a young man, bursting into animated dance. How thrilling it was when my father recreated the dancing teacher using only his gestures, as he remained sprawled on the sofa.

In my mind's eye a picture appears: Nyomke, a mischievous smile on his face, coming home from heder with a cluster of children and impressing them with his repertoire—I can assume that he was already eager to appear and perform before a crowd—walking on his hands, tumbling like a circus clown, making frightening leaps from a great height.

Once this leap ended badly for him.

They found him with his tongue bleeding and he was incapable of uttering a word. At home they were horrified at the thought that the boy might, God forbid, remain mute. Several hours later, he already managed to say his first words, although they were punctuated by lengthy silences. Periods of stammering continued to plague him intermittently for the rest of his life.

Nyomke did not learn his lesson from the accident and went on as before. Wherever there was a crowd, shouting, laughter, brawling, chattering, Nyomke was always there! Running, climbing, joking, soaking up the atmosphere, taking in a juicy expression from the peddlers in the market-place, memorizing the melodies of the worshippers, and always coming back to mimic each and every one of them, together and separately.

Still, he did not forget to march in time with the times: In 1905,[4] when he was six, there was a big demonstration, and policemen made efforts to disperse it. Nyomke's uncle was then living in their house and shar-ing a room with Nyomke. The kid pulled the pistol peeking out from under Uncle's pillow, and ever since—although Uncle immediately took the gun back from him—had become in his own eyes a revolutionary. He scrabbled in his pockets, found a few coins, and at a shop that sold toys, bought a toy pistol.

The day after the demonstration was dispersed, police forces sur-rounded all of the houses, even the teacher's house which held the heder, and carried out searches. "Master," whispered Nyomke to Reb Genokh, "I have a weapon." The child was genuinely frightened. The police officer overheard it, frisked the boy, found the toy gun, and burst into laughter. Later the teacher and the pupil staged a performance based on this incident.

My father told the "pistol story" many times; it was the crown jewel in the ME series. The first time I heard it was when I was sick, and since the daylight bothered me, I was lying in the dark and imagining that it wasn't Nyomke who had hidden the pistol under the pillow but I myself, and at any moment, a frightening police officer might appear at the door.

Several years later a search was conducted in our house following my father's arrest. Those who conducted the search were much more fright-ening than the police officer in my father's ME story. As then, I was lying in the dark, this time the dark of night, and the dread that gripped me reminded me of the story of the gun.

Who knows how deeply that "pistol story" was etched in Father's soul? That sense of fear that brought a sensitive and vulnerable child to the abyss of despair must have awoken in Zuskin under the conditions of his deten-tion and trial. Is it possible that he mentioned it there when he was granted the right of a "free speech"?

Shall I talk about days, or nights?
About people? About just things?[5]

"Just things," inanimate objects, frequently served as important milestones in my father's life as though he had entered "the colossal world of law-like regularity through the small world of concrete concepts."[6] And indeed, the ungraspable cannot be grasped.

Nyomke continued his mischievous behavior, a child who had a hand in everything.

At home, too, there was no lack of interesting attractions. At home Reb Genokh danced, many other guests came to visit, the sounds of machinery and the apprentices' lively chatter drifted in from the sewing workshop.

Occasionally, at home in the evening, when his father Leybe had finally finished his work and perusal of medical texts, he began to read aloud the works of Sholem Aleichem. On those evenings, everyone, including mother, left everything, the apprentices did not rush home, the teacher came, too, and the neighbors. Leybe looked at those surrounding him, excited at the prospect of anticipated pleasure. "Listen my children and I will tell you the story of a penknife; a story that is not fiction, but real, that happened to me myself."[7] The absolute silence that prevailed during the reading was interrupted now and again by a peal of laughter or sighs and sobs.

When Nyomke learned to read, he began to read the stories of Sholem Aleichem aloud in the backyard. No less than reading aloud he loved to observe the expressions on the faces of the listeners. "I would ascend the stage and feel the breathing of the audience,"[8] he would confess many years later.

My father's mother had a very young sister, Minna, who was only slightly older than Nyomke and, thus, was his childhood friend and, afterward, a "star" in the ME stories. Only when I read her memoirs did I understand that by giving me the content of the Sholem Aleichem stories, my father was actually pointing to his own childhood. "The happy times of childhood were the Shabbosim and holidays . . . When one holiday came to an end, we waited for the next one . . . One must read Sholem Aleichem in order to understand this,"[9] writes Minna.

Nyomke found purpose in reading aloud to his illiterate neighbors, but he aspired to more tangible deeds. His father Leybe understood this. The child was young, of course, not even eight years old, but proficient enough in reading, writing, and arithmetic and so it paid to test him. Leybe entrusted Nyomke with managing the account books of his charity society.

The boy was delighted. He not only helped his father, something which by itself filled him with pride, he submerged himself totally in the thick of life, learned to know the people whose existence until now made only a slight impression upon him. Tragedy, pain, poverty, weddings, circumcisions, and a sense of no-exit alongside unbounded cheerfulness—all these passed before him. How many characters there were! What "pollen"! It would yet become a work of art.

Certainly Zuskin's childhood and youth were spent at the hub of Jewish lives. In that hub another matter was refined and tested which was important for Zuskin's future.

The theater.

There was no theater in Ponievezh although there were actors like Grandfather and Reb Genokh; there were holidays and weddings whose customs were very theatrical and were experienced as theater. In addition, at least once a year, on Purim, a circus troupe or itinerant theater company would give a performance. Perhaps all of these inflamed his child's imagination; perhaps a spark of the dreams had been burning in the depth of his soul from creation, and what he saw and absorbed breathed life into it. This speculation belongs to that same realm of the ungraspable that cannot be grasped.

Nyomke occasionally managed to filch a loaf of bread or delicacy from the kitchen and give it out to the hungry actors who played the supporting roles. He loved to watch the actors as they put on their makeup and got dressed; he also loved to put a wig on his own head or to attach a beard to his face.

Nyomke's attraction to the theater pleased the actors and actresses, his enthusiasm at their performance flattered them, and his gift for mimicry aroused their excitement. They laughed and said with great approval, "This child is going to be an actor yet!"

Nyomke staged plays in his house. He received an invitation to play the role of a child in some play. He learned the role by heart, but at the last minute, he got stage fright and ran away. Nyomke would grow up.

The boy's talent would become the adult's art. But then, too, he would be frightened whenever he had to mount the stage: he would never rid himself of the sense of responsibility nor the lack of confidence.

It was time for Nyomke to become Benjamin, and the family was planning the next stage of his studies. From ME stories I know that because of the shortage of money, Father was the only one of the six children who got an education. Leybe Zuskin was not pious and he hoped that his son would study in a secular school to acquire an occupation that carried prestige—his son should be a doctor. Thus, Nyomke tried to be accepted to the "reali school"—the secondary school that focused mostly on math and natural science studies. His application was rejected several times because of the "numerus clausus" system—for every ten non-Jewish students, they accepted one Jewish student, and preferably a wealthy one. He started to give private lessons, but one day Leybe came home and told him, "Mazel tov, son, you were accepted to the reali school."

In the heder, Nyomke did not distinguish himself particularly at his studies because he was impatient; now he wanted to prove that he was capable, along the lines of "Ah! So you didn't want me? Look at this!" and he became one of the best pupils in the school. He explained to his father, who was surprised by the discipline his fun-loving son had imposed upon himself, "I will show them to discriminate against Jews!" Although among the teachers there were also anti-Semites, Nyomke rose to the head of the class with a certificate of excellence.

One of the non-anti-Semitic teachers taught Russian language and literature. Benjamin Zuskin was his favorite pupil. The teacher, who dearly loved classical Russian poetry, was filled with amazement at hearing this Jewish boy recite a Russian poem with profound understanding and great feeling. In parallel to his studies at the reali school, the boy acted in a troupe of amateurs.

The young Zuskin who lived in the city, which was largely Jewish (of twenty-seven thousand inhabitants of Ponievezh, twenty-three thousand were Jews), knew about outbursts of anti-Semitism, naturally, but, as I understand it, never considered them other than one facet of life. He first related to anti-Semitism as a phenomenon in 1913 during the Beilis Affair.[10] He knew everything that happened in that trial down to the last detail, since every day he read to his father's apprentices the reports of the trial as they appeared in the newspapers. The case touched him and he was delighted when Beilis was acquitted of all guilt.

In 1914 World War I broke out, and in June 1915 the Supreme Commander of the Russian Army ordered that the Jewish population be deported from areas near the Russian-German border. Among these towns was Ponievezh.

The Zuskin family arrived at the railroad station and found there a great crowd of people from Ponievezh and from the surrounding towns, but no train. Meanwhile, people were sitting on the ground under the open sky. Night fell and, with it, rain. And the next day was the same.

Nyomke could not settle down, and full of curiosity, he moved among the seated people. Suddenly, not far off, amidst the weeping of the women, the shrieking of those giving birth, the wailing of the children, and the groans of the dying, he heard laughter. As he approached the circle where the laughter burst from, his glance fell upon a tattered pamphlet of the stories of Sholem Aleichem. Someone was reading aloud from it.

And so, the young boy personally experienced the horrors of suffering that Jews undergo only because they are Jews. He learned to understand the spirit of the nation, where pain and joy are mixed, and the everlasting power of creativity.

World War I brought to an end the childhood of Benjamin Zuskin.

Benjamin

A young boy approaches me with quick steps. I look at him. This is Benjamin, who has bid farewell to Nyomke forever.

His childhood in Ponievezh is replaced by a life of wandering.

The Zuskin family arrived in the city of Vitebsk. After a short time, the family was joined by the parents of the mother Chaya and her sister Minna. Even under such conditions, young people found a reason to laugh and to have fun, but not the adults—there was no livelihood, no future. One of Leybe's acquaintances gave him a letter of recommendation to his relative who owned a clothing store in Penza. The Zuskin family again packed its bags and traveled to Penza.

Penza, which is considered a large city, is located in the eastern part of European Russia, approximately one thousand five hundred kilometers from Ponievezh, which is in western part of Russia. These facts are known to all, but very few know that Penza is a theater town. In the eighteenth and nineteenth centuries there was a widespread phenomenon of having in-house theaters on the estates of the Russian nobility. If we are to judge by the number of theaters of this kind, Penza held third place in Russia, after Moscow and St. Petersburg.[11] Penza also had a connection to twentieth-century theater, in its prime and in its decline. That was the birthplace and first appearance on stage of a person who was to reveal himself as an innovator in Russian theatrical art, Vsevolod Meyerhold. There, too, mounting the stage, albeit a stage of amateurs, was a person who was to reveal himself as a unique Jewish actor, Benjamin Zuskin. The same end lay in wait for both of them: Meyerhold was executed in 1941, Zuskin in 1952.

When the family arrived in Penza, Benjamin's father Leybe was offered unreasonable terms of employment. And now fortune smiled on Benjamin's brother Yitshak; he, too, was a tailor, like his father, and he managed to acquire a sewing machine and the two of them, Leybe and Yitshak, began to work together at home.

The family just has begun to recover from all the blows when an induction order arrived for Yitshak who, with Leybe, was responsible for the family's livelihood. Now Benjamin had to go to work. And so, along with his studies, he gave private lessons.

At the reali school he was accepted into the ninth grade. He studied languages: Russian, French, and German; mathematics, algebra, and geometry; natural sciences and physics; political economics, draftsmanship, and drawing; as well as the craft of bookbinding.

My father loved to cover my schoolbooks and the results were a work of art. How amazing it was to what extent all of the experiences he had undergone and soaked up in his childhood and adolescence had become so rooted in his innermost soul. Incidentally, as the scion of a dynasty of tailors, he always sewed on his own buttons. Always.

He was recommended as a private teacher at the home of a well-to-do merchant. Now Benjamin had some money and for the first time in his life, he could allow himself to go to a real theater, a good Russian theater where the actors impressed him. From then on he went to the theater regularly, twice a week, and took his place in the upper balcony. Only now did he begin to see professional theater and to understand the nature of the acting profession.

At the same time it was not in his nature to remain a passive spectator, even in a professional theater. In Penza, a city of many refugees, a committee for the refugees was established and theater groups operated alongside it, among these, also groups of Jews. From September 1916 on, Benjamin took part in Yiddish plays.

At the end of 1915 or the beginning of 1916, Benjamin met a lovely modest girl by the name of Rachel Holand. She was also from Lithuania, from the town of Vilkomir. She attended the high school and intended to become a doctor. A spark was lit between them, youthful love.

After the February Revolution of 1917,[12] Benjamin was caught up in the enthusiasm of the events taking place around him. The youth became very active. In Penza they set up a cultural society for young people. This society also had a library and publishing house in the Yiddish language, which served as a source of information for Benjamin, so thirsty for knowledge. He was among the most active members of the society and as such, he organized a club for devotees of Yiddish theater, where, of course, he himself acted.

A Russian theatrical director invited him to his theater as a regular actor. Benjamin refused. As someone who strove for excellence, he was worried lest his performance in Russian might not be natural enough. Years later it would become clear that Zuskin, the renowned actor, was not eager to play the roles of non-Jewish characters, not even in performances in Yiddish.

As an amateur he continued to appear on stage as the opportunities arose. And now he was invited to an appearance on the stage of a large social club, which was almost a theater!

An evening was being organized there under the title of *An Evening of Sholem Aleichem*. It is interesting that Zuskin's first performance on the stage of the Moscow State Jewish Theater would also be as part of *An*

Evening of Sholem Aleichem. So surprising how things in his life are so intertwined!

Of his performance at the club, a review was published that would be preserved for years and would miraculously survive. What was in it? If Zuskin took such pains for thirty years to make sure that it did not get lost, and even wrote about it in his "Curriculum Vitae," there must have been something in it important for him. What was it? It was written that a glowing career as an actor and a director lay in store for him, on condition that he didn't get sidetracked into slapstick.

The newspaper where this review was published was printed on the very same night that in Petrograd, the October Revolution was taking place. Thus the two most significant events in Benjamin Zuskin's life took place on the same night: the review of his acting which contained a prophecy of his future as a renowned actor, and the Revolution that created the conditions for the fulfillment of the prophecy in the realm of his life.

And in the realm of his death . . . The connection between these things is fairly straightforward, without any sidetracking, and certainly not in the direction of slapstick.

Benjamin found work as a clerk in the Prison Service. It did not interfere with his studies because classes were held in the afternoons. The pressure at work was not great and the director of the Prison Service had an excellent library with many books on theater. Benjamin spent long hours in the library, hungrily devouring the books.

In 1918, Benjamin completed the six basic years of study at the reali school, but to complete his secondary school education, he had to study additionally in the senior division. In order to extricate himself as quickly as possible from the status of pupil, he completed the two-year study program in one year and, in 1919, he received his diploma.

Even before that, in 1918, the Soviet regime was established in Lithuania, the Zuskin family's homeland. Many of its former residents, Leybe Zuskin among them, submitted applications to be allowed to return. Leybe's application was accepted, and at the beginning of January 1919, he returned to Lithuania. A week later Benjamin brought his mother and two of his sisters there and returned to Penza. Two brothers and the oldest of his sisters already lived apart. He had no plans to leave Soviet Russia. He clearly remembered that during his stay in Lithuania he felt stifled and humiliated. He was full of youthful hope.

During the civil war that broke out in Russia after the October Revolution, the Red Army of the Ural Mountains District established its military headquarters in Penza. Benjamin, after graduating secondary school, began to combine his work in the Prison Service with a job in those headquarters, first working in the recruitment office and later in the political division as an instructor in the theater department. This department was considered very important because it was officially defined as part of the "ideological front." Sometime later, because the headquarters was moved, Benjamin found himself together with the political division in the city of Yekaterinburg.

In Yekaterinburg he was accepted to the College of Mine Engineering. The conditions of life were difficult for everyone, and studies were organized so as to allow the students to earn a living. Between six and nine in the morning, they attend lectures and then they went to work; between six and eleven at night back at the college again, they had workshops and did lab experiments.

Tala, Mikhoels's daughter, was positive that Zuskin went to study mine engineering because of some misunderstanding. Tala knew my father as an actor in every fiber of his being, and she took in his personality from this perspective only. His pursuit of any other field seemed strange to her.

In truth, there was no misunderstanding here. When they left for Lithuania, Benjamin's parents made him swear that he would acquire a "real profession." His parents, who were theater lovers, excused their son's attraction to the theater but did not agree that acting would be his main occupation. They saw it as unacceptable, while Benjamin tried at first to fulfill the oath he had sworn to his parents.

And yet, why among all the "real professions," did he choose mine engineering? I presume that the young man from Lithuania, the land of flat plains, who was blessed with a sense for beauty and a talent for drawing, was very thrilled by the colorful richness of gemstones found in such abundance in the mountainous region of the Urals, and by the fantastic shapes created on their surface. It is possible. Yet if one may consider his occupation as a mine engineer as a milestone in his life, then again what is noticeable is that at the center is an inanimate object. Here—stone.

At times Benjamin left Yekaterinburg to pay a visit to his relatives and friends in Penza. He loved to stay with Minna. After her fiancé was drafted into the army, Minna went to Petrograd where she studied and worked. She returned to Penza to collect her parents and join the Zuskin family in Lithuania. Various reasons delayed them, and in the meanwhile, Minna was working in a Soviet governmental office and even rewarded with a room of her own to live in. Benjamin admired her, approved of her independence.

One evening, Benjamin wanted to know what Minna would say if he were to leave the college and go to Moscow in order to become an actor. He pressed her to give him an answer immediately. Minna, without hesitation, answered: "A wonderful idea. Go. Anyone can study engineering but not everyone can be an actor."[13]

In time when it becomes clear that it was Minna's encouragement of Benjamin that would turn out to be the catalyst in his fulfilling his own wishes, Leybe Zuskin would write her an angry letter: "May the children you have in the future cause you the worries that I have with Benjamin. After all, it was you who pushed him off the track into acting."[14]

A short time after Benjamin moved to Yekaterinburg, his beloved Rachel joined him there. She was accepted to medical school. They were married.

In 1920, Benjamin received a letter from Moscow, from Abraham Baslavsky, a friend from the days when they were both actors in the amateur theater in Penza. Abraham had been urging Benjamin to come to Moscow, writing about the theaters and acting schools that were so plentiful there, and also notified him that there was the Academy for Mine Engineering where Benjamin could transfer without any difficulty. If fortune smiled on him, he would become an actor. If not, he would continue to study engineering.

The letter helped Benjamin make the final decision. The reorganization of the college in Yekaterinburg reinforced Benjamin's decision; if he had to move to another higher education institution in any case, then Moscow was preferable above all others, especially considering the fact that Moscow also had a medical school.

At the end of the summer of 1920, Benjamin and Rachel moved to Moscow. They were expecting a child.

Benjamin continued his studies at the Academy for Mine Engineering and worked at odd jobs. At the same time he collected information about the theaters and he arrived at the decision that seemed final: he would try to get accepted by Vakhtangov who was directing two studios—the Russian and the Hebrew[15]—both affiliated with the Moscow Art Theater, the most famous of the Russian theaters.

His dream of being a Yiddish actor would presumably remain a dream, because the Yiddish stage there was so pitiful. Benjamin had already outgrown the juvenile ideas of a youth from Ponievezh who was willing to swallow whatever he was served; had he not already had a taste of real theater? Now he was unwilling to sacrifice his studies at the Academy just to act in an amateur capacity, especially now that he had a family and was obligated to ensure its future.

Time passed. Benjamin was torn between his studies and pursuing a living—and his home. At home there was no money, and there were day-to-day difficulties of life. Nevertheless, he was full of hope and he believed that things would change.

One day in November 1920, Zuskin went to visit Abraham. By virtue of his being a friend, he opened the door without knocking. Abraham was not there. In his room, Benjamin met an unknown person.

This meeting proved to be fateful.

3

First Interlude

JUNE 11–12, 1952
TRIAL
TESTIMONY BY BENJAMIN ZUSKIN

ZUSKIN. In Moscow I went to my friend; he was not at home. In his room I found a stranger.[1]

JANUARY 19, 1949
PRELIMINARY INVESTIGATION
INTERROGATION OF BENJAMIN ZUSKIN

INVESTIGATOR. What was your relationship with Mikhoels?
ZUSKIN. Friendship and work relations.[2]

JUNE 11–12, 1952
TRIAL
TESTIMONY BY BENJAMIN ZUSKIN

CHAIRMAN. Do express your opinion of Mikhoels.
ZUSKIN. Mikhoels was a wonderful actor.
CHAIRMAN. Are you giving truthful testimony?
ZUSKIN. The absolute truth.[3]

MARCH 17, 1949
PRELIMINARY INVESTIGATION
INTERROGATION OF BENJAMIN ZUSKIN

INVESTIGATOR. You continued to be connected with Mikhoels in a
criminal relationship?
ZUSKIN. I came to share his opinions.[4]

JUNE 11–12, 1952
TRIAL
TESTIMONY BY BENJAMIN ZUSKIN

ZUSKIN. I would like to recount . . .
CHAIRMAN. In brief.[5]
ZUSKIN. I'd like to describe . . . things that are not found in the forty-
two volumes of the Investigation File . . . [6]
So, I found a stranger speaking on the telephone, and I un-
derstood that he needed a typist. So I said: I know how to type.[7]

4

Act Two
(1921–1928)

Novice

A young man in a threadbare student's uniform is seated in front of a typewriter, a student's cap with a cracked visor perched on his head; on his feet are galoshes, laced with rope. His bearing is erect and graceful; his appearance is elegant despite these signs of poverty. He types quickly without inquiring into the contents of the document, finishes, extends the typed sheet to the man for whom it was typed. He tells the man his name:

Zuskin.

The man thanks him and introduces himself:

Mikhoels.

Greek tragedy with its climaxes, its vast amphitheaters, its heroes cloaked in gold-broidered tunics—can it reach highlight of the encounter between these two, clothed in the garb of poverty, brought together in a wretched room in forlorn post-Revolution Moscow, before a typewriter with broken keys? Can it match their dizzying flight, the perfect understanding between them, their quarrels that went to the point of hatred, the devotion of one to the other to the point of love, their unbelievable end, an end ungraspable by the mind?

At Zuskin's crossroads again lies an inanimate object—this time it is a typewriter.

When Zuskin learned of his companion's involvement in the theatrical arts, he asked if he could perform something in order to get Mikhoels's opinion of his abilities. He recited from Chekhov's stories, performed from melodramas and other plays. Mikhoels said that Zuskin certainly would be accepted in his theatrical school, founded and directed by Granovsky.

The next day Zuskin was introduced to Granovsky. He mustered up his courage and presented before the omnipotent director the same selection that had won Mikhoels's approval. Despite his nervousness and lack of confidence, he detected glints of encouragement in Granovsky's gaze.

Granovsky explained that the Soviet regime allowed the Jewish theater to be rebuilt, that for the first time in the history of the Jewish people a state Jewish theater was being established. He also said that it was not at all clear what awaited Zuskin in Vakhtangov's studio.

Zuskin was invited to an audition several days later. But he was still hesitant; he would prefer to see Granovsky's studio from inside, to see at least some rehearsal. "Please do so!" At a rehearsal, the acting, by Mikhoels, was very impressive and also made him laugh to the point of tears. Little by little he understood that these were not tears of laughter. He wept. Until this point he did not know that art had the power to thoroughly unsettle a person.

He agreed to audition. Along with reciting aloud, he had to prepare a piece that included singing, movement, and facial expressiveness. Expressiveness? Facial? If he knew anything about that, it was only the vaguest notion. What could he do? Aha, he got an idea: Grandfather! If this audition was going to determine his beginnings on the stage, then why not go back to the very beginning of beginnings?

Arriving at the audition, he makes a heartfelt cry: "Grandfather, help me." Then he stands in the center of the room, bows his head over an imaginary table, winks his right eye, whispers to himself, rubs his hands together, takes a pair of imaginary glasses of his pocket, places them on his nose, takes them off, cleans them with the corner of his jacket, puts them on again, moving them to the end of his nose, and at that moment, becomes an old man. On the invisible table, he smoothes out a piece of invisible cloth, takes an imaginary measuring tape, and humming, begins to measure the cloth up and down, with an invisible bit of broken chalk. Then the climax, the stage of cutting. But where are the scissors? The sounds of his humming intensify, they resemble a scream, Where the hell are the scissors?! He bangs on what is meant to be a table. Here, thank God! The humming turns into the sounds of victory, I found them! He cuts. The act of cutting ends. The tailor chuckles with satisfaction. From the lapel of his cape, he takes out a needle, threads it, not without difficulty, and begins to sew. That's it! A sigh of relief. And now, no table, no scissors, no cloth, no thread, not even a needle, no cape, no old man. A young man in a threadbare student uniform stands in front of the judges and they see with their very eyes that a miracle has just transpired.

The room is full of spectators. Even if the person being auditioned is engrossed in his own actions, his eye catches a flicker of movement in the space around him. These are students, actors, and even theater employees. It is hard to describe their enthusiasm.

Zuskin would appear again and again in the piece *The Old Tailor* (*Der alte shnayder*) for many more years. The skit would be so popular that every time he was invited to participate in any artistic event, he would be asked to bring a "needle and thread."

One after the other, the following important events took place:

In March 1921, Zuskin was accepted to Granovsky's studio.

On April 19, 1921, his daughter Tamara was born.

In June 1921, three months after he began to study at the studio, Zuskin left the Academy of Mine Engineering, and joined the theater troupe as a regular actor.

And if things had been different? If he had continued to study engineering? There is no reason to have regrets on that account. Many engineers, including mine engineers, traveled a path of suffering, such as in the Mining Engineers Trial in 1928, or the Industrial Party Trial in 1930.[1] In the twentieth-century game of roulette is there any winning number?

Now Zuskin could consider himself lucky. Here he was, an actor! Nonetheless, he did not give up the tasks that had occupied him from his first day at acting school: writing and illustrating posters, typing, serving as secretary, running the warehouse, and his devotion to these tasks was no less than his devotion to acting.

So now, Zuskin was in Moscow, at the Jewish theater. Where did this theater spring up from?

Many of the intellectuals who had welcomed the October Revolution aspired to reevaluate and to fashion new artistic forms. On the other hand, the Jews, intoxicated with freedom, burst out of the Pale of Settlement into the big cities in order to quench their thirst for self-expression. Eduard Bagritsky, a Russian poet of Jewish descent, expressed this feeling clearly: "Open the door wide!"[2] Could they have imagined that the wide-open door would lead to nowhere?

Moyshe Litvakov, one of the central figures at Yevsektsia,[3] and in charge of all Jewish culture in the new Russia, was an enthusiastic supporter of the renewed Jewish theater.

In Petrograd in March 1918, the Jewish School of Acting was established, the first of its kind in history. Alexei Granovsky was appointed to be the director.

In January 1919 the studio opened its doors to an audience, and in honor of the important event, it was given the status of a theater, even though in fact it continued to serve as a school.

At approximately the same time, there were attempts to establish a Jewish acting studio in Moscow, but these failed. After one of the people behind the initiative, Abram Efros, was negotiating with Granovsky and the relevant institutions, a decision was made that the theater had to move from Petrograd to Moscow. That was in October 1920.

At the end of that same year, an order was issued by the People's Commissariat[4] of Enlightenment, which changed the status of the Petrograd studio-theater and determined that it would be the State Jewish Chamber Theater, GOSEKT,[5] in Moscow. Thus was born the first Jewish theater in history that was subsidized by the state.

Twenty years later Zuskin would say that dreams of such a theater "could be fulfilled only in our country."[6] This statement may be understood as though it had been dictated by the official authorities but Zuskin sincerely thought so. Furthermore, it was absolutely true. Only "our country," the Soviet one, of course, funded theaters and other institutions whose function was "to give self-expression to small nations."[7] Yes, only "our country" in its aspiration to supervise everything that was identified with the "ideological front," could have established such a theater, dominated it, and ultimately cast it into the abyss. Only "our country" could have executed the actors.

After the theater moved to Moscow, uniting the Petrograd and Moscow troupes, accepting new actors, and planning the repertoire took a bit over two months.

On January 1, 1921, the debut performance opened on the stage of the theater in Moscow.

Actually, Zuskin joined the theater at a time when it was in the first stages of formation. "To seek—that is the byword we will place at the top of our plan":[8] that is what Alexei Granovsky, the artistic director of GOSEKT, used to say repeatedly.

Granovsky, born in Russia to an assimilated Jewish family, studied in Germany with the eminent director Max Reinhardt. Under him he learned styles of modern theater and was powerfully drawn to establish a new Jewish theater—not just that but to create it ex nihilo.

Ex nihilo? Out of nothing? No, that was not possible. It was clear that without the decision and support of the government institutions on the one hand and without the unique personality of Granovsky on the other, the theater would never have achieved what it did.

But the history of Jewish theater started much earlier.

Among the conditions of acceptance to Granovsky's studio was one firm principle—not to register candidates who already had experience in the old Jewish theater, because of the concern that they might infect the newborn theater with the old routines.

However, the old theater had not only routine patterns but also a connection to the tradition and history of the people. As early as the second century, there had been a theatrical production of the *Book of Esther*. In the Middle Ages, when the holiday of Purim was celebrated joyfully and festively, the performances known as the *Purimshpiel* had begun and they are familiar to us to this day.

A Jewish theater with a regular repertoire was first established in 1876 in Romania by Abraham Goldfaden. His own plays are still performed on Jewish stages around the world until this very day. With this, no worthy successor to Goldfaden had since appeared, and the conditions were not created to give rise to Jewish theater.

For his education, for his experience, and talent, Granovsky was received as a shining star, as a dazzling director. The man who perhaps lacked knowledge of Jewish tradition was gifted with a spark of genius, and he apparently had a feeling that was described by Osip Mandelstam: "The body language of the Jew is an expression of the senses . . . which has all of the characteristics of a fashion that has not become obsolete in thousands of years."[9]

Granovsky felt: "The basis of every performance is the rhythm."[10] Granovsky, it may be assumed, knew how to perceive "the pulsations of the heart of the people and its blood."[11] He turned around, skipping over the shtetl and the *Purimshpiel* groups, and inserted a primordial rhythm. Without this rhythm, the theater would not have become The Theater.

Granovsky had the talent "to read a play like an event,"[12] and he did not hesitate to shorten or revise the text as necessary. "The word is an event, while silence is more natural than the word,"[13] and the gesture, more strong than it. The stylization of gestures is not used for any external stunt but rather makes it possible "to overcome the tedium of daily life."[14] Granovsky used to design a play not as an operetta embedded with separate passages of speech and song but as a symphony where "musical elements that come in uninterrupted succession are replaced by the text, the acting, the stage-set, the lighting, the song, the mise-en-scene, and the pause."[15] Like the conductor of an orchestra, "he knew how to conduct the throng on the stage so that each one has his own character and at the same time, is part of the whole."[16] An interesting parallel statement was made with reference to Zuskin: "In every role that he played, Zuskin was perceived as a whole,"[17] even if every detail of his acting was an event unto itself.

In Moscow the theater is allocated a three-story building at 12 Stankevich Street. The first and third stories are used as dormitories for the theater's actors and employees. Mikhoels lives on the third floor, and Zuskin moves in to live on the first floor.

Until 1936 they would both live in these dormitories with one kitchen, one lavatory, and one bath for fifteen to sixteen families. Many of the other tenants would continue to live there for much longer.

The theater was on the second story. "From the day the theater was opened in Moscow until April 1922, it mounted its performances on a tiny stage, which had only ninety seats in the audience,"[18] wrote Zuskin in one of his articles.

This auditorium was decorated by Marc Chagall. Chagall also designed the scenery and the costumes for the first performance in Moscow.

According to Chagall's concept, flesh and blood actors, dressed in costumes that he designed and made-up with the makeup that he styled, would move among the objects of the stage-set that he created, and would become one with the images he drew on the curtain, the walls, and the ceiling. Furthermore, "the actors would express traditional Jewish emotions in a modern style,"[19] like the painted images.

Covering the entire wall along the auditorium was a mural, entitled *Introduction to the Jewish Theater,* and in it, geometric shapes blended with fantastic images and portraits of living people such as: Granovsky, Efros, Chagall himself, Mikhoels. Although the mural was already mounted in place, Chagall made changes and added touches all the time. Zuskin, too, would yet be added to this mural.

On the opposite wall, between the windows, four pictures were mounted: *Music, Dance, Drama, Literature,* which comprised the series called *The Arts.* On the frieze above them was a narrow picture as long as the wall: *The Wedding Banquet,* and it created a connection between the four arts and the art of theater on the opposite wall. In his mind, Chagall connected these arts with the Revolution. He saw the Revolution as a wonderful holiday like the theater, like a wedding. In 1922, when he understood that the "revolution is a blood wedding that begins as a holiday and ends with knife fights,"[20] Chagall would leave Soviet Russia forever.

That same year, 1922, when the theater was to move to its new abode, the mural and paintings would be hung in the foyer. The renovation work in this building several years later would be a pretext for getting rid of the works of a person who was considered a traitor.

In the top right part of the mural appeared the element of two women. "The women play the lyre and the tambourine. Their instruments recall those taken up by Miriam . . . after the parting of the Red Sea . . . To balance this turn to the distant pass, these women are led by Zuskin into modern drama."[21] It might be that Chagall entrusted Zuskin of all people with leading the women from the remote past to the modern Jewish theater, because he observed that Zuskin's style, while the most modern, was rooted in a memory of the past.

"This paradoxical theater," wrote Mandelstam, "when it sees a Jew, it loses its head . . . and immediately pulls him into its workshop."[22] In this "paradoxical theater," Benjamin Zuskin was given his first role.

Debutant

Working on his first role, Zuskin invested his heart and soul. Whatever worries he had, the people around him saw a cheerful man, good-natured and open, and in the small theater or in the crowded dormitories, the shout was frequently heard: "Zus! Zusa! Zuska!"

What does the name mean?

In moving from childhood to adolescence, Nyomke became Benjamin. But for some reason, this name did not stick to him in the theater, and after a casual joke, the people close to him began to call him by a shortened version of his family name, Zus or Zusa or Zuska.

He was prepared at every opportunity to enthrall his friends with endless tales, mostly funny, and always related to his childhood. Before long most of the actors knew his childhood friends and exchanged among themselves bits that they had taken from them. "The most significant and important impressions he took from his childhood,"[23] Mikhoels was to say of Zuskin. Many of his fellow actors recall that Zuskin surrounded them with the world of his childhood.

An Evening of Sholem Aleichem (*Sholem Aleichem ovnt*) on January 1, 1921, signaled the opening of the first season of the theater in Moscow. The *Evening* consisted of three acts: two short plays *Agents* (*Agentn*) and *Congratulations!* (*Mazel tov!*) and a monologue *The Spoiled Celebration* (*A farshterter peysech*). All were based on the writings of Sholem Aleichem, and all were directed by Granovsky and designed by Chagall. The two plays were the more impressive, while afterward it was decided to replace the monologue with another play entitled *It's a Lie!* (*S'a lign!*), also from Sholem Aleichem's writings. In the new play there were only two characters. Zuskin was accepted to the theater just as this decision was made, and he was offered one of these two.

In his debut performance, "Zuskin proved himself a great talent, from the moment he appeared on stage."[24] And let us not forget the date of this appearance; it is the date that marks the beginning of Benjamin Zuskin's career as an actor: September 24, 1921.

The content of the play is rather simple: Two Jews are sitting on a bench in a railroad car, as though nailed to it, and chatting between themselves. The First Jew by his appearance is a matchmaker, and he tries to wheedle details out of the Second Jew about the fortune and daughters of a wealthy Jew in the town of Kolomie, because it turns out that the Second Jew comes from that town.

To every query of the First Jew, the Second Jew answers by beginning with a story, "Some people say . . ." then he interrupts himself immediately with the categorical words, "It's a lie!," as if he is trying to say, "Let them talk!" And then he continues exuberantly with the gossip. The First Jew listens to him most attentively and takes an interest in the details. Every question and every answer is accompanied by deliberately exaggerated gestures, like the movements of marionettes, and the play ends when the two figures conversing are transformed into a petrified tableau. That is all.

In the debut performance, Zuskin played the First Jew, but after that first performance and in all the subsequent ones, he appeared as the Second Jew, the one who pretends that his stories are lies.

The Jew from Kolomie was very familiar to Zuskin. So, he knew who the type was that he had to enact, although he didn't know how to portray him. He was still inexperienced, being pushed without any preparation into the river of European modernity. Granovsky explained nothing but demanded mathematical precision in styling the Jewish gestures. How did it happen that the performance was nevertheless a success? "Zuskin's originality overcame the graphic sketch,"[25] and despite innovations, he remained faithful to his inner sense.

Even so, Zuskin understood that his intuition alone was not enough here and tried to decipher what he was being asked to do. These thoughts gave him no peace.

What to do? Perhaps leave everything and go away?

The option of leaving was discussed and rehashed among the members of his household. According to Rachel's parents, Moscow did not have the right conditions for raising the little child Tamara. Rachel's parents pressured them to return to Lithuania. Zuskin, despite the difficulties, was not willing to give up his dream of being an actor. They finally reached a compromise. Rachel would go away with her baby daughter and with the adults to Lithuania, and after some time they would return to Moscow, on condition that Zuskin's status was more defined. If not, he would join them.

Rachel, Tamara, and the relatives left, as had been agreed. In time, matters would become complicated: Lithuania became an independent country, and the border between Russia and Lithuania would be closed. Rachel would obtain a divorce, remarry, and build a new family.

What would have happened to Zuskin had he gone away with Rachel, and lived with the family in Lithuania? During World War II, Rachel perished in the ghetto. Here again a twist of fate, again a turn of the "real twentieth century."

The Sorceress

In April 1922 the GOSEKT theater moved from its location on Stankevich Street, with its tiny auditorium, to its new abode on Malaya Bronnaya Street. The auditorium in the new building seated not ninety but five hundred people in its audience. The new stage was also much larger and the repertory had to be adapted.

Although the GOSEKT performances were successful, Granovsky understood that the theater had not yet achieved its potential. He wanted to stage a performance that would amaze, that would dazzle, that could be considered the theater's manifest. Granovsky chose the play *The Sorceress* (*di Kishefmakherin*) by Goldfaden, a play that never was taken off the repertory of the old Yiddish theater.

In the old theater there was a sentimental attitude to the life of the shtetl. The modern Yiddish theater would emphasize social commentary, would ridicule a "bourgeois" desire for wealth. There were already a composer, stage decorator, costume designer, and actors had been cast in most of the roles. But one matter remained. Who would play the Sorceress? Granovsky, although he challenged most of the customs of the past, was not willing to give up one custom—the role of the Sorceress must be played by a man.

Granovsky's beautiful and clever wife, Alexandra, shrugged in astonishment, "What is there to think about so hard? After all, we are dealing with a real sorceress, one of those described in the folk tales as flying, riding on brooms . . . Take Zuskin. Try him at least. Every movement he makes is divine."[26]

Zuskin considered himself an actor, a genuine actor, ever since the play *The Sorceress*.

Let's read the ad from up close: *"The Sorceress.* A Humorous Jewish Game. Concept and direction: Alexei Granovsky. Musical adaptation: Joseph Akhron. Text adaptation: Moyshe Litvakov, Yekhezkel Dobrushin. Set and costume design: Yitshak Rabinovich. Cast: The Sorceress—Benjamin Zuskin . . ."

Benjamin Zuskin? Who is that?

The play *It's a Lie!* was one of three parts of a performance; Zuskin played one of the two only characters in the third part, and he was unknown to the general public. And now, the day after the debut performance of *The Sorceress*, which took place on December 2, 1922, Zuskin's name was on the lips of everyone in Moscow. Zuskin's name was now connected with fame.

Let us also take a look at the play:

In the shtetl there is a widower by the name of Avremtse who lives with his daughter Mirele. He gets married. His wife Basia is the embodiment of the stepmother, with all the bad this implies. She hates Mirele, and in order to be rid of her, turns to the local sorceress. The Sorceress succeeds in convincing Mirele to visit her, and with the help of the evil Elyokum, sells her into the harem of the Turkish Sultan. Finally, as happens in folk tales, the good ones—Marcus, Mirele's intended groom, and Hotsmakh, an itinerant merchant and leader of the market crowd—triumph over the evil: Basia, Elyokum, and the Sorceress are soundly defeated.

That is the content of the play. "It was merely the thread on which the characters and episodes are strung . . . The grotesques presented everything with great intensity and poke fun at everything that was presented."[27] And everything was presented in all directions. The actors were on the ceiling, in the windows, on the right and on the left, in front and in the back.

The critics and artists, thrilled, gave voice to their excitement. They spoke highly of the play in general and of Zuskin in particular, competing with each other to shower them both with praise:

EFROS. *The Sorceress* was received with accolades.[28]

LIUBOMIRSKY. The audience was as intoxicated as though they had drunk wine.[29]

GOLDBLATT. Zuskin's appearance in the role of the Sorceress was a genuine revelation.[30]

DEUTSCH. The pace and the joy were exhilarating.[31]

MARKOV, less than thirty years later: The presentation of *The Sorceress* stunned the spectator with sparks of fire, somersaults, turns, falls, a total submission to the laws of music, the cadence of the words. Of all the troupes that have visited Moscow, the closest to Granovsky's style of directing was the black troupe in *Porgy and Bess.*[32]

Pavel Markov must have seen *Porgy and Bess* in Moscow at the same time that I saw it, in 1956. I attended this thrilling performance with my mother, and I noticed that her elation was mixed with sadness. Yes, she too had noticed the resemblance between what we had just seen and the style in her theater, even though the production of *The Sorceress* was more dazzling, more exciting, more tempestuous, more theatrical.

The characters in the play *The Sorceress* were planned as masks. For example, the mask of the leader of the marketplace crowd—Hotsmakh (Mikhoels). The mask of the cruel, sanctimonious old woman—the Sorceress (Zuskin).

Zuskin created a kind of a seasoned merchant woman. This is true also for the character's manner of speech: bass notes when she is insisting alternate with notes of tittering when she is fawning. Zuskin recalled his grandfather who knew how to play with his voice. He also remembered Ponievezh: Two peddler women sat opposite the heder. One spoke in a bass voice, the other in a thin, high-pitched voice.

For the musical score of the role Zuskin called to mind the memory of prayers in synagogues, or of a discordant crowd's intonations in Jewish marketplaces.

And what about his movements? Before *The Sorceress*, in *It's a Lie!*, the hero was motionless, only his hands moved, albeit with full expressiveness, but without much variety, while here a very broad range of gestures and contortions were required, like of an acrobat in the circus.

I still haven't said anything about the appearance of the Sorceress.

The costume.

Granovsky meant to design the Sorceress as she is described in the European folktales. In order to show the aspect of fortunetelling, cards were sewn on the costume, and to hint that she was Jewish, her left leg was wrapped in tefillin straps.[33] A real desecration of God's name! Tefillin!? On the foot!? On the foot of a woman!? And not just any woman but a fortuneteller! So she is neither honest nor moral!

The makeup.

As everyone knows, Zuskin knew how to draw. When he prepared for a role, he drew the portrait of his character, drew it again, and modified it until he achieved a satisfactory result. The portrait was used as the basis for the makeup. For his Sorceress he specified a long nose sharpened at the tip and owl-like eyes. The production designer Yitshak Rabinovich did not spare his praise. Zuskin also designed, with great art, the hands of the Sorceress so that they appeared elongated.

From my mother I learned that during theater performances in Paris in 1928, one of the renowned cosmeticians there, after seeing *The Sorceress*, began to use Zuskin's method of making up hands—and thus, her lady-clients' fingers seemed longer and more elegant. So, one might declare somewhat jocularly that even the acclaimed Parisian world of fashion was not able to manage without Zuskin.

The highpoint in the play *The Sorceress*—in Zuskin's appearance and in the entire performance—is the scene of the seduction of Mirele.

"I-I-I . . ." The Sorceress draws out her voice. Pause. "I-I-I a-m t-h-e S-o-r-c-e-r-e-s-s . . ." She continues to draw out her voice and gradually moves from singing to song-like speech. "I have come to you at a good time. I . . ." her speech becomes liquid, until it is streaming, fluent, uninterrupted, "I read the cards, I deal in rags, I gossip, keen, whisper, divine." Pause. Continuing, very slowly: "I am the only sorceress in the entire world; the most important thing is making a living, Jews. Money is the most important thing."

The orchestra falls silent. Against a backdrop of the colorful, tumultuous crowd in the marketplace, Mirele appears. The Sorceress calls out to her and in an attempt to bring the girl to her house, she swaddles her in lies, persuasively introducing herself as a family member. And so on. Mirele refuses the invitation and the Sorceress does not cease. Finally she again begins to draw out her voice: "Come home with me, I will offer you d-e-l-i-c-a-c-i-e-s." The orchestra picks up, and with the first notes, the Sorceress begins her famous song, *"Kum kum kum tsu mir, kum tsu mir, tokhter meine."* Mirele answers her, *"Nein, Nein. Kum, kum! Nein, nein! K-u-u-m!"*[34]

A hop. The Sorceress stretches out in her flight and extends her hands to Mirele, fingers spread apart—remember how these fingers have been made up—like the predatory vulture that swoops down to carry off a vulnerable chick.

The spectator hears and sees—as I would hear from the audio record many years later—the Sorceress with all of her "enchanting" manners will not hoodwink him, because of the actor's ironic, even spiteful attitude to the character he is playing. "The chance to make fun of the shtetl which has become a thing of the past charmed me. On top of it all, I enjoyed amusing myself at the expense of the earthy Yiddish theater";[35] in this way Zuskin related to the role of the Sorceress.

In this play the acting troupe won acclaim. Mikhoels's enactment of Hotsmakh proved that he acted brilliantly. At the same time, in Efros's words, "Zuskin is more impressive; his acting is more engraved on the mind."[36] While Mikhoels tried to give expression to Granovsky's teachings, Zuskin "unintentionally, with the hot temperament of an untrained novice, rips the flimsy fabric of the script and reaches the heights."[37] "The Sorceress was like that! It was like this! What is not learned in any classroom . . . Even the slightest breeze and he is already air-bound! It was . . . something from the heavens."[38] Zuskin was not aware of it, and did not expect such dizzying success.

Mikhoels did not expect it either. Thirty years were to pass, and Zuskin would recount that the mention of his name in the theater reviews before Mikhoels wounded the master artist, and Zuskin was quite sensitive to it. It would be natural to assume that there were expressions of jealousy, the type that is so commonplace among actors, had we not been dealing with people who were in no way commonplace.

With this, Zuskin continued to polish his role, working diligently to bring every detail to perfection.

The tension had its effect. In 1924, in one of the performances of *The Sorceress*, after a long monologue, Zuskin fell from the upper stage and suddenly felt that he was unable to pronounce even one word. His mouth was wide open; from his throat a roar burst forth. The spectators rolled with laughter, assuming that the scene was part of the play. And then Zuskin managed to blurt out a word, in Russian, "Zanaves!" (Curtain!) The curtain fell. The audience was informed that due to Zuskin's sudden illness, the performance was postponed to another time. But Zuskin was unable to act. The role of the Sorceress was given temporarily to another actor.

Everything happened the way it had happened in his childhood. Now, he was afraid to come back to the stage, feeling then like a person being brought to the gallows. Yes, that was the debt he owed to his fame, a fame that according to popular opinion he earned easily.

Zuskin had a nervous breakdown. His illness lasted a few months. In the beginning the doctors were unable to diagnose it but finally he was pushed back onto the stage, full of energy and confidence, and returned with great inspiration to cheerful exuberant Zusa and to the flying Sorceress.

Soloveychik the Shadkhen (Matchmaker)

In 1923 the theater again turned to Sholem Aleichem's works, this time his play *The Big Win* (*Dos groise gevins*), whose title was changed to *Two Hundred Thousand* (*Tzvei hundert toyzent*). Dobrushin adapted the text according to Granovsky's concept. Granovsky also directed the play.

The hero of the play, a poor tailor named Shimele Soroker, played by Mikhoels, wins a lottery with a prize of two hundred thousand rubles. The newly wealthy man is suddenly surrounded by a conspiracy of scoundrels, and as quickly as Soroker becomes rich, he becomes poor again.

The essence of the production is: Preserving human dignity is more important than pursuing wealth. Granovsky strove for an appropriate theatrical expression and therefore he expanded the use of mise-en-scenes in relation to the verbal part. It was not disrespect for the classic but a wish to serve up the classic work on the tray of modern theater.

Zuskin plays the role of the matchmaker Soloveychik.

When he first appears in the play, all of the other characters are already on stage. He does not make a bland entrance, but parachutes in from the upper stage using a red umbrella. He lands, sings an amusing song, skips around a series of characters, and is already up high again, on the opposite upper stage.

Parachuting with an umbrella, excessive pestering, a dancing gait, a rush of words instead of conversation—all of these are techniques to represent a person who has no ground under his feet but also the specific profession of this person. The matchmaker must know how to dance at all the weddings, to ingratiate himself, and to convince with glib speech. For Zuskin, the abstract and the concrete, the general and the specific are always intertwined.

In the course of working on the role, Zuskin found in childhood memories a shop owner who used to skip-dance between his customers and to speak in an idiosyncratic manner. To refresh these memories, Zuskin visited a toy shop near his theater in Moscow, to see the wing-like movements of the shopkeeper's hands. All this was not enough for him: "If the basis of the role is the flow of movement, so its climax is the fluttering of the fingers."[39]

In the play, the transitions that Soloveychik makes from one situation to the other are very impressive. For example, his obsequious smile when he is received by the newly rich Soroker gives way to a bitterness and pained expression when he is rejected by Soroker as a worthless object; when at a ball he is forced to dance with a chair since there is no lady for him, he is no longer a mechanical doll but a suffering human being; the same suit at one moment gives Soloveychik an elegant appearance, and at another his trousers seem too wide, his coat too short and tight; by the end of the play the submissive expression on Soloveychik's face is swiftly replaced by his usual look.

Sholem the Shadkhen

That same year Zuskin played another matchmaker, this time named Sholem.

A comparison between the two roles shows that Sholem the Shadkhen is the more reserved of the two, something that is reflected in gestures, movements, the way of speaking.

Sholem the Shadkhen is a character in the play *The Divorce Paper* (*Der get*), which was added on to the *Evening of Sholem Aleichem* as the fourth act. It is based on Granovsky's concept as adapted from Sholem Aleichem by Dobrushin.

The play *The Divorce Paper* is a satire with elements of tragedy mixed with the grotesque. For example, the main character Reuben-Hirsch commits suicide by hanging, and his body remains hanging from a rope in the middle of the stage.

Zuskin, too, uses the grotesque. It is particularly noticeable on the occasion when his hero's wife, busy running from her shop, where she earns a living, to her home, where she runs the household, surprises her husband as he is studying the Mishnah with Reuben-Hirsch. "The wife appears and calls her husband's name. He doesn't respond. She takes a broom and sweeps, and Zuskin flies toward the audience in the theater. It cannot even be called a skip because a skip requires a certain effort. And here . . . Everything he did was done consummately, everything!"[40]

Prince von Flasco Drigo and Others

In 1922–1923 Zuskin appeared in a few small supporting roles, and between them in the role of Shlomke in the play *God of Vengeance* (*Got fun nekomeh*) by Sholem Asch.

In 1924, when both the actors and the audience began to show signs of weariness with the plays filled with sophisticated effects and even more sophisticated insinuations, a respite was required, and the theater presented *Three Jewish Raisins* (*Drai yidishe pintelekh*).[41]

In this play, the theater makes fun of both an Odessan ostensibly historical musical, its vulgarity and poor taste, and of a strident, insipid American musical. In addition, it also ridicules prejudices that are expressed in a mystical performance.

So, to the first raisin: *Prince von Flasco Drigo. A tragedy. Jewish Theater in Odessa.* "It has, as they say, everything you could want: Tzipke-Dripke the sultan's wife, robbers, grooms that are switched, the Wandering Jew, and the aristocrat Prince von Flasco Drigo. The characters are lampooned with sharp ridicule, although an amazing sense of proportion is maintained."[42] Zuskin appeared in the role of Prince von Flasco Drigo. Finally the young actor earned a role in a play that was "merely" a joyous performance.

Second raisin: *The Jewish Musical in America.* Here are only dance and song. The non-rhymed talking parts are used only to bridge between the dancing and the singing. All of the participants have a synchronized rhythm, and they are happy to dance and to infect the audience with their laughter. Zuskin plays an African American. When we spoke of the resemblance between two plays, *The Sorceress* and *Porgy and Bess*, it was mentioned that both groups of actors resembled each other in being connected to the heartbeat of their people. Here Zuskin the Jew succeeds in "being the both"—he tap-dances and he does it with the precision of an African American, born and bred.

Third raisin: *A Night at a Hassidic Rebbe.* Almost every scene here is a crowd scene. And there the precision and sense of beauty befit the craft of a jeweler.

The actors exult wholeheartedly. Apparently, as real Hassidim know, "by dancing and clapping, the harsh sentence is mitigated."[43] But neither the dancing nor the applause that Zuskin won in abundance helped to mitigate his own sentence.

The Second Badkhen

In 1925, the Moscow State Jewish Chamber Theater (GOSEKT) was promoted a notch: the theater's trade union decided, on September 15, 1924, to drop the word "Chamber," which denotes narrow goals and a limited audience; the decision was approved by the authorities, and from 1925 onward the theater was given the name: The Moscow State Jewish Theater, or GOSET[44] for short.

The same year, 1925, the theater put on the play *By Night at the Old Marketplace* (*Bay nakht afn altn mark*), based on the romantic-symbolic drama by Yitshak Leybush Peretz.

The play is a kind of "carnival of ghosts." There are a dying city and a graveyard coming to life. In the dying city are living people: the gatekeeper, prostitutes, religious, elderly women, drunks, children, shouting and running, and in the middle of all this, people stop each other, exchange a few words, hum, laugh, shout, pray, wail, and return to their poor, falling-down homes through the old marketplace. The Badkhens scatter them and repeat their mirthful roar: "The dead will rise!" A parade of the dead, adults and children, appears. The dead dance at the entrance to a black wedding. Then they are carried away by a breeze and vanish. The mocking laughter of the Badkhens accompanies them.

Such is the "amusing" plot. The mise-en-scenes, the music, the scenery, all join together in a powerful performance. The rhythm richly accentuates everything here: sound, movements, illumination—a light beam may draw out a single personage, or his face or hands, or one foot, the speech—a sentence of three words may be divided up among three actors.

When Granovsky adapted the original play according to his concept, he split into two the character of the Badkhen, who is Peretz's central character. Granovsky placed at the center of the play two Badkhens.

The First Badkhen (Mikhoels) is the "bearer of the denial."[45] He seems to be an unambiguous symbol. Nonetheless, he sends a double message: he denies the very existence of the vanishing shadow world, and simultaneously he mocks it, as though it really does exist.

The Second Badkhen (Zuskin) has no text of his own, because he doesn't exist at all in Peretz's work. His cues are an echo of the cues of the First Badkhen, and he quickly repeats his intonations, as the words fly and whizz like balls from one to the other, and the Second Badkhen turns to the First like a pinwheel. Even so, Zuskin acts independently, as well in the scenes of frivolity as in those of tragedy.

When the two Badkhens stand and face each other, the Second Bad-khen on the stage floor and the First on the upper platform, the former, with his speech and movements, is perceived as a reflection of the latter. The situation that has been created could be funny and amusing but, in fact, the Second Badkhen's behavior acts to soften the sharp gestures of the First and makes his words of sarcasm more humane.

It is difficult to explain why Granovsky split the character of the Bad-khen into two. Perhaps he guessed that the "ego" and the "alter ego" would appear as a recurrent theme in many GOSET productions. It is also likely that in *The Sorceress*, Granovsky understood that the incorporation of bril-liant contrasts between the mathematically precise actions of Mikhoels-Hotsmakh and the floating of Zuskin-Sorceress conveys something that has no rational explanation. And he was tempted to gamble: What would the two come up with now?

In truth, all of the inspiration, all of the feelings of trust and mistrust, the sense of being wounded by fate, and even death would fly between Mikhoels and Zuskin just as the words whizzed like balls between the two Badkhens. The double message in the First Badkhen's behavior would reveal itself more than once in the heroes that Mikhoels played. More than once Zuskin would be sorry to see it in Mikhoels the man. More than once the impression would be created that Zuskin, in reality as in the plays, was like the "alter ego," but actually he would never be anything other than himself.

The play *By Night at the Old Marketplace* amazed theatergoers and critics throughout Europe. One of the most eminent and influential of the theater critics, Alfred Kerr, wrote: "This is tremendous art. Tremendous art . . . eternity reflected through pantomime . . . Stunning."[46]

Within this play there was something hidden, something with an ungraspable depth. It is interesting that after a performance in Vienna, a certain person came to the theater office and asked to convey to Granovsky, who was absent, that the play had shaken him as something that went beyond all imagination. To the question, "How shall we present you?" he answered: "Sigmund Freud."

In 1968 a list was published in the U.S. of the hundred best theater presentations in the world during the previous fifty years since the end of

World War I. The list included two presentations put on by the GOSET under Granovsky's direction: *By Night at the Old Marketplace* and *The Travels of Benjamin the Third*.

Husband

Before the opening of the new season of 1925–1926, much paperwork accumulated at the theater and even before rehearsals began, Zuskin was asked to help out in the office, as he once did.

In the theater's new status, it was given new standards, and the troupe expected reinforcements, especially of professional dancers, given that here the art of movement was very important. For almost two years a college preparing dancers for drama theaters had been operating in Moscow. This year some of the graduates were directed to GOSET.

One morning in September 1925, Zuskin was sitting in the theater office. On the table in front of him were blank application forms and a typewriter. Graduates of the college of dance were waiting in the corridor, and they approached the window opposite the table one by one, as Zuskin, most painstakingly, typed their information onto the application forms.

Now the turn had come for one of the girls. Zuskin, his eyes fixed on the form, asked: Name? Eda. Family name? Berkovskaya. For a fraction of a second he tore himself away from the typewriter and looked up . . . Two months later they are married. At this crossroads in Zuskin's life, too, an inanimate object was involved, again a typewriter.

My mother Eda Berkovskaya came to Moscow from her birthplace Minsk in 1922. In Minsk Eda graduated with a degree in classical studies at the Russian gymnasium, and in Moscow she began her studies at the college of dance, taking day classes and at the same time night classes in art history at the university. After being accepted to the GOSET, she, like my father in the past, stopped studying at the university.

My mother worked at the GOSET until it was closed in 1949. She began her career there as a dancer. Afterward she also became an actress, but she never abandoned the dance: she danced by herself and served as a choreographer's assistant.

My parents' marriage lasted twenty-three years, from November 22, 1925, until December 15, 1948, when Mother left their apartment for a tour with the theater, and once back, found out that in her absence Father was arrested. I could have ended this paragraph the way fairy tales end: "they lived happily ever after until death separated them," except for the fact that what actually separated them was much more horrifying than death.

Friedl the Good Angel

In 1926, Granovsky staged *The Tenth Commandment* (*Dos tsehnte gebot*) based on work by Goldfaden in Dobrushin's adaptation, directing it as a kind of a variety show. It somewhat recalls the play *Three Jewish Raisins*, but there is a significant difference between the two works: In *Raisins* they make fun of the old-fashioned Yiddish theater, and here they satirize the complacent, self-important bourgeoisie.

Goldfaden's work is used only as the basis for adaptation. Instead of a "Jewish-shtetl-style" play dealing with morality of the tenth commandment "Thou shalt not covet the neighbor's . . . wife," in this production they make jokes and jest at Paradise, Hell, and the tasteless self-righteousness that exists on earth, all in a wealth of sparkling color.

The leading figures are Mikhoels and Zuskin: Mikhoels is the intelligent, rational, Evil Angel, while Zuskin is the quiet, bashful, Good Angel.

Before we deal with angels, let's remain close to earth and add that in the play *The Tenth Commandment*, my mother Eda Berkovskaya made her debut performance.

The plot of *The Tenth Commandment* begins in heaven where the Angels, the Good and the Evil, make a bet with each other over the question, What determines the way the world is run? In their wanderings over the earth, the Bad Angel is Ahitoyfel, who serves the wealthy man Ludwig in Berlin, and the Good Angel is Friedl, who serves the wealthy man Genokh from the town of Nemirov. Since these two wealthy men were chosen to resolve their dispute, Ahitoyfel convinces them, as a start, to swap their wives with each other. The plot takes place in Eastern Europe, Berlin, Paris, Palestine, and Heaven.

In each of these places, Zuskin's hero assumes a different character: that of the Good Angel in Heaven; of the simple servant Friedl on the road in East Europe; of the Entertainer dressed in European elegance at a cabaret show in a prestigious café in Paris.

In his role as the Angel, he slides effortlessly and rhythmically around the stage, like the fluttering of angels in the air. This gait also is continued in the character of Friedl, so that the audience does not forget his role as the Angel. Consider Friedl's profile in a photograph in this book: his feet are placed side by side and in profile to the audience, positioned one slightly in front of the other; imagine him walking this way rapidly, and then you will understand his style of "fluttering."

In this role there is a combination of clownery and obsequiousness. Here is also irony—Zuskin likes Friedl and also pokes some fun at him.

Toward the end of the play, Friedl understands that there is neither justice nor honesty in the world, and he abandons the role of Angel. The other characters flee paradise for hell because it's merrier there, and they hang a sign: "Thou shalt not covet . . ." They decorate the sign with lit electric bulbs. Unfortunately, though, the word "not" remains darkened. The plot is the tenth commandment in reverse.

As to Zuskin, he once more plunged into the atmosphere of a variety show. But the important thing is that in Friedl's character, there is the basis for Zuskin's greatest role of all—Senderl.

Senderl

On April 20, 1927, a first performance of a new production, *The Travels of Benjamin the Third* (*Massoes Binyomin Hashlishi*), takes place. In 1946, after twenty-five years of his acting on stage and in the cinema, Zuskin would say, "*The Travels of Benjamin the Third* is the best thing that I was ever able to do."[47]

So, the reader will understand why I devote such special attention to this play.

The play is based on the Yiddish version of the novella by Mendele Moykher Sforim,[48] dramatized and directed by Alexei Granovsky, with scenery by Robert Falk and music by Lev Pulver. At the heart of the plot are two Jews, Benjamin and Senderl, known in the literary world as the "Jewish Don Quixote and Sancho Panza." They are the poorest and most despised of the townspeople of Tuneyadevke.[49] Everyone, even their own wives, scorn them, but primarily Senderl who is called Senderl-the-Housewife, for his spinelessness. Senderl, wretched and reviled, follows Benjamin the dreamer far away, on a journey that ends, to their astonishment, with their return to Tuneyadevke.

The novella is a sharply satirical work; even in its title there is satire: traveling around a small town is called "travels," and the hero Benjamin earns the title of Benjamin the Third, ostensibly the successor to two previous famous travelers, Benjamin of Tudela of the twelfth century known as Benjamin the First, and Joseph Israel of the nineteenth century who called himself Benjamin the Second, in memory of the First.

The play blunts the satire of the original story and the performance softens it even further: "Behind Mendele Moykher Sforim's sarcasm one may see all the Benjamins and Senderls illuminated by a nobility of soul."[50] This is Zuskin's interpretation.

Once on stage Zuskin's hero has an outlandish appearance: a beardless face like that of a woman, large mole on the left cheek out of which grow three-four long hairs, the right cheek bandaged as bloated from the slaps he suffered at the hands of his wife, the innocent eyes of a child, a belly swollen from hunger, bowed legs; clothing that might be either a man's or a woman's: trousers with a cotton lining that thicken the thighs to look like a woman's, a woman's shawl on his shoulders at the beginning of the play and a woman's coat later on, and to complete the picture, a big man's hat with a cracked visor. To ensure that "Sancho Panza" would be lower than "Don Quixote," Zuskin, who was taller than Mikhoels in real life, had to reduce his height. "So, as I was working on Senderl, I once saw a wagon driver with bowlegs like after rickets . . . I realized that I needed just those legs,"[51] recalls Zuskin.

The blend of a comical and pitiable appearance with behavior that shows nobility of spirit undoubtedly creates a powerful effect, but the impression made by the external look gradually dissolves as the play develops.

Although the role of Senderl is a very verbal one and does not allow for replacing almost any word by gesture or facial expression, which are always preferred by Zuskin, the actor manages to find moments when he sneaks in a "speaking" gesture.

Zuskin's Senderl is a person with a tender soul, and with this, "if there is any sentimentalism here, it belongs to Senderl, not to the actor Zuskin."[52] In order to show the comic side of sentimentalism, Zuskin chooses grotesquerie.

The play was not taken off the stage for some fifteen years. I did not see the play because its debut performance took place before I was born, and in its last years, I was still a little child. But I always knew that for my father, none of his accomplishments meant as much as the character of Senderl.

This play and the name "Senderl" are also connected to my life story. According to Jewish tradition, the son is named after a deceased grandfather, and in my case, the first names of my sons do reflect two facets of their grandfather's personality: Alexander (Russian parallel to Senderl in Yiddish)—the peak of his being an actor—and Benjamin, his human being. And in my opinion, there is no more fitting name for this book than *The Travels of Benjamin Zuskin*.

May it be on the right foot! That is how a Jew wishes his fellow Jew a successful journey. And these are the opening words of Benjamin and Senderl on their journey. When GOSET went on tour as far as Europe, the phrase, *On the Right Foot!* would be used in one of the newspapers there as the title of the column reviewing the GOSET performances. When any one in our family is standing before a journey or some important beginning, there are no better wishes than, "On the right foot, Senderl!"

On stage, when Senderl hears these words of blessing from Benjamin, he takes a step with his right foot and walks right into the heart of the spectator. Here he is unforgettable.

Here both of them are unforgettable, Mikhoel-Benjamin and Zuskin-Senderl.

Their duo is so cohesive, so united, so perfect, and so amazing in their perfection—and in the difference between them. While Benjamin envisages that somewhere it will be good for all of mankind, Senderl who is devoted to him, is enchanted by his dream but knows in his heart that these are futile dreams. He is not detached from reality and does not cease to guard his pack containing their entire "wealth"—scraps of food and a handful of kopeks. In the future Mikhoels would work assiduously for the welfare of all of mankind while Zuskin, devoted to his friend, would never stop guarding his pack with their spiritual wealth, which he believed was the genuine wealth.

The way they look one beside the other highlights both the resemblance and the difference: Benjamin marches with his head held aloft, his walking stick grasped in his right hand, his entire being like a taut string. Senderl, who also clutches a walking stick in his right hand, drags himself after him, and his gaze is focused downward, at the ground. How appropriate are those bowlegs!

Where are they walking? Where are their feet taking them? They ask which way to turn of the farmers in the fields, of whomever they meet, in the bathhouse, in the marketplace: Which is the way to the Land of Israel? And they plod on and on, walking stick in hand, their profiles turned to the audience.

The weary travelers reach the inn and plan to rest. They roll over on the hard wooden benches. "Oi! Ai!" in the deep voice of Benjamin. "Oi! Ai!" Senderl repeats these exclamations in his gentle voice. The sounds of the orchestra create a presaging of every intonation and close it. "Benjamin, do you hear? I'm hungry. I could eat something before going to sleep. And you, Benjamin?" "Me?" And Benjamin, though his voice is gripped with hunger, continues to act the hero: "No, good night." "Good night. Benjamin! Are you asleep?" From the orchestra, which was silent during their conversation, the high thin notes of the oboe and the bassoon come to life as though replicating the intonations of the question and answer. "I'm asleep," Benjamin replies. "Senderl, so, are you asleep?" "I'm asleep." Senderl's voice, along with the thin high notes of the bassoon, can scarcely be heard. The companions then again wish each other a good night and finally fall asleep.[53]

In their dream they see themselves in a fantasy land. Some creature, who suspiciously resembles the attendant in the bathhouse that they had visited on the way, brings them to Alexander the Great, and he anoints

Benjamin to be king of the Redheaded Jews and marries him off to his daughter, Rahab the Whore.[54] Everyone joins in the celebration. Food and wine are plentiful. In the midst of the dancing that follows the feast, the wives of Benjamin and Senderl appear and shower them with vigorous blows.

The festive music changes to groans from Senderl: "Oi Ai!" "What's the matter, Senderl?" asks Benjamin. "I had a bad dream, Benjamin," Senderl answers despondently. "So did I." Benjamin is also sad, and each of them tells his dream to his companion, and lo and behold, it is the very same dream.

All right, then. Let's get on with our journey. "On the right foot, Senderl!" "On the right foot, Benjamin!" murmurs Senderl, devotedly but hopelessly. The orchestra plays a reprisal, and the two of them set off again, trudging ever forward, staff in hand, profiles turned to the audience.

Now the music changes to a slow march that enables the audience to feel how plodding is the gait of the two companions and to imagine themselves actually there. "We see the town through the eyes of that wretched pair, and together with them we pass through the marketplace and wash up at the bathhouse. Together with them we ask the farmer our ultimate question: Which way to the Land of Israel? The way out lies here, and leads to eternity because Mikhoels and Zuskin invest their very souls in their Oi! and Ai!"[55] writes a Jewish-Austrian critic.

Suddenly the movement and the music stop.

And the travelers find themselves back in their own town. "There's nothing to be done, Senderl," says Benjamin. "After all, the world is round." "Yes," replies Senderl in despair, "but what will we tell our wives?" He has already noticed that their angry wives are looming nearby.

"No matter what, we had a wonderful dream, didn't we, Senderl?" "What a dream! What a dream!" Senderl repeats in a voice, which expresses the transition from despair to enthusiasm and then to helplessness.

The music thunders again, and the companions sing their famous song, "What a dream":

BENJAMIN: We sat before a luscious plate.
SENDERL: We sat and saw but never ate.[56]

The sounds of the orchestra seem to make their magical performance perfect. A symphony without equal! "The preposterous exploits of the inspired duo of Mikhoels-Benjamin and Zuskin-Senderl began to pale in contrast to the plots of their noble and tragic souls. At the end of the premiere, the audience rose like one person, and the theater erupted,"[57] wrote the critic.

To my regret, I never saw this "inspired duo" except as part of a program in memory of Mendele Moykher Sforim in 1947. My parents brought me there to see with my own eyes that there are miracles in the world, even if only in a brief performance.

The two appeared dressed in black evening suits, and my father had a starched shirt, bowtie, and patent leather shoes. I knew he did not like to appear in formal attire when portraying a character in a program such as this. "I prefer to appear not 'in white tie and tails,' but in costume and makeup of the character,"[58] my father wrote in his article "Curriculum Vitae." However, from the moment that I heard their "Oi" and "Ai" I forgot about the bowtie, and I saw before me two luckless individuals dreaming lofty dreams that could never be realized. The sense of touching something hopelessly unattainable haunted not only those two up there on the stage, it haunted me as well as I sat among the audience beside my mother in her festive dress. The feeling was supported by Mikhoels's voice, deep and full of pathos, and my father's, gentle and kindly: "What a dream!"

And what an awakening.

The Benjamin-and-Senderl performance was in the second half of the program. The first part consisted of speeches. Mikhoels's speech is etched in my memory because it was so picturesque. He spoke of, among other things, how Mendele did not disqualify in his text words from other languages. In the version of the novella he wrote in Yiddish, Benjamin and Senderl ask the farmer on the road their question in Russian: "Kudy doroga na Eretz-Yisroel?" (Which way to the Land of Israel?) But in Mendele's day, that question had no answer. Not long ago, though, continued Mikhoels, Comrade Gromyko answered the question from the podium of the UN General Assembly.[59] And upon hearing those words, the audience burst into uncontrolled cheering.

It should be noted that the program in memory of Mendele Moykher Sforim took place in December 1947, and Mikhoels was referring in his speech to the 29th of November of that year, when the Soviet representative to the UN, Andrei Gromyko, declared his country's support for the Partition of Palestine which led to the establishment of the State of Israel.

When Mikhoels went the next day following the Mendele memorial program to obtain a recording of his speech, which he had been promised in advance, he was told that the recording had been destroyed. Just an accident, they told him.

It was a bad omen.

We sat before a luscious plate.
We sat and saw but never ate.

Great Actor in Minor Roles

Following the dizzying success of the play, *The Travels of Benjamin the Third*, the authorities decided to send GOSET abroad in order to promote the art of the Soviet Union, especially of the small nationality living within it that had been discriminated against in the past. The relevant Soviet institutions began negotiations with Western theatrical agents, and meanwhile the theater put on a few more plays.

One of these plays was designed to pay off the theater's debts to the Central Repertory Committee, which demanded that the theater put on plays on Revolution-related subjects. Thus on November 27, 1927, ten years after the October Revolution, the theater opened with the premiere of *The Uprising (Oyfshtand)* by the Soviet playwright Lipe Reznik. The Repertory Committee was not satisfied: despite the fact that there is a reference to the revolt of oppressed people against those who rule over them, it takes place on the distant Java Islands which was not especially relevant for Soviet Russia. Still it was better than nothing.

Zuskin was offered a small role in this play, as one of the leaders of the uprising.

The Uprising is not the first show based on a Soviet play: a year before *The Travels*, in April 1926, the theater presented the play *One Hundred*

Thirty-seven Children's Houses (*Hundert-zibn-un-draysik kinderhayzer*), which is an adaptation of a story written by Soviet author Abraham Veviorke.

The reader's attention should now be directed to a very characteristic nuance for GOSET. The reason for naming the play "Children's Houses" (Orphanages) is totally obvious, because at the heart of the production is an appeal for donations on behalf of the orphanages. But why was the number 137 chosen specifically? Here is the answer: despite the many concessions made in GOSET in response to the demands of the era, the theater still wished to remind the devotees and cognoscenti in its audience of the words of the fourth verse in Psalms 137: "If I forget thee o Jerusalem, may my right hand forget its cunning."

Zuskin struck it lucky that his role as the town Lunatic was a small role and bore no ideological label. Incidentally Eda Berkovskaya played the role of a wild boy who provokes the Lunatic.

In early 1927 before it set out for Europe, the theater put on a play, which was completely European: *Trouhadec*. This play was written by Jules Romain, a twentieth-century French playwright, and the play was translated into Yiddish. Although Zuskin was offered an interesting part, the role of Trestaillon, he rejected it emphatically. It is true that he had come a long way since he was a young amateur actor, but despite the experience he had acquired, he was not yet ready to play the part of a non-Jew. Much later I read Romain's writings and I didn't like them much. Then I thought that perhaps the additional reason for my father's refusal to participate in the play stemmed from his well-developed aesthetic taste and his striving for perfection.

The last play put on before the European tour was a play of a writer considered by the GOSET to be like one of the family, Sholem Aleichem. And this time, the play was *Luftmentsch*. Mikhoels had the main role, Menakhem-Mendel, a *luftmentsch* who is a matchmaker-broker. Granovsky, faithful to himself, split the character of this hero into two. The role of Menakhem-Mendel's double, Kapote, is played, naturally, by Zuskin who "decided to create a character who is the opposite of Menakhem Mendel."[60]

The audience, which was familiar with the acrobatic antics of the Sorceress, which remembered Soloveychik walking on tip-toe, and the fluttering of Friedl, was now shocked at the sight of not a luftmentsch, meaning a person who is "suspended in air," but rather "air without a man."[61]

Two months after the premiere of the play *Luftmentsch*, the GOSET theater set out for tour in Europe. At the end of the last performance before their trip, the actors were impatiently waiting for something. Zuskin finally provided it:

> We're packing our bags today
> We're traveling far away.[62]

When they heard the song, the actors removing makeup in their dressing rooms, the theater students loitering behind the scenes, and the stage hands taking down the stage sets all left what they were doing and joined in the singing.

Europe

On April 2, 1928, the excited and enthusiastic GOSET troupe took their places on the train for Europe.

The first station was Warsaw. They would remain there a few days. No performances were planned there for now, perhaps on their way back to Moscow.

The actors disembarked onto the railroad platform and at once found themselves surrounded by people of distinguished appearance. They came especially to welcome the members of the acting troupe. The well-wishers on the platform were the representatives of the Jewish community in Poland: actors, writers, public figures, and members of the Jewish leadership.

The entire GOSET ensemble was invited that evening to the Passover Seder. God in heaven! In the vanity of daily life in the Soviet Union, some of the actors forgot the Jewish holidays and even Passover, the holiday closest to the soul of every Jew, and they didn't know that Passover eve was that very night. At the evening, they took their seats at a round table. Booklets containing the Haggadah in Hebrew and Yiddish were handed out to everyone. They read the text with their eyes and felt their spirits soar as the Chief Rabbi of Warsaw read it aloud.

The journey westward continued. The actors fell silent. They were thinking that while they considered Europe a modern place of elegantly dressed people, well-kept cities, luxurious shops with tantalizing shop windows, on their first step there, they had actually met their own Jewish past, which was unfamiliar to some of them, and which had made them laugh in the plays they put on. They found it hard to digest the magnitude of the impression.

In Berlin, where they put on their premiere performance of this tour, they were already not so sure that their chuckling was only for the sake of chuckling. "Outwardly it seemed that the theater was making fun of tradition, but that was not the case, for the laughter of Jews at their own tradition is an ancient Jewish tradition."[63] This is how Joseph Roth, a well-known Austrian author of Jewish descent, responded to this debut performance.

The first free day in Berlin, the entire troupe was invited for a luncheon organized in their honor. The huge auditorium sparkled and was colored in all the shining colors of the rainbow from the crystal of the chandelier and the tableware. Here a surprise awaited the troupe, although of a different kind. The actors who were accustomed to a modest life under the Soviet regime felt ill at ease in the luxurious atmosphere. But how great was their amazement when it turned out that Granovsky, in contrast to them, felt at home in this environment: he easily held his own in conversation, on an equal footing with his hosts who were prominent cultural personages in Europe. If in Warsaw the actors were suddenly made aware of their connection to Jewish tradition, here in Berlin they began to understand that the artistic style that they so admired, without devoting much thought to its sources, was created by Granovsky who was part and parcel of European culture. Their style was actually a symbiosis of two cultures, and they realized this fact only now.

On April 11, the GOSET began its appearances in Europe in Berlin, in the impressive and imposing edifice of Des Westens Theater, presenting *Two Hundred Thousand*. The next day they performed *The Travels of Benjamin the Third*. More than forty theater reviews in the Berlin press were devoted to both performances: "The acting . . . we have never seen the like."[64]

In the words of praise written about Granovsky's stage direction, there were even hints that Granovsky was greater than his teacher Max Reinhardt, the unchallenged luminary of European theater. To surpass the latter's accomplishment was considered impossible; to be accepted to his troupe was the dream that even well-known German actors almost didn't dare to aspire to. "If they heard in Europe of an actor who had turned down Reinhardt's invitation to act under him, they would be astonished, and more than that, they would make of him a laughingstock."[65] Can one even imagine someone that weird? Well: "Reinhardt invited me to join his troupe, and I turned him down,"[66] Zuskin was to have said.

After a few weeks when the theater reaped successes in Berlin, the troupe turned to the German cities considered "Jewish"—Frankfurt and Mannheim. "We arrived in Frankfurt on the Shavuoth holiday, and our performances were boycotted. We arrive in Mannheim. The Jewish organizations arrange a festive luncheon for us. Representatives of all of the Jewish organizations in the city participated, from the Orthodox Jews at one end to the workers organizations and Communists at the other . . . Not one word was uttered in criticism of the Soviet regime. The opposite was the case."[67] These words Zuskin was to write later, from Vienna, and address them to Litvakov in Moscow in order to reject the accusations against the GOSET that it did not show loyalty to its Soviet homeland.

Finally, their first tour in Germany was behind them. And in front of them—Paris! The theater was a Jewish theater, of course, but living and operating in the Russian milieu, where every educated person had always felt the deep cultural bond between Russia and France, and for Zuskin Paris was cloaked in a fog of mystery and charm.

In Paris they appeared in the theater Porte Saint-Martin, located in the neighborhood of La Marais. The population there was largely Jewish even though not only Jews came to the theater. The GOSET's success in its appearances in Paris was so great that the Paris police was once called to bring reinforcements to direct the traffic near the theater.

In Paris the troupe met theater people as well as writers, poets, and painters. Marc Chagall saw all the plays and was enthused. The encounters of the GOSET people with him and other so-called "traitors"—those who had emigrated from the Soviet Union and never returned—the sense of freedom that they felt there without being fully aware; the dubbing of the theater "Granovsky's" rather than the "Soviet State's," all of these enraged the Soviet authorities.

In the letter to Moscow, Zuskin rejected the accusations that they purportedly had connections with the right-wingers: "Believe me, my dear Moisei Il'ich [Litvakov] . . . Someone fed you false information."[68] What is interesting here, of course, is "someone": informer, or informers, appointed or planted to report everything to the secret police. True, the conflict between the artist and the regime is eternal but under Soviet conditions it took on its ugliest and most frightening form.

In mid-July, the GOSET stopped the performances for a month and the actors went on vacations. Zusa and Eda and several other friends chose a fishing village, which is also a resort, Les Sables-d'Olonne, on the Atlantic coast.

The group of vacationers left Paris on July 12, while Zuskin was forced to postpone his leaving because of some important meeting, and afterward he decided to stay in Paris until after July 14, Bastille Day, the French national holiday. On July 16, he joined Eda. The next day, he received a telegram from his father Leybe stating that he, Leybe, and Benjamin's sister Sonia were coming to Paris. The date of their arrival was close to the date when the theater's performances were supposed to resume.

When they met, Leybe, who was sixty at the time, explained that under a bourgeois regime in Lithuania, they beat him because his son was employed in a Soviet theater. Brother Yitshak the tailor with his family had settled in Canada, and he invited their father, mother, and sisters to come to him. Since Leybe did not find work there, he was planning to seek his fortune in South Africa. On the way from Canada to South Africa, he found the opportunity to meet his famous son in Paris.

Rumors of a visit by Zusa's father and sister spread quickly among the GOSET people who had just returned to Paris and stirred great excitement. Leybe was excited. He was filled with pride to see that all of Paris was cheering his son. And thrilled by his son's talent, he wrote to his sister-in-law Minna: "May the children that you have in the future give you as much *nakhes* [satisfaction, pleasure] as my son Benjamin has given me now. After all, it was you who encouraged him to become an actor."[69] How different is what he wrote now from what he wrote her in the past.

After a break, the theater appeared in Paris for two weeks more. Every evening, at the end of the show, the audience was in no rush to disperse. There were theatergoers who went behind the scenes. Once Chaim Weizmann, chairman of the World Jewish Congress and future President of the State of Israel, went backstage. "At the end of the performance, Chaim Weizmann visited us. He thanked us for the show and expressed his enthusiasm . . . What were we supposed to do? Turn our backs on him and walk away?"[70] Zuskin would justify himself in the letter previously mentioned. Whether Weizmann proposed that they go to Palestine or just sent regards to his brother and sister in Moscow, or both, is unknown.

After Paris, they went to Belgium—Brussels and Antwerp—and then to Holland—Amsterdam and Rotterdam. They move from country to country and from city to city. The scenery changed, but wherever they went, GOSET and its actors won the crowd's admiration and acclamation. After Belgium, Holland, and once more Paris, they arrived in Vienna.

On the train to Vienna, Zuskin joked as usual, and not everyone noticed the worry gnawing at his heart. He was always excited when facing an unfamiliar audience, but Vienna, according to the rumors, was the most critical and the haughtiest city of them all. Would they be well-received there, too?

Zuskin's unease had some connection with the letter from Litvakov, which reached the theater in Vienna. In fact, Moscow's admonitory wag of the finger had been directed at the theater throughout its tour of Europe, but this time it was much more threatening. In his reply to Litvakov, of which excerpts were quoted previously, Zuskin concludes with these words: "And now, as to the behavior of our actors in Europe. I swear on my honor that we are all behaving properly. We are working beyond our capacity . . . What did they write to you about us? . . . And the most insulting is that on the one hand, unbelievable success and on the other . . . instead of being proud of us and wishing us success in the future, you accuse us of things that are totally unfounded."[71] Zuskin could not calm himself. The meeting with his father left an open wound. Deep down in the recesses of his consciousness there were thoughts about Reinhardt's offer, about Chaim Weizmann. But what kind of future awaited him in the West? Take, for example, Mikhail Chekhov, the greatest Russian actor of all and the most admired by Zuskin. But after he emigrated from Russia his performances on stage were never accorded the same acclaim that he had known in his homeland.[72] No, Zuskin felt himself an integral part of Granovsky and of all the theater. It is true that there were rumors that Granovsky may not return to Russia. And what then? Nonsense! Those were wicked rumors. Still Zuskin could not find peace for his troubled spirit because he felt that the Soviet regime, which had previously breathed life into the theater, now did not trust the theater troupe.

If Zuskin had stayed in Germany in 1928, who knows what would have happened to him five years later, in 1933, when Hitler came to power? In the twentieth-century game of roulette, there was no winning number.

Critics of the West—and it must be said, left-wingers among them— assumed that it was the Soviet regime that shaped the theater in its own spirit. And what did the non-leftist critics think? "What does this marvelous theater have that so astounded the German critics?" asks one of them, "What did Lenin's and Stalin's blessing and their long arm contribute? Nothing. The theater appears to us well-formulated thanks to the director's talent, daring in its attitude to tradition and convention; the theater where under the ethnic costumes there beats a living human heart. The entire troupe has a sense of rhythm which is unique and totally alien to the Bolshevist atmosphere."[73]

Why was it Zuskin of all people who was asked to write the letter to Moscow? On the one hand, he continued to work in the secretarial job during the theater's tour in Europe. On the other hand, and this is the main thing, no aspersion was cast on his pure intentions. "I have good reasons to believe that you believe in me now as you believed in me then, so I ask you to believe me today as well. I am writing the truth."[74] With these words, Zuskin begins his letter to Litvakov.

Zuskin's words generally reflect his loyalty as a Soviet citizen. And yet he did not notice that the rhythm inside him was loyal only to its own world and was "totally alien" . . . And then again, perhaps Zuskin did notice this? Is it possible that his impending doubts and fears were already stealing into his heart?

Tension and fatigue were already having their effect. Zuskin appeared on stage, thrilling the audience. And again, collapse. For several performances there was a stand-in. Granovsky's new acquaintance, Sigmund Freud, examined Zuskin but did not detect any abnormality save the fact that he was a sensitive soul with an exaggerated sense of responsibility. After a few days of rest, Zuskin's energies were renewed.

At the end of September, the appearances in Vienna came to an end. In October the troupe appeared in Berlin and in the small towns surrounding: Magdeburg and Cottbus, in November, Hamburg in Northern Germany, Berlin again, and then Leipzig and Dresden.

All this time, as the trip continued, Granovsky was negotiating with American impresarios about inviting the theater to the United States. He was offered excellent terms, but the Soviet functionaries were filled with fears and distrust. In the end the troupe was permitted neither to travel to the U.S. nor to continue its European tour. In early December the theater returned to Berlin, staged the closing performances of the tour, and left on its journey back to Moscow.

Although the tour ended unexpectedly, Zuskin managed to arrange for himself a quick trip to Kovno in Lithuania to meet Rachel, and particularly to make the acquaintance of his daughter Tamara, already seven years old.

At first, Tamara did not approach him but then, she started to be captivated by the charm of his personality. She held her breath as she listened to his colorful stories about the theater, the performances, while he was still enveloped in the exhilaration of the European tour and the applause of the audiences in Berlin, Paris, and Vienna. Parting with Tamara, Zuskin promised to write to her and asked her to write to him.

I wish to examine in retrospect the GOSET's triumphant tour of Europe, a tour that marked the end of the first, and brilliant, phase of this theater, rich in accomplishments.

Along with *Two Hundred Thousand* and *The Travels of Benjamin the Third*, GOSET also put on in Europe *By Night at the Old Marketplace*,

Trouhadec, The Sorceress, Luftmentsch, and *The Tenth Commandment.* In the cities where GOSET was given additional, small stages, such as in Berlin, it also staged skit performances: *A Night at a Hassidic Rebbe* taken from *Three Jewish Raisins* and *Mazel Tov* and *The Divorce Paper,* taken from *An Evening of Sholem Aleichem.*

The European press, with very few exceptions, gave highly enthused reviews, expressing powerful impressions of "Granovsky's theater":

> BERLIN. This is truly theater of international stature.[75] In front of our eyes, we see the emergence of theater, entertainment, circus, and also the soul of man. Dazzling![76]
>
> PARIS. This theater troupe is the most cohesive of any I have had the fortune to see until now. In the ensemble, the soul is a collective soul while the spirit is individual.[77]
>
> ROTTERDAM. The toughest, most difficult-to-please audience is demonstrating sweeping exhilaration.[78]
>
> BRUSSELS. Great art, tremendous art. It is an example to us all![79]
>
> LONDON. How fortunate that I was able to see all this before I returned to London.[80]

The reviews were not content with heaping praises on the theater in general but praised every single play individually:

> *The Sorceress.* A play that arouses exultation and thunderous applause.[81]
>
> *By Night at the Old Marketplace* is an unsurpassed miracle. Everything moves so quickly, spinning, fluctuating, climbing, rambling, rolling, laughing and weeping, falling and rising. Fascinating. This is not a play. It's an act of enchantment.[82]
>
> *The Travels of Benjamin the Third.* You will find there neither conventional principles of directing nor any Jewish features such as prayer, dybbuk, cholent, or any mention of Tisha B'av . . . [83] Still, it is a theatrical performance par excellence, and it is Jewish to an extent no mortal can surpass.[84]

So what did the critics write about the hero of this book, Benjamin Zuskin?

> Zuskin is truly a discovery for us. Elegant precision, intelligence, innocence, and intuition . . . He stands out from the whole ensemble. His heroes are a mixture of mortal and marionette. Zuskin's acting has moments that cannot ever be forgotten . . . He skips and jumps and rejoices like a child. Blessed is the theater which has such children![85]

Europe, mesmerized, took its farewell of the GOSET theater with great regret: "All of this flows so fast and passes us by, and we will be able to assess it only in our finest memories."[86] Granovsky also took his leave of the theater with great sorrow. He was signed on a contract in Germany, and officially he was delayed in Europe until the contract expired. In truth, he was afraid to return to Moscow, to the atmosphere of distrust and dictates.

He was to remain there and thereby escape the tragic destiny of his two stars, but he too was doomed to a bitter fate. The West would quickly forget his theater's bravura tour of Europe, and the artist would live in poverty and die in March 1937 at the age of forty-seven of some illness. There is no correlation between genius and the twentieth century. Besides, for Granovsky, artistic creativity cannot be reconciled with any kind of pressure, be it ideological or wheeling and dealing. "As suddenly as he had appeared in the Jewish theater, so too he left it suddenly. He had not only directed sixteen stunning plays but he also established, for the first time in history, a Jewish acting studio—a school of acting that had an impact on the Jewish stage and its character."[87]

Thus in January 1929, the GOSET ensemble returned to Moscow, without Granovsky.

5

Second Interlude

OCTOBER 4, 1951
PRELIMINARY INVESTIGATION
INTERROGATION OF BENJAMIN ZUSKIN

ZUSKIN. After the European tour, Granovsky . . . never went back to
the Soviet Union.[1]

JUNE 11–12, 1952
TRIAL
TESTIMONY BY BENJAMIN ZUSKIN

CHAIRMAN. And the repertory stayed as it had been?
ZUSKIN. The Theater began to put on plays written by Soviet
playwrights.[2]

MARCH 4, 1952
PRELIMINARY INVESTIGATION
INTERROGATION OF BENJAMIN ZUSKIN

INVESTIGATOR. How did the Jewish Theater spread its ideas of
nationalism?
ZUSKIN. Through old plays with . . . a distorted notion that the Jews
are a unique nation, ostensibly.[3]

JUNE 11–12, 1952
TRIAL
TESTIMONY BY BENJAMIN ZUSKIN

CHAIRMAN. But you were one of the leading actors?
ZUSKIN. My roles . . . I played a workman . . . a Party member . . .
an educated Russian . . . None of this fits in with my being a
nationalist.[4]
CHAIRMAN. You described Mikhoels . . .
ZUSKIN. The talk is of Mikhoels but I knew Vovsi, and between them
there is a colossal difference.[5]

MARCH 17, 1949
PRELIMINARY INVESTIGATION
INTERROGATION OF BENJAMIN ZUSKIN

INVESTIGATOR. Was Mikhoels a Jewish nationalist?
ZUSKIN. I tried not to pay attention to his negative traits.[6]

JUNE 11–12, 1952
TRIAL
TESTIMONY BY BENJAMIN ZUSKIN

CHAIRMAN. What about Markish? Tell.
ZUSKIN. In the most difficult periods of my life, Markish was a good
friend and adviser to me. I am referring to 1938.
CHAIRMAN. 1938?
ZUSKIN. In 1938 I submitted a request to resign . . . I felt stifled in the
theater.
CHAIRMAN. You should have left.
ZUSKIN. If I had left, the theater would have fallen apart.[7] Besides the
Committee of Artistic Affairs didn't allow me to.[8]
    I'd like to describe . . . things that are not found in the forty-
two volumes of the Investigation File.[9]
    I fought to portray a Soviet character.[10]

6

Act Three
(1929–1938)

Man of His Times

In January 1929, the GOSET returned from Europe.

Solomon Mikhoels was appointed artistic director. The difficulties arose already from the beginning.

First, there were problems with the repertory. In order to prove its loyalty to the regime, the theater was forced to stage Soviet plays. However, in these plays the so-called enemies of the people who were presented in an impressive and colorful manner face off the "decent heroes" who rebel against their old lives, or enthusiastically build new ones, and these are likewise dull. An artist who senses the inanity of a concept will not dare admit it, sometimes not even to himself.

> I never sold my lyre but when surrounded
> By menaces from implacable fate
> Then I brushed the lyre so that it sounded
> A false note . . . [1]

The Russian poet Nikolai Nekrasov who penned these lines during the Tsarist era had no trouble saying what he did. In the present age, and for Jews, everything is more complicated. "The false note" may be due not only to dread at the fate menacing them but also to the artists' desire to be loyal to the Soviet authority that provided them with the conditions that caused the flowering of Jewish culture. They still did not know that this flowering would be short-lived.

They still did not feel, as Ostap Bender, the hero of a very popular Russian satirical work, described: "An atmospheric column weighing two hundred and fourteen kilograms presses down on every single person, even Party members."[2] So what is a director supposed to do when subject to such pressure?

And the actors? "The actors of this wonderful theater were adept at flying and grotesquerie."[3] Let us assume that they would change their comical colored patches for uniforms of workers but how would they move on stage? After all, it would not do to tumble and flip head-over-heels between the building scaffolds or production lines.

Now the artistic style had to be the style of realism. The actors were forced to increase restraint in movement, or try new forms of self-expression, new acting techniques. This tempering, which in conditions of absolute freedom would not have been necessary, would bear fruit, though not at once.

Naftole Hoz

The curtain rises and the play *Court Is in Session* (*Der gericht geit*) by Dobrushin begins. And it opens not only the new season at the GOSET after its return from Europe, but also marks the new era in its history.

On stage the scenery is still interesting, but this time the working-class audience sees "silhouettes of themselves in their workplace."[4] The hero of *Court Is in Session* sets out to rebuild an old mill and marry a non-Jewish woman. Thus, to the new Soviet audience, they present a new Jew—the Soviet Jew.

Zuskin's protagonist, the carpenter Naftole Hoz, is the first manual laborer on the GOSET stage. He is an old man but he is on the side of the young people building a new life. To rescue the role from shallowness, Zuskin knows how to open.

An elderly Jew stands there and works, exchanges a plane for a saw that he intends to sharpen. But wait a minute, what's going on here? The whetstone has disappeared!

This scene recalls the search for the scissors in *The Old Tailor*, although here the actor and his moves are more sharply honed. The scene is etched in the audience's memory, and now Zuskin goes on to cast a spell on the audience.

In general, the press welcomes the play as a first swallow of the Soviet repertory, but it is not happy that here is a craftsman who is working alone and not as part of a team of workers in a factory, and who is not even a member of the Communist Party.

Good Hero

In 1930–1933, the GOSET's new plays were written by Soviet playwrights only. But the old plays continued to run and to guarantee the box office revenues of the theater.

In the play *The Dams* (*Grobers*) based upon the novel by Hershel Orland, which was staged beginning in 1930, Jews and non-Jews, workers and farmers, all of them enthusiastic, dry the swamps and build dams. Add to this disputes between Jews and Ukrainians, between men and women, between foremen and workers, mix this all with a love triangle, and you get the required dose of socialist realism coated with a few Jewish characteristics.

Zuskin played the role of Yossi the hunchback who at the beginning works as an independent carriage driver and draws apart from society, and in the end rallies and—it goes without saying—enthusiastically joins the dam builders.

The 1930–31 season ended with the play *Don't Grieve!* (*Nit gedayget!*) by Perets Markish, poet and playwright.

Markish and my father. If the saying is correct that the degree of kinship between people is determined by the blood flowing not in but out of their veins, so there is no kinship closer than between Zuskin and Markish, who were executed together.

The plot of the play takes place in a shtetl and focuses on the struggle between the inhabitants who join a Jewish kolkhoz in the Crimean peninsula[5] and those who continue to cling to the values of the shtetl.

Here Zuskin is Mendel the independent water-carrier who becomes, with great joy—could it be otherwise?—a member of the kolkhoz.

In order to adapt the character of Mendel to the rules of the theater, Zuskin embellishes his manner of walking by using grotesque methods, and in addition inserts a lullaby as a recurrent motif.

In November 1931, in honor of the fourteenth anniversary of the October Revolution, the theater staged the play *Four Days* (*Fir teg*) by Mark Daniel who adapted it from his own novel about a real-life personality, an underground revolutionary activist named Yulis Shimelyovich.

The play has been considered as an attempt to create a new genre in plays, the Soviet tragedy, because the heroes of the play prefer to commit suicide rather than to fall into captivity. In 1952, Yulis's brother Boris Shimelyovich was to be executed as a member of the Jewish Anti-Fascist Committee, together with my father. In 1966, Mark Daniel's son, the writer Yulii Daniel, would be sentenced to imprisonment under difficult conditions for having published a satiric book in the West. One might say that the attempt to create Soviet tragedy was incredibly successful.

Zuskin appeared in one of the main roles as Stanislav Bronievsky, a Polish revolutionary and comrade-in-arms of Yulis (Mikhoels).

The Pole Stanislav Bronievsky was the first non-Jew whom Zuskin played, and it required a special approach to the role and in particular to the utterance: not to speak with an accent but to stud the speech "with a word of a national tone."[6]

The climax of the role is when Stanislav, like his comrades in the underground, prepares to commit suicide. With meticulous precision he straightens the hem of his coat, pulls himself erect, and goes down to the basement to shoot himself.

Would my father remember his Stanislav years later and envy him?

Bad Hero

The two plays that the GOSET staged afterward also describe Soviet experiences, albeit experiences that were considered negative according to the official propaganda line.

In 1932, the GOSET put on the play *Spets* by Yekhezkel Dobrushin and Yitshak Nusinov.

In this period's reality, "spets" was the nickname for "specialist," and it stuck to the engineers, the remnants of the Tsarist regime who were drafted into the Soviet industry and suspected of sabotaging the building of socialism.

Mikhoels played the part of the Specialist, "Spets," and he did it brilliantly. This was also the first play that he directed. The prevailing opinion was that the directing was not similarly successful, but Zuskin saw in it a basis for the future.

Zuskin had a small role as Uncle Misha. In a party given by the engineer Berg, Misha chats with those who ostensibly are sabotaging the building of socialism, and he woos the pretty ladies and dances with them.

Zuskin's other hero is also a person who does not accept the Revolution: Doctor Babitsky in the play *The Measure of Strictness* (*Midas hadin*) by David Bergelson. The play was staged in 1933.

Zuskin constructed the character around the sentence "I am a marginal person." He walks close to the wall, wears an overly long coat, and a wide-brimmed hat. Long hair and a thick moustache almost completely hide the part of his face not concealed by his hat brim. All this underlines his "marginality" in relation to the life around him.

Every bad hero that Zuskin played, no less than every good hero, was not fashioned as a stereotype of good or evil, because Zuskin showed not a formula but a human being. This gave him a sense of satisfaction, of course, but deep in his heart, he felt that such roles did not do him justice.

Film Hero

In the period between 1930 and 1933, Zuskin acted not only in the theater but also in films.

The Soviet film in Russian, *The Small Town Man* (*Cheloviek iz mestechka*), which was directed by Grigorii Roshal and Vera Stroeva, based on the screenplay that they wrote, was first screened at the end of 1930. This was Zuskin's first movie, if you don't count the silent film *Jewish Luck* (*Yevreyskoye schastye*) from 1925, where he appears in a scene that lasts only a few seconds.

In *The Small Town Man* Zuskin appears in the main role, David Gorelik. Like Yossi in the play *The Dams* and Mendel in *Don't Grieve!,* David is transformed from a small man—an apprentice in a sewing workshop who dreams of his own business—to the status of a big man, the manager of a Soviet shoe factory.

Why, in the Soviet era, which promises happiness to everyone, does a sewing workshop apprentice find his happiness in shoemaking? That is not so clear, but it is clear that Gorelik is successful in imparting, on a propaganda-paved conveyor belt, his inner truth.

In 1933, in the cinema studio in Leningrad,[7] the movie *Border (Granitsa)* was made based on a script by Mikhail Dobson and directed by him, with Zuskin in the main role of Arieh the young clerk.

The film's plot takes place in an Eastern European shtetl near the border with the Soviet Union. The shtetl's residents are split between the good and the bad. The "good" ones, poor Jews, aspire to the life on the Soviet side of the border, a life that seems wonderful to them. The "bad" ones, the town's wealthy man and his henchmen, do their best to annoy the good ones.

Arieh works in the wealthy man's office. The audience first becomes acquainted with Arieh as he sits at his desk, calculates figures with an abacus, and hums an improvised tune where words are replaced by numbers, and the pauses emphasize his total engrossment in his calculations.

During the plot it becomes clear that the subject of bureaucracy was chosen to show a dedicated, loyal, serious person. These qualities are expressed also in Arieh's underground activities.

In the closing segment symbolizing the victory of the socialist forces of light over the capitalist forces of darkness, and of the ethnic brotherhood as well, Zuskin has an opportunity to try out his beloved way of expressing the feeling by using music or song. Arieh, excited at the underground campaign, bursts into a song without words. First it is a quiet Jewish melody. Then it becomes louder, and when Arieh's Russian comrade begins to accompany the singing with his harmonica, the song, gradually through small musical passages, becoming something that could be either Russian or Jewish, resounds triumphantly.

The filming of the movie ended in 1933, but it was screened only in 1935.

Even though the plot is based on strict ideological rules, Zuskin did not allow himself to remain in a routine. He tried not to use grotesquerie too obviously, because that did not sit well with the Soviet authorities, but he found unique ways of portrayal that only he knew. He also discovered that the cinema even more than the theater required a concentration of all an actor's possibilities.

And so my father's long-standing love flowered into cinema art.

Yosl Bobtses

Although my story has already arrived at the year 1933, I am stopping and going backward. The play *The Deaf Man* (*Der toyber*) by David Bergelson based on his novel of the same name was staged by GOSET in 1930. I skipped over this intentionally because although Bergelson was a Soviet writer and playwright, the play refers to an era before the Revolution.

Zuskin's protagonist, Yosl Bobtses, is a person who demeans every-one—himself before the rich mill owner whom he serves as a clerk as well as those who are lower on the pecking order than himself. The actor delves into the personality of Bobtses, and in the end he arrives at this conclusion, that for Bobtses he can choose nothing but dark colors.

As usual, Zuskin paid attention to the external components. Bobtses comes out slightly hunched over, walks as though sneaking along, and his costume and makeup are also carefully thought out. Zuskin gave Bobtses protruding and even elongated ears, hinting at his habit of eavesdropping everywhere.

Bobtses is brought face to face with the Deaf Man, who is played by Mikhoels. The Deaf Man is a worker in the rich man's mill who has lost his hearing there. He is full of dignity and restraint, until his instincts burst forth and cause him to rebel. And again, edgy Soviet critics accused the theater of representing the rebellion by one man and not by an orga-nized group.

The confrontation between Bobtses and the Deaf Man is given em-phatic expression in the scene where Bobtses, using humiliating gestures, hints that the belly of Esther—the Deaf Man's daughter—is beginning to bulge, and not without the responsibility of the mill owner's son. Bobtses's laughter is malicious, a blend of screeching and wailing, so that the Deaf Man "hears" him by his appearance; then he bursts out of his restraint, jumps on Bobtses, catches him by the throat, and tries to choke him. The tragedy is highlighted by the force of the contrast between his strangling grip, which is potentially murderous, and the ceaselessly quivering, twitching movements of Bobtses.

Granovsky, it seems, not only understood the unique quality of the Mikhoels–Zuskin duo; he also guessed that the impressive power it had would become more powerful over time.

Anatole

The limited success of the plays by Soviet playwrights tormented Mikhoels and spurred him on to seek new ideas. Would it be worth trying something from the European classics? Even something lightweight, to be a litmus test for the troupe?

Eventually they chose the vaudeville play *The Millionaire, the Dentist, and the Pauper*[8] (*Der milioner, der tsahndokter un der oreman*) by Eugène Labiche, a nineteenth-century French playwright. Zuskin, as other actors, began to study: one must understand what a vaudeville play is and what was the social atmosphere in France of the nineteenth century and how to detach the actors from Jewish gestures and intonations.

The actors were actually happy because the play was supposed to be cheerful, and here they could act crazy on the stage and really feel themselves released from the Soviet tedium and especially, for the first time, act outside of themselves, rub up against the European experience.

The GOSET invited the director Léon Moussinac, Communist and Jew, from France. As his assistant, Alexandra Azarkh-Granovskaya, Granovsky's ex-wife, was chosen. The Granovsky couple separated while still in Western Europe, and in 1933, she returned to the Soviet Union. She worked as an acting teacher in the Acting School and was very familiar with the French theater.

During the first reading of the play, Zuskin immediately fell in love with the character Anatole-the-Pauper. He discovered that deeply etched into his memory were the idlers who loitered in Paris on the Saint-Martin

Boulevard opposite the theater where the GOSET appeared. Zuskin wanted to give free rein to these idlers, as in previous roles, he had done for characters from his childhood.

And indeed, Zuskin took the part of Anatole-the-Pauper, and Mikhoels, the role of Gredan-the-Dentist.

Eda was given a wonderful role, Agnes. She had been in the theater for nine years. She was accepted as a dancer, but now there were nearly no plays with dancing roles, and she played small parts. And now there was a big part that had a combination of speaking and dancing, and for Eda, it was a bridge between the world of dance and the world of acting.

Zuskin already ignored the fact that he was playing a non-Jew. After all, Anatole is that same little man so beloved by him, even if this fellow does feel at ease in a well-tailored dinner jacket, bow tie, and foppish moustache.

A wonderful friendship was forged between Moussinac and the troupe. In the spring of 1934, they began rehearsals for *The Millionaire, the Dentist, and the Pauper*, and in the summer, they stopped the rehearsals. They set out on a tour of appearances throughout the Soviet Union. Moussinac asked to join the tour. Afterward he would describe this tour with explosive enthusiasm.

On November 14, 1924, the premiere of *The Millionaire, the Dentist, and the Pauper* opened. Success! In those days the first convention of Soviet writers was held in Moscow, and left-wing writers from the West were also invited. The French writer and journalist Jean-Richard Bloch went to see the play and afterward he wrote a review brimming with compliments for Anatole, which were not connected in any way to the "proletarian ethic": "If only old Labiche were here now in Moscow! It seems to me that the elderly playwright would be captivated by the charm of this actor in the role of Anatole. Comrade Zuskin creates a character which has in it farce, and it is as though Pierrot had just stepped off the moon; this character is laced with clownish grace and melancholy."[9] The Communist Bloch apparently did not manage to escape his attachment to the concepts of the "corrupt West."

And Eda, what of her acting? "Agnes as portrayed by Berkovskaya is fantastic and young,"[10] Bloch notes in the same article.

Fool

When Mikhoels discovered that on the list of classical plays that were permitted to be shown on Soviet stages the Shakespearean tragedy *King Lear* was included, he announced to the actors that he intended to stage it. Most of them protested vigorously, and so did Zuskin.

Why is that? Zuskin pondered the matter. There was no shortage of talents in their theater. If the actors were not familiar with European culture, eminent lecturers could always be invited. As to the ban to portray a non-Jew he had placed on himself in the past, it had already expired. Perhaps a lack of self-confidence? Well, it is true that he was not always sure of himself, but deep down he was convinced that he could cope with a task of this nature. Is it possible that an actor who loves challenges as he did would not be won over by such an enormous challenge?

Zuskin had nothing at all against Shakespeare. Yet, he felt in his heart that Mikhoels's concept did not sit well with the very bones of Jewish theater as Zuskin perceived it in his mind's eye. When many years later a documentary movie about GOSET had been planned in Israel, as one of the options for the movie title they proposed *Shakespeare in Yiddish*. Then I understood immediately that this attitude—Yiddish is something inferior and Shakespeare is something sublime—could have offended my father who was proud of the Yiddish language. He didn't want his theater to prove that Jews are "also" human beings, to prove anything at all; he aspired to have the theater be true to itself.

Eventually Zuskin and the actors who were opposed gave in and accepted Mikhoels's idea and the opinion of the other actors supporting him, such as my mother.

When the roles were decided upon, there was no doubt as to who was going to be King Lear, that was Mikhoels; and it was clear to everyone that Zuskin would be the Fool, since Mikhoels and Zuskin had already proved themselves as a wonderful duo.

Zuskin suppressed his bitter thoughts and started to work. Bit by bit the role of the Fool began to captivate him.

According to Mikhoels, "Zuskin, an actor blessed with brilliant talent . . . is applying all of his artistic techniques in this role, one of the most difficult roles in the world repertory."[11] Zuskin, as we have seen, always sought a model to imitate. As the first prototype for the role of the Fool, he used the Russian writer Yuri Olesha. Afterward, he almost completely abandoned this first impression, and yet something of it was left.

I cannot bypass this first impression without skipping ahead. In 1969, the year of the seventieth anniversary of Benjamin Zuskin, in the Actors House in Moscow they organized an evening in his memory. Since publishing the name of a Jewish actor would not be encouraged by "the powers-that-be," the evening was within the framework of the series, We Knew Them Well, in memory of two different artists. On the outside posters only the name of the event was mentioned, leaving the names of the honorees to the playbills.

And the honorees were Zuskin and Olesha. I am not sure that the organizers knew of the connection in the hidden triangle—Zuskin, Olesha, the Fool. After all, this connection was coincidental. And yet there are no coincidences in the world.

Along with hunting down models to imitate, Zuskin rummaged around in his personal baggage and in passing found Jewish nuances that he could use in the character of the Fool. Sergei Radlov, director of the production of King Lear, agreed that the Fool would be Anglo-Jewish.

Zuskin was convinced that the Fool really did look bi-national, but this is only partially true. Zuskin was not aware of the fact that his Fool was portrayed as a universal character.

The noted actor and director Leonid Leonidov describes in his diary his impression of that play: "Yesterday I saw Lear at the GOSET. Very interesting . . . Zuskin brings his Fool to the forefront . . . I felt an urge to direct Shakespeare, perhaps Hamlet . . . and who could play Hamlet? . . . Zuskin."[12] A knowledgeable person like Leonidov was able to detect in Zuskin's Fool, behind the clownish mannerisms, the nobility of spirit and profundity of thought which were right also for Hamlet, the most profound and sophisticated of Shakespeare's characters.

And now let us also try to become captivated by the King who gives up his throne and the Fool who carries the throne with a bashful and loving heart; let us be entranced by the extraordinary performance described in scores of books and innumerable articles.

Let us imagine that today is February 10, 1935, and we arrive at the opening of *King Lear* at the Moscow State Jewish Theater.

The red and black curtain rises, the gate of the King's palace above the stage level gradually opens, and in front of the audience's eyes, the throne appears. Into the throne hall empty of its occupant, the Fool hurls himself with a leap. Another leap, and he is sitting cross-legged on the King's throne. The King enters. Quietly he pinches the Fool's ear between his fingers and slowly lifts him off the throne. At the same slow pace, the Fool slowly straightens one leg, then the other, and submitting to the King's hand, he slides down delicately to the feet of the throne, and placidly crosses his legs.

The Fool responds swiftly to whatever happens. His facial expression and body language reflect his feelings and thoughts, his attitude to the events surrounding him: He pats the King's arm to express his sympathy; he scratches his ear and smiles ironically when Regan and Goneril falsely flatter their father the King; he clutches his head with both hands when Cordelia the youngest refuses to answer her father the King's question of how much she loves him; he flies off the floor, straightening like a spring just released, and as a sign of farewell, extends his hand toward the banished King's subject Kent, and returns to his place and weeps mutely.

About fools one must speak seriously.

They do appear in ancient myths, in popular story-telling tradition. "In all of these legends, he is not foolish but rather clever, and he is also as innocent as a child and is always regarded as a holy character whom it is forbidden to harm."[13]

Shakespeare's plays are populated with the clowns or jesters—or fools as he called them—of the medieval royal courts. According to many historians, these fools were revealed to be wise. They were very involved both in the life of the people and the life of the royal court, and they had a noticeable influence on the king and his immediate environment. Zuskin adopted these characterizing traits for the Fool whom he was playing. "Presenting *King Lear* at the GOSET reflects history, and a commitment to history is also expressed in Zuskin's approach to the character of the Fool,"[14] a critic claimed.

In Shakespeare's plays fools always have some hidden meaning. In tarot card play, too. The tarot cards in their main pack are numbered according to a certain hierarchy. Only the card with the picture of the fool is not given a number: he is everywhere and at the same time, nowhere, but so long as the fool exists, the game is not over. "The fool gives the strength to continue."[15] In the play *King Lear*, the end begins when the Fool totally disappears off the stage. The end of Jewish theater in the Soviet Union arrived with the disappearance of the Jewish Fool, Zuskin. In tarot cards the fool is traditionally shown as he walks toward the abyss, and this reminds me of what my father said: "In the play *King Lear* I feel that I am walking on the blade of a knife."[16]

But let us return to the play.

The Fool is still weeping, but when the Duke of Burgundy gives up Cordelia who has been disinherited, the Fool's face clears. He leaves his spot at the foot of the throne, approaches Cordelia in the forefront of the stage, and kisses the hem of her gown.

The connection between the Fool and Cordelia is worth a story of its own. Why does Shakespeare not have any text for the Fool when Cordelia speaks and vice versa? It is known that in Great Britain during the rule of Queen Elizabeth the First, the period when Shakespeare lived and wrote, women were forbidden to appear on stage, and the female roles were played by men. "The actor who played Cordelia also played the Fool,"[17] was the theory of A. C. Bradley, the British Shakespeare scholar.

Giorgio Strehler, a twentieth-century Italian director who was renowned for being a commentator and director of Shakespeare's plays, says: "In the connection between the Fool and Cordelia, there is something of a mystery concealed from the eye but it awakens a suspicion that the Fool is in love with the King's daughter. In general, the subject of the Fool and Cordelia is most astonishing. It is hardly comprehended, it slips between your fingers."[18] Strehler says about the Fool's love for Cordelia that despite the fact that in Shakespeare, Cordelia and the Fool never appear on the stage at the same time, they do in the GOSET's play.

For me the subject of a connection between the Fool and Cordelia is very personal. After all, Cordelia was played by my mother. Unlike the relations between the Fool and Cordelia, my parents' love for each other was not concealed, but known to all.

During the GOSET performances in Paris, after a rehearsal, Mother was walking toward the hotel, and on the way, she met the French poet Louis Aragon and his wife, the writer Elsa Triolet. They were acquainted from before (Elsa was a Jew born in Russia). The three stopped to chat. Suddenly my father came running toward them, pulled out of his coat pouch a small bouquet of light blue flowers, and handed them to my mother. "Is it Eda's birthday?" Elsa asked. "No, nothing special, I saw pretty flowers." "It turns out that you are not only a consummate actor," said Aragon with great emotion, as Elsa translated, "You are also a painter! You chose flowers that match the color of your wife's eyes."

Zuskin studied from the books how other actors played the Fool in *King Lear*, including the greatest of all, the German actor Joseph Keinz. And to his surprise, he discovered that his own interpretation of the role was completely different. Unfortunately, Zuskin did not know what the philosopher Hegel wrote: "Shakespeare's fools are astonishing in their understanding of what is happening and in their genius humor . . . They are just playing the fool."[19] One may speak about Zuskin's intuition, while in truth, intuition and the quest for a model to imitate are only the starting points for Zuskin's work on his role. "Fool . . . indescribable, unbelievable! Only a rare talent is capable of such a thing."[20]

Zuskin-Fool and Mikhoels-Lear. Much has been written about this pair, but a study of this enigmatic connection has not yet been exhausted.

The contrast between them reaches a climax in the tempest scene. King Lear is standing and raises his arms to heaven, and in a loud voice, demands mercy. The Fool is silent but circles the King rhythmically, twisting and turning. The Fool's convolutions recall a whip lashing through the air, and they highlight the resolute stance of Lear. Thus they show the audience that the real tempest is not in the environment but in their hearts.

The Armenian actor Vagram Papazian says: "I don't want and I am not able to compare anyone to Mikhoels-Lear or Zuskin-Fool. Perhaps there were not worse than them and there might even be better than them, but like them—there never were and there never will be."[21] Gordon Craig, the British director and scholar of theater in general and Shakespeare in particular, notes: "Zuskin is excellent as the Fool, in no way secondary to Lear but an independent character in all respects"[22] after having seen the play in Moscow.

Each of them, the King and the Fool, has a unique personality, as the actors who play them have, although they are always side by side, on stage, in life, in death, and even post mortem.

Was it the right decision for the GOSET to stage *King Lear?*

Yes, and also no.

Yes, because *King Lear* brought dizzying success to the theater and changed it from a theater with a specific identity to a universal theater. Even as the years passed, when the GOSET was spoken of, they would speak of this play, of the King and the Fool.

No, because Zuskin's intuition was not playing tricks on him. The wave of the King's scepter and the jingling of the Fool's bells herald the beginning of the end. "In the King-Fool duo was reflected the tragic development of the personal fate of each member of the duo."[23]

The beginning of the end would come only thirteen years later: "First they murdered King Lear. They murdered King Lear in the city of Minsk, and the running of the theater fell to the King's Fool . . . For an entire year the Fool waited for his inevitable arrest. Later the family would learn of his execution. There was once a King's Fool . . . He once was and he is no longer."[24]

Mikhoels and Zuskin were to be treated as the King and the Fool so many times that the term "the King and the Fool" would cling to them. Under this title a play, a documentary film, articles, and studies of the two actors and their fate were presented, as well as the fate of their theater and of Soviet Jewry.

With this, it seems that no one would be able to get inside the relationship of "Lear-Fool" through which shines the connection between Mikhoels-Zuskin, than did Zuskin: in his article "King Lear's Fool," appearing near the end of this book, and through his Fool's song:

No joy awaits you but the pain,
My King, my blind man, my wise man.[25]

Who is the fortune teller here—the Fool or my father?

On March 5, 1935, Benjamin Zuskin was awarded the title: Distinguished Artist of the Russian Soviet Federal Socialistic Republic.

Pinia

1935 was a very busy year.

The play *King Lear* was already running, but Zuskin continued to work on the character of the Fool after having tested it through the audience's response. And naturally he continued to work on other roles as well. In addition to all this, he was compelled to leave the theater once in a while and without even dropping by his own home; he would rush to the railroad station in order to travel by night train to another city where filming was taking place for the Russian-language film *Seekers of Happiness* (*Iskateli schast'ia*). At the end of the filming, he retraced his route.

I was about six when my father said, "We are going to see a movie." Today, children don't understand that in those days there was no television and no video, and if there were children's films, they were very rudimentary. For that reason, I had never been to the cinema.

My father and I enter the cinema hall. So what's this? Father sits down next to me; he is not dressed up for the play and he is not wearing any makeup. The movie is about to start and here he is, sitting next to me as though he had nothing to do with it! Father, hurry, you won't make it in time! And my father is silent and smiles with great satisfaction. The last ring of the bell.

The lights go off. On the screen the subtitles appear and disappear, and a beautiful, slow song is heard against the background of endless expanses, replaced by the picture of a river with a steamer sailing on it. On the deck sitting on a ladder rung is a Jew of middle age in a shabby suit of European cut and a black hat that covers his forehead. That is Pinia.

As of that moment I sat entranced. I don't know what astounded me more, my father's acting or the fact that he was sitting next to me in everyday attire, and I could touch him and still see him up there, on screen. A few years later, Father told me that the opening of this role was his invention. In this opening, Pinia is asking a man standing nearby, "How much could a ship like this cost?" and to the question of his interlocutor, "What, do you want to buy it?" Pinia answers, "No, just wondering."

The question does not square with the speaker's appearance, which proclaims him as a man without a penny in his pocket, something that creates an obvious contrast, and the audience rolls with laughter.

My mother told me that when the theater was on tour in Odessa, a city known for its inhabitants' sense of humor, every morning a group of wiseacre children used to wake my father thusly: "Comrade Zuskin! We want to ask you something." My father would go out to the balcony of his hotel room, still half-asleep after his late-night appearance the previous evening. "Comrade Zuskin, tell us please, how much could a ship like this cost?" And the group of mischief-makers would laugh and scatter.

The movie tells the story of a Jewish family that arrives from abroad in the Soviet Union to the area bordering China. In 1928, this forsaken area began to become populated with Jews who came from all over Russia and even from outside, following a proclamation by the Soviet government, and in 1934, the area was declared the Jewish Autonomous Oblast (region), which received the same name as its capital city, Birobidzhan. The movie's plot takes place that very year, 1934.

The family at the center of the plot consists of the elderly woman Dvoyra, her son Lyova, her two daughters Basia and Rosa, and Pinia, the husband of Basia. They become members of a kolkhoz.

Everyone, except for Pinia, eagerly throws themselves into their new lives. Pinia, whom life in the capitalist world has "spoiled," refuses to work like everyone else and prefers to search for gold that, according to the rumors, abounds in the area. The search for gold does not bring Pinia happiness. The particles of gold that he seeks so avidly within the grains of sand reveal themselves to be particles of simple metal; he himself is arrested when he attempts to cross the China border.

The message of the movie: happiness can be achieved only through work on behalf of the Soviet homeland, as Dvoyra and her children do.

The happiness that was promised to people, who believed, like Dvoyra and her children, in Birobidzhan as an alternative to Palestine within the territory of the socialist state—the nature of that happiness is all too familiar. In real life the "good" heroes of the film, including Kornei, the non-Jewish fiancé of Rosa, would certainly have been arrested on a charge of "Jewish bourgeois nationalism."

Meanwhile the plot continues.

Rain deluges the shack that seems like a house of cards where Dvoyra's family is living temporarily. In the Soviet Union, it should be noted, difficulties were with no end but were always defined as temporary. Pinia sits curled up covered with the newspaper, and in a tone tinged with spite, he says, "What a beautiful apartment! Such a cozy summer home!"

When my mother and I were to encounter housing difficulties in the Soviet Union, temporary difficulties of course, or during the Persian Gulf War when my sister's home in Israel was damaged by an Iraqi missile, we would say, "Such a cozy summer home!"

Every morning Pinia furtively takes from the house a shovel and a large bowl, and on the pretext that he is going to guard the vegetable garden, he heads for the forest and goes down to the riverbank to pan for gold. One day Lyova comes to the forest, and completely by coincidence, he comes across Pinia exactly at the moment that Pinia is all excited at the sight of a bottle containing glittering sand. When Lyova asks Pinia what he plans to do with the gold, Pinia mulls over his answer since he has not yet decided, but after a short while he has an idea: he would buy a factory for shleykes,[26] and so, would become "Pinia Kopman—King of Shleykes!"

Zuskin-Pinia accompanies these words with his head held high and upraised hands—one signaling victory, another holding the bottle of "gold." But then his pants start to slip down because Pinia has no money to buy even shleykes.

In spite of the fact that we have moved away from Pinia Kopman a distance of many years, people who saw the movie *Seekers of Happiness* still remember, with a smile, the King of Shleykes who enriched the history of art with the unforgettable phrase, "How much could a ship like this cost?"

This propaganda film was to be remembered not because of the Soviet heroes, even though they are played by outstanding actors, but by virtue of the character who is rejected by the Soviet heroes. "The role of Pinia was easy to play by using all of the regular techniques, but I have seen Zuskin at the peak of the flowering of his rare talent, in the role of the Fool, so I am positive that to portray Pinia as Zuskin did, nobody else could have done that,"[27] writes director Leonid Trauberg. The connection to the Fool here is appropriate even though the comparison seems paradoxical. The common denominator between the Fool and Pinia is that both are supposed to make you laugh, but they both have an additional dimension, and they arouse poignant reflections about the cruelty of the world. The movie was screened countless times and eventually its quality was damaged. In 1987 it was restored, but I thought that to a modern viewer, especially a young one, it would seem not modern, and therefore, boring. So I was very happy that a young Israeli actor at the end of his watching the film in the late 1990s, and another one who watched it in 2013, were excited precisely by the contemporary quality evident in my father's acting.

In Moscow the film was shown from time to time at a movie house designed for the repeated screening of old movies. I lived close to this movie house, and used to see it very often. I remember that movie well, of course, and know almost all of the roles by heart, not just my father's.

When I imagine the moment when my father heard his death sentence, I see Pinia in close-up with the secret police officer. I see Pinia, his shoulders slumped, despair in his appearance. I hear the tone that cannot be imitated in his last line in the film—and perhaps also in the last line in his life?—"I don't understand anything."

Father

In 1934 fifteen years had passed since the establishment of the GOSET theater, and in early 1935 official celebrations were held in honor of this occasion.

Mikhoels and Zuskin were living all this time in the cramped dormitory on Stankevich Street. But the success of the play *King Lear* and the celebrations in honor of the GOSET had their effect, and in early 1936, the city of Moscow awarded both of them apartments on 12 Tverskoi Boulevard, close to the GOSET theater. Mikhoels was given one large room in an apartment shared with several neighbors, on the ground floor in the first entrance to the building—for him and his wife Asia; and a two-bedroom apartment on the third floor in the second entrance for his daughters and their deceased mother's sister. Exactly above them, on the fourth floor, was Zuskin's one-bedroom apartment.

On February 17, in the late afternoon, Eda was taken to the maternity hospital. By night, Zusa's mother-in-law and sisters-in-law received the longed-for phone call. We have a daughter! The daughter was me, the author of this book. I was born a quarter of an hour before midnight, and my official birthday in the records is February 17. However, since because of some respiratory problem my first breath was taken only after midnight, Father decided that we would celebrate my birthday on February 18, because 18 stands for the Hebrew letters *chai*, meaning *life*.

Eda was still in the maternity hospital, but workers from the furniture factory, admirers of the occupant's talent, were already bringing the furnishings and setting each item in place in the apartment. They did this in advance, secretly, so that Eda would not find out, taking measures and then manufacturing everything according to the spot where it would stand.

Eda had left for the maternity hospital from her previous residence, and returned with an infant to a new one. Zusa, beaming with joy and with a mischievous glint in his eyes, opened the door wide before her. Eda stepped in . . . her lips parted in amazement, but she could not utter a word. What a surprise! And the apartment immediately began to fill up with actors and friends carrying bouquets of golden mimosas. At this time of year, these flowers were brought to Moscow from the Caucasus and sold on every street corner.

Now a new way of life began, with three, and in conditions of comfort.

And yet, Zusa never stopped thinking of Tamara.

He corresponded with her and could not find peace for himself because due to the political circumstances, he was not able to visit her. He started making inquiries to find a way to invite Tamara to come to him. Eventually, even though there was no free passage between Lithuania and the Soviet Union, with the help of one of the members of the Soviet government, a Jew and Zuskin's ardent fan, an entry permit was obtained for Tamara. In the fall of 1936, she arrived in Moscow, at the age of fifteen.

Zuskin welcomed her at the railroad station. At home, Tamara became acquainted with Eda and with her little sister.

The new conditions astonished Tamara. In Lithuania she had a room of her own, and she assumed that if that were the case in her mother's modest apartment, then with her father, a famous much-lauded actor, the conditions would be no less. It turned out that her father's apartment was comfortable only from the Soviet point of view. The unique bedroom was used by the parents and the baby. The living room was also a dining room, father's work room, and the place where he rested between rehearsals. Now it would also hold a bed for Tamara.

From the first day Tamara proved to be a dedicated girl, bright and amazingly well-behaved. She played with her sister, embroidered decorations on her dresses, helped with the housework, and exceled at school.

Eda's worries about the projected difficulties in Zusa having to share his paternal affection with two daughters turned out to be groundless.

Zuskin pampered his baby daughter, while the older was like a friend to him. Tamara was still an adolescent but she grew up in the West and saw the Soviet propaganda as deliberate deception. Suddenly, Zuskin felt that he has a strong desire to pour out his heart to her, to be precise, to himself in her presence. So, he involved her in his doubts: With the sharp sense of belonging to everything Jewish, he was tormented by the theater forsaking its expression of this belonging; no, he could not allow himself to oppose the Soviet regime even in his thoughts, the regime that gave him his own theater, but "the heart and the wit do not meet."[28]

The younger generation was entering Zuskin's life and not only at home.

Teacher (Beginning)

As I have already written, in 1920 Granovsky's theater-studio was moved from Petrograd to Moscow, where it then received the name "The State Jewish Chamber Theater" (GOSEKT), which in 1925 was changed to "The State Jewish Theater" (GOSET). Although the theater's names, both the first and second, made no mention of the word "studio," the studio, or the Jewish School of Acting, continued to operate alongside it. This situation did not change until the GOSET went on tour in Europe in 1928. During the period of the tour, the studio ceased to function.

While the theater was on tour outside the Soviet Union, the Soviet regime did not remain idle. Institutes of education were reorganized according to a uniform method. In the fall of 1929, less than a year after the theater returned from its tour of Europe, the State Jewish School of Acting opened; its function was to prepare a reserve of actors, not only for the Moscow-based GOSET, but also for Jewish theaters throughout the Soviet Union.

It was incredible how many applicants there were for the school. They were mainly young people who had grown up in a Jewish environment. Even the auditions were held largely during the times that the theater appeared in areas with a dense Jewish population. These young people dreamed of becoming Jewish actors but generally had no concept of theatrical arts or culture in general.

Solomon Mikhoels, the school's art director, and Moyshe Belenky, its general manager, were convinced that anyone who intended to become an actor had to be an educated person. They put together a course of study taking into consideration this view. In addition to subjects such as acting, diction, music and singing, and movement, which are the building blocks of theatrical arts, the school also taught the history of art; Russian and Jewish theater and literature; likewise they taught languages. There also was no escape from teaching ideological courses as instructed by the regime, and so they also taught both types of materialism—dialectical and historical. What exactly the difference between them was—no one was quite sure. In addition to the regular teachers and lecturers on staff, there were also guest lecturers, some among the best in Moscow. Several of the courses were taught by the school directors, Mikhoels and Belenky.

Zuskin followed developments at the school with great interest. The high standard of instruction made him happy, and he was especially delighted with the way Yiddish was taught.

Students came from different regions, each one speaking a different variety of Yiddish, which was far from the literary Yiddish required by the GOSET. Zuskin spoke a Lithuanian Yiddish, and in GOSET it was considered the standard for linguistic correctness. Later Zuskin would write with pride: "In our theater, we work hard on vocabulary, on pronunciation, on the musical aspect of the language."[29]

Mikhoels and Belenky tried to convince Zuskin to join the teaching faculty, while Zuskin, despite his inner conviction of the need to create a reserve of actors from the younger generation, was hesitant. His prior experience in giving private lessons as a youth and an insufficient (from his point of view) knowledge of artistic theory, were not enough to allow him to teach, a matter of great responsibility to him. Nonetheless, he began to accustom himself to the idea that in the future, he would teach at the School of Acting.

And so, when after the first class, which was a three-year course from 1929 to 1932, graduated, the second class entered and the curriculum was expanded to four years, 1932–1936, Zuskin did begin to teach. In the meanwhile he was not on the regular staff: he practiced with a student or two, sometimes with a slightly larger group. He was as devoted to these practice sessions as he was to his roles on stage. And just as the audience took pleasure in his nimble movements on stage and was not aware of how exhausting it was to achieve this agility, so too his students enjoyed Zuskin's smiles peppered with jokes and did not realize that they were being drained to the last drop.

Occasionally Zuskin was asked to speak to the students. He referred in these talks to the actor's duties. He stressed that acting in the theater was a type of "sacred mission."

In 1936 Zuskin became a regular teacher. He was responsible for a regular class throughout their entire period of studies. In this class he would teach the art of acting and supervise all steps of his class's studies.

A true intimacy was created between Zuskin and his students. A glint of satisfaction in his eyes was more important to his students than their official grades. Zuskin taught at a stiff pace and his demands were many and uncompromising, yet he knew how to create a relaxed, informal, and friendly atmosphere, and peals of laughter frequently rose from his classroom.

The final year of the class, 1939–1940, chronologically belongs to the next act, Act Four, but because I wish to describe the academic course of this class in full, I will allow myself to digress from the chronology.

So, the last year of studies began. It would be devoted to preparing the final performance, and Zuskin had to choose the play. It was better not to choose one long play but rather several short and distinctly different ones, Zuskin mused, and that way every student could express himself on stage in diverse styles as part of one final project. He looked for appropriate plays in classic Yiddish literature, aiming to inculcate good taste in the students and to try to ensure that a rich literary language would live and breathe through their speech.

He decided on four works of Y. L. Peretz: a story *The Death of a Musician* (*A klezmer toyt*); two one-act plays, *Champagne* (*Shampanier*) and *Fire!* (*S'brent!*); and a symbolic romantic drama in blank verse called *Chained in the Synagogue's Anteroom* (*In poylish af der keit*).

Before the academic year began, Yekhezkel Dobrushin adapted the story to a play and abridged the plays and the drama. In the first lesson of this last school year, Zuskin announced to his students that the final production would be called *An Evening of Peretz* (*A Peretz ovnt*).

Zuskin built the work with his students on *An Evening of Peretz* as he built his own roles in the theater. How interesting! He was surprised to discover that he had some kind of systematic method.

Zuskin was eager to introduce his students to the dazzling world of Peretz and the enchanted world of the stage.

The final production was held on April 3, 1940, exactly twenty-five years after Peretz's death. *An Evening of Peretz* was very successful, and for a short period, they added it to the GOSET repertory. After this short period, most of the graduates were no longer in Moscow: they were invited to work in the Jewish theaters in other cities, including Birobidzhan.

Chaim Boytre

Poet and writer Moyshe Kulbak offered the theater a play that he had written, *Boytre the Bandit* (*Boytre der gazlen*).

The play had everything one could ask for: a Soviet playwright, Jewish atmosphere, devoted love, just struggle, historical setting. The plot takes place in 1829, during the reign of Tzar Nikolai the First, and it faithfully reflects a portrait of the period. The play also suits the world tradition of literary-folklore legendary heroes, such as the English Robin Hood, the Russian Stepan Razin, the German Karl Moor, who is the hero of *The*

Robbers, a play by German poet Friedrich Schiller. A song in *Boytre the Bandit* whose words were taken from *The Robbers* alludes to the connection between the two plays.

The plot begins the moment Boytre (Zuskin), having escaped from the army, returns to his hometown and finds refuge in the forest, in a shed that was once used as a small tar-producing factory. In his time Boytre was drafted into the army as a recruit.[30] This forced recruitment was initiated by Aaron Wolf, the town's wealthy man who wished to protect his only daughter Sterke from the courtship of Boytre the orphan.

Boytre disguises himself as a klezmer (Jewish musician) and enters a hall where the wedding of his beloved is taking place, and after having observed the scene silently, he takes Sterke away from the wedding hall, and hides with her in the forest.

This action by Boytre and his next steps, such as punishing one of Aaron Wolf's cohorts and attempting to seize the public coffers to help the needy sick people, attest that Boytre is capable of performing deeds of daring.

However, at night in the forest when Sterke and Boytre's friends fall asleep, there he is a different man. He is dreamy and sad, and he sings a lyric song. It is clear to the audience that Zuskin is trying to "present Boytre as a little man, an ordinary person who because of circumstances is forced to do extraordinary things."[31] By nature he is not a bandit at all.

In general, the play was given positive reviews, and Zuskin was praised for his role. With this, he became aware that his acting had ups and downs. In recent times he felt fatigue: rehearsals and performances, film shoots, teaching at the school, worries related to his disputes with Mikhoels, distressing thoughts about the fate of the theater, hesitations about his own course, and uncertainty about life surrounding him. Not everyone is able to cope with all of that, not even someone less emotional than Zuskin. "He said that he can't go on acting anymore and that he was leaving the theater,"[32] wrote film director Sergei Yutkevich while mentioning a recent meeting with Zuskin, who seemed to him like someone on the verge of a nervous breakdown.

About his wish to leave the theater, Zuskin was speaking for now in the heat of the moment. Very quickly he overcame his crisis.

On October 14, 1936, the GOSET began the new season with *Boytre the Bandit*, and in the audience was also Lazar Kaganovich, a Jew and a prominent figure in the Central Committee of the Communist Party and also a member of the government. He expressed his dissatisfaction with the play. "Where did you ever see warped Jews like these, with side-curls? He shouted furiously, and his words are given added power by the intensity that lay in the strength of his muscles and his towering stature."[33] Kaganovich's response to the performance also included a call to show genuine heroes on stage, the heroes of the past, like the Maccabees, Bar Kokhba. This component of Kaganovich's words affected the theater's repertory in days to come.

Boytre the Bandit did not have a long run.

Two months before the premiere, in August 1936, the media published the indictment in the case known as the Trial of the Terrorist Center. This was revealed as the beginning of the great wave of purges. Although in the Soviet Union there was never any period without purges, the new wave was like a tidal wave. Something was lurking, threatening, something that had not yet been conceived of, hovering over the country, and over the theater and its actors too, of course. The persecutions were not directed particularly against the Jews but rather against the elite of Soviet society, where the percentage of Jews was high since they took an active role in the Revolution and the institutions set up in its aftermath.

Of all the criminal cases throughout the Soviet State in this period, a minimum was directed against Jews just because they were Jews. Within the framework of one such case, the so-called Jewish Terrorist Center of Minsk, Moyshe Kulbak, the playwright of *Boytre the Bandit*, would be arrested in 1937 and several years later would disappear from this world. The play would be removed from the repertory of the GOSET.

Stage Director (Beginning)

For the first time in his life, Zuskin was about to work as a director. He had to direct the production based on the play by Mikhail Gershenson, *Hershele Ostropoler*. This play was inspired by Jewish folktales that were well known to Zuskin from the time he was a young child. Hershele is a merry, sly clown, trickster, and prankster who tells jokes, and with many wily tricks manages to take money from the rich and divide it munificently among the poor. The wise Hassidim praise him because according to their belief, "it is a great mitzvah to be always happy."[34] The same approach to Hershele appears in a work by Isaac Babel, one of the greatest Soviet writers who, although he wrote in Russian, related mainly to Jewish subjects, because of his Jewish origins: "What does a Jew do for a living? The rebbe asked, lifting his eyelids. I am writing the tales of Hershele Ostropoler in verse. A great deed, whispered the rebbe and closed his eyelids . . . What is a Jew looking for? Joy. Reb Mordechai, said the righteous man . . . let the young man sit down at the table . . . and let him be joyful that he is alive and not dead."[35] This is what Babel wrote in his short story *Rebbe*, where a Jewish cavalryman from the Red Army happens upon the house of an old rebbe.

Zuskin tried to breathe some joy into the play.

Most of the critics were convinced that the tyro director Zuskin could and should be a director. They remark favorably on the mise-en-scenes, the tastefulness, the humor, the rhythm, the fidelity to the eternal spirit of the people, as well as on the traditional GOSET's combining humor and hints to grotesquerie. At the same time, they ascribe these qualities mostly to every scene separately yet claim that there is something missing in the production as an integral whole—because of either the play, which is built from a collection of separate pieces, or the director's inexperience.

Zuskin was aware of his shortcomings as a director. After all, he would rather work with separate actors than with an entire production. Of the further directing attempts made by Benjamin Zuskin in GOSET as well as in other realms, the reader will learn later on in this book.

Gripped by Fear

The years 1936 and 1937 followed each other in rapid succession.

During those years, the arrests increased, particularly among Party activists who were not favored by the regime or who had incurred their envy. Among the detainees are sharks, whose names in the past had aroused reverence and fear, along with the small fish.

The Yevsektsia, the Jewish Division among the supreme institutions of the Communist Party, was disbanded already in the early 1930s. In 1937 Moyshe Litvakov was arrested and after him, Ida Lashevich, the administrative director of the GOSET and a member of many years' standing in the Party, and afterward two students at the Jewish School of Acting who blurted out something that was not allowed to be said in a large gathering.

After the superior authorities meted out severe sentences, applied efficiently, to the Party activists and to other people, they approached the intellectuals.

Actually, that is not accurate. The educated people in the field of engineering, the specialists (remember *Spets!*), had been dealt with previously. The writers had been instructed from the podium in their convention held in 1934 about what and how to write, because if they didn't . . . well, many others who wrote differently disappeared. Music was punished in January, and painting in March 1936. Now in 1937–38, they started to round up the last remnants.

The time of the theaters had also come. There were too many theaters, and so every theater conducted itself in its own way: one tried one thing; another invented a different thing. What was left to invent? Everything had to be just as in real life. If the Soviet theaters had insisted on showing everything exactly as in real life, they would have been showing mainly horror shows.

The extraordinary, unconventional-style theater under the artistic direction of Vsevolod Meyerhold was closed down conclusively in 1938. One year later Meyerhold would be arrested, and two more years would pass until he was executed.

GOSET seemed besieged on all sides. It would not be forgiven neither for the "terrorist" Kulbak and his *Boytre the Bandit* nor for the primal sin—Granovsky's defection from the motherland. Failure to understand what was happening around them and anxiety about the unexpected took up residence in people's hearts, and did not let up, even within the walls of their own homes.

Zuskin is no different now than others. However, more than many others he is consumed by fear for the fate of the theater: in the worst case, there will be nothing left to think about. More accurately, there will not be anyone left to think. And in the best case? Then what? What is projected for the theater if it manages to pull through? After all, their theater is different by its very definition. And now the theater has been ordered to fall into line and to be like everyone else. There is no point in staging Soviet or foreign plays, whose roles can be played by actors from any theater speaking any language. Another actor would be lacking that "something" that was passed on from generation to generation; without that "something," Shakespeare's familiar, universally admired characters, or unfamiliar characters such as the unknown Naftole Hoz from the play *Court Is In Session*, would never achieve such a thrilling portrayal as at the GOSET. And yet, see what happens in a mosaic: replace a few shapes with other shapes, and the picture might be less beautiful but it will survive.

And if he is wrong? If he just doesn't understand the spirit of the age?

Perhaps Eda is right? He knows that she is no less terrified and despairing than he is, but she has a strong instinct for survival and tries to convince Zusa and herself that there is apparently some need for what is happening and that he shouldn't see everything in such a gloomy light.

He recalls the period of Granovsky. Then, at the beginning, he didn't fully understand his style, and finally became enthused with it. The statement that Granovsky's theater was, beside its language, not Jewish, is wrong; it is precisely now that the theater is close to such a situation. Granovsky was wise enough to decipher the spirit of the nation. It is true, Granovsky's theater was ruled by an iron discipline, but this way the theater was able to achieve perfection, not today's punishments for every lateness to rehearsal. Granovsky? Even thinking about him is forbidden.

And Mikhoels? Mikhoels has too many public obligations now, beyond his work at the theater. He is too conspicuous. Perhaps he is gradually distancing himself from "the fashion that does not become obsolete over thousands of years."[36]

Mikhoels, for his part, precisely because of his adherence to a two-thousand-year-old fashion, cut corners where others tried to toe the line. He admitted to no guilt. He relinquished nothing of his worldview. Yet he did throw "them" a bone. He was required to condemn religion? Very well: "Socialist realism cannot reconcile itself to religion,"[37] Mikhoels says in one of his speeches, so that he can say in another one: "Man has no greater aspiration than the aspiration to knowledge, and no greater joy than the joy of knowing. That is written in the oldest book in the world, and the name of that book is the Bible."[38] There was a duty to demonstrate loyalty to the Party? Have it your way: "Our art has to serve human happiness. That is what we learn from our Party."[39] Except for the mention of the Party as necessary lip service, everything here is true—who could object to human happiness? Mikhoels was rewarded: the threats against the theater were removed.

It also helped that the GOSET acted as a kind of ace in the hole to repel the slanders of the West: Look, in the West, in Nazi Germany, all Jewish institutions of culture were wiped out, while here in the Soviet Union, they encourage the theater which is the center of Jewish culture.

Now the repertory had to be dealt with. Mikhoels decided to stick to the policy he had chosen: to continue to appear to conform while actually following "the old fashion," and with all of these acrobatics, not to lose a sense of proportion. Of all the statements in the field of art, he chose the one whereby the mold of artistic creations would be a national mold, while its content would be socialist. It would be possible to add to such a "mold" allusions to the glorious past or national values. "After the elimination of the censors of Jewish origin, who were knowledgeable about Jewish history and tradition, there nobody would be left among the political censors capable of deciphering the theater's national codes."[40] The new censors would see only what was on the surface.

If Zuskin is momentarily reassured, then it is only partially since because of the forced process of assimilation, most of the Jews in the audience would not understand this code, just as the new censors do not.

And what about Mikhoels as a public figure? Gradually but without reservation, Mikhoels is becoming an unchallenged figure of authority to the general public. Is it possible that gradually and without reservation, Mikhoels is becoming Vovsi?

"Running back and forth, as though we had been sentenced to it, moving was for Father a symbol of his existence split into two parts."[41] In these words, Tala, Mikhoels's daughter, would react to Mikhoels's living "between" apartments, hers and his own.

Zuskin tried very hard not to have those around him see him as chronically bitter. Similarly, his love of life and proclivity to joke, at home and at the theater, occasionally triumphed over his melancholy moods.

Rabbi Akiva

Mikhoels did not forget Kaganovich's demand to show strong and attractive heroes from the past. From the poet Shmuel Halkin, the wonderful translator of *King Lear* into Yiddish, he commissioned an adaptation of two plays by Goldfaden: *Shulamis* and *Bar Kokhba*.

From April 1937 onward, the GOSET staged the play *Shulamis*, based on a homiletic tale from the Talmud and reflecting the theater's attempt to arrive straight into historical Judea.

The play *Shulamis* had a long run on stage. Since there were also roles of animals, in my childhood I saw it several times, as matinees, and was enthused by its beauty, and by my mother's acting and dancing in the role of Abigail. "Eda Berkovskaya creates an impressive image . . . Her dance reflects the actress's ability to convey psychological nuances."[42] It was only the deceitfulness of Abigail that saddened me; after all, to me, the heroine portrayed by my mother should be irreproachable.

The subject of the drama *Bar Kokhba* is the story about the revolt of the Judeans against Rome in 132–135 CE. The revolt, led by Bar Kokhba, is a historical fact, and a revolt against oppressors is close to Soviet ideology. To even further highlight the theater's adherence to ideology, a certain modification was also introduced: the struggle of the Jews for their freedom was presented not as a national struggle but as a war for independence of all nationalities living in Judea. In the performance, this aspect is more obscured than in the written play: The scenes where combatants who represent Jews and other nationalities appear are accompanied by Hassidic melodies and dances. The concept is clear—if the audience's familiarity with tunes of the past is called into question, then the Hassidic melodies would bring them around to a state where the connection to the Jewish people is unquestionable.

The premiere of *Bar Kokhba* took place in March 1938. Zuskin appeared in it, in the role of Rabbi Akiva.

To prepare for the role, Zuskin had to refresh his memory and read things over again. Now he was already imagining in great detail the character of Akiva who was born a shepherd and became an esteemed rabbi, philosopher, and the mastermind of the rebels.

The text here, as in *King Lear*, is rhymed and full of hidden meanings. For example, when Rabbi Akiva addresses Rabbi Eliezer who believes the promises of the Romans:

You are, Eliezer, a blind man or a cripple:
Who will need the Torah if there are no people?[43]

In these words Zuskin's thoughts were also reflected: Who needs Jewish theater if the Jewish spirit is not still deeply rooted in the hearts of the audience?

In the meanwhile the theatergoer could enjoy the performance and the character of Rabbi Akiva. "Zuskin's protagonist," writes a critic, "has the dignity of the Biblical heroes, and like them, his movements are measured and imposing."[44]

Eda also acted in Bar Kokhba in the role of Zagyr the Greek woman who waits on Bar Kokhba's beloved, and she combined her talent as a dancer with her dramatic temperament, and also won praise.

The fears of Zuskin and Eda were somewhat set aside thanks to their success and satisfaction with work.

Motke

On November 7, 1937, the GOSET put on the premiere performance of *The Family Ovadis* (*Die Ovadis mishpokhe*) based on the play by Perets Markish to mark the twentieth anniversary of the October Revolution.

In this play, Markish succeeded in emphasizing one of the important values in Jewish tradition—family life. Ever afterward, in the GOSET Soviet plays, the socialist content would be poured into the national mold represented by family. In these plays it would be impossible to replace a Jewish actor with another actor, because there is a difference between family life and building dams or toiling away in a factory.

The father of the Ovadis Family, the elderly Zeyvl (Mikhoels) is trapped in the past. Yet he secretly pays heed to the opinions of his sons who are swept up, each in his own way, in the current of modern life. The plot takes place in Birobidzhan. Zuskin is familiar with this Soviet Jewish "paradise" from the days of filming *Seekers of Happiness*, but in the film, Zuskin-Pinia tries to flee the paradise while in this play, Zuskin-Motke, secretary of the regional council of the Communist Party, tries to shape it.

The role of Motke, I think, appealed to my father—he had an urge to appear in the role of a totally different character, one who was erect, attractive, neat, distinct from his previous heroes.

I would speculate that behind all this, he felt a need to play a man who was in control of things. Since he was in the habit of deciphering the essence of a character while working on it, perhaps he hoped to unravel the essence of an avowed Communist, and perhaps also what it represents. If so, he would get to the roots of things.

Shapiro

Zuskin was now participating simultaneously in theater rehearsals and film shoots, as he had been two and a half years earlier. In the period between the end of 1937 and the beginning of 1938, at the Detfilm[45] Studio in Moscow, they were filming *The Blue and the Pink* (*Goluboye i rozovoye*).

Zuskin returned to the cinema with a great will, and he loved the role of Shapiro. It was just when, before the start of the shooting, he received the sketches for Shapiro's image, he was disappointed with the proposed makeup—Shapiro looked like Pinia in the film *Seekers of Happiness*. In Zuskin's opinion, any resemblance of Shapiro to Pinia, even the slightest, might lessen the uniqueness of Shapiro.

Eventually, everything worked out with the makeup. And yet, the film, to the sorrow of its creators, was not screened. Some "someone" on some committee did not like the film.

They announced the end of filming in spring 1938. Not long before that, Zuskin was invited to the Commissariat of the Food Industries, which also supervised cosmetics factories. The Commissar Polina

Zhemchuzhina belonged to the Soviet elite by virtue of being the wife of Viacheslav Molotov, the second most important personage after Stalin at the head of the Party and the state. She was Jewish, loved GOSET as well as the actor Zuskin, and knew that he put on his makeup by himself; thus, she asked her guest to volunteer to be a guinea pig for the stage makeup products that they had just started manufacturing in the Soviet Union.

Zuskin hoped to benefit from his acquaintance with such a high-placed person in order to cancel the ban on *The Blue and the Pink* but Zhemchuzhina "claimed that she had to go somewhere" and couldn't—or didn't want to—even watch the movie.

Gripped by Despair

In 1937–1938, the years of the purges and the fear, festive events were frequently held much like parties given in London in the seventeenth century during plague years. In the clubhouses of the writers' and artists' associations, all kinds of happenings were organized. And those who were in charge of the artists' loyalty were happy to lend an attentive ear. After all, it was easier to eavesdrop on conversations conducted out loud and in a relaxed atmosphere. The male artists bought evening jackets; their wives, or the women artists who aspired to flaunt themselves before their acquaintances, ordered evening gowns at the prestigious sewing shops. These shops, owned by the service division of the writers' and artists' associations, were ideal places for eavesdropping.

During this time, Zuskin happened to meet some prominent Russian actors, and he suddenly felt like distancing himself from the subject of the shtetl. Actually, he wanted to distance himself not from the subject but from the cliché that was inevitably attached to the subject.

Zuskin feels trapped.

The theater that is still the top priority for him changes its mission statement. The truth is leading the way out of the "Jewish mission" there was Shakespeare. Thanks to *King Lear*, they achieved fame, as well as the possibility of inserting Jewish concepts in a creation that is universal. Through Shakespeare, the theater was raised . . . wait, stop! That is exactly the rub.

Through Shakespeare, the theater was raised to the heights? Absolutely. But Zuskin sees in his mind's eye specifically one line in an old and generally favorable review on the production of *King Lear*: "The GOSET theater has apparently entered a period of self-abnegation."[46] At the time, he ignored that line, but it remained buried somewhere in his mind.

Zuskin continues to muse: if it is impossible to fuse his being an actor and a Jew, and if dealing with a Shakespearean play is to some extent an escape—really, why not escape? For instance, into the field of cinema.

Zuskin was interested in becoming a part of the film industry as a regular actor, and therefore he wanted to speak to the President of the Committee of Cinematography, Semyon Dukelsky.

A representative of the Party's Central Committee that oversaw cinema received him. President Dukelsky was also present at the meeting. He told Zuskin that the Party's Central Committee had seen excerpts of his films which were specially chosen for this purpose, and that the Party's supervisor and he himself had no objection to Zuskin moving from the field of theater to cinema.

Boyarsky, the representative of the Committee of Artistic Affairs who was responsible for the GOSET, was not willing to even hear of Zuskin's resigning because the GOSET repertory and the prestige of the theater depended upon him. Boyarsky refused to approve Zuskin's request, but as a friend, suggested that he take a long vacation. This polite but definitive "No," which left no room for appeal, cast Zuskin into despair.

Eight months pass and Zuskin refuses offers of new roles, and he also appears infrequently on stage. He continues to work full time only at the School of Acting. At home, he is undertaking a therapeutic process and at the end of the process again finds himself back on stage. At the beginning of this eight-month period, Zuskin is filled with a sharp bitterness because of the refusal to release him from the theater.

If he had left, he would be far from the stress inside the theater, from the dread of the unexpected in its future; he would not be upset because of the absences of Mikhoels. The fact that Mikhoels gives expression to his gifts in official areas outside the theater may be explained by his desires to bring salvation to the theater and to his people. It is possible. Until the appointed time. But Zuskin, who is indifferent to social connections, is bothered by Mikhoels's involvement and that of his wife Asia in societal life. Is Mikhoels swept into this only as the escort of his beloved wife or perhaps is he himself seeking glory? Or is this how Mikhoels is trying to divert himself?

With time the hue of Zuskin's thoughts grow paler and become less gloomy. In his mind's eye, he ponders his career in the theater. He never had it easy, and yet he had times of exultation, of a sense of soaring and of freedom to create. When was the climax of his happiness in the GOSET? Ah, yes, of course! In the performances of *The Travels of Benjamin the Third*. What song was sung there? Here it is:

> We sat before a luscious plate
> We sat and saw but never ate.

We. How did he dare forget the "we"? If he had left, he would not be facing a most brilliant partner. "The greater the actor opposite whom you act, the greater is his contribution to the way that you act. I was fortunate: fate brought Solomon Mikhoels to be my partner on stage."[47] Zuskin would write these words in 1946, close to the end of his life, a real life and not that which was forced upon him during the interrogations and trial.

Spectator

After *The Family Ovadis* was staged, GOSET intended to present an additional play whose plot also takes place in the bosom of the family.

But the theater had to stop the process of designing the family history and deal with a fairly tedious play that they were "recommended" to stage. The play in question is entitled *Restless Old Age* (*Umruike elter*), and it is about a scientist who was serving the tsar and after the Revolution devotes his knowledge to the welfare of the proletariat. This play, whose production was by way of paying off some kind of ideological debt, was not a success.

We have no interest in it either, since Zuskin did not act there, but what is interesting is his role as a spectator. My mother told me, in retrospect, that Father was not happy with the interpretation given by his colleague Daniel Finkelkraut to the colleague's protagonist, Scientist Polezhaev, the play's hero. Father did not see in Scientist Polezhaev as portrayed by this actor any passion for plants, while Polezhaev was a researcher in the field of botany. According to Mother, Father used to remember how his elderly mathematics teacher in Yekaterinburg's college would treat utterly abstract, extremely small variables as though they were living souls or the heroes of a drama, this one a hero, the other a heroine. So, Father was sorry that Polezhaev had demonstrated no similar emotion.

On November 27, 1938, the GOSET staged the premier of *Tevye the Dairyman* (*Tevye der milkhiker*) based on Sholem Aleichem. Mikhoels directed the performance and played the main character, Tevye.

The role of Tevye, the aging, clever dairyman, was the last role of the great Jewish actor Solomon Mikhoels, and in it he reached the peak of his achievements on the theater stage.

Zuskin did not act here, he was just evaluating the play, and he was positive that the theater created an impressive production. With this, something was bothering him—the hall. What was disturbing about the hall? Where was that noise coming from? Although it was minor, even muffled, it didn't stop. Why, it was clear! In the play *Tevye the Dairyman* every word is a pearl. But the most of the audience did not understand Yiddish, while others in the audience were translating the pearls in the play and at the same time, explaining some concepts, or the meaning of some movements. For example, Mikhoels "cries out to the national memory"[48] by raising his arms in a gesture reminiscent of prayer. But for the spectator, the traces leading to the roots of national tradition had already been wiped out of memory.

Now the men and women of the GOSET were already preparing for the twentieth anniversary of the GOSET. Rumors flew that there were to be great celebrations, that titles would be handed out, and awards of distinction.

So perhaps he, Zuskin, was mistaken? Perhaps nevertheless there was yet a place for the theater?

7

Third Interlude

MARCH 4, 1952
PRELIMINARY INVESTIGATION
INTERROGATION OF BENJAMIN ZUSKIN

INVESTIGATOR. You said that the theater is a nest of nationalism.
ZUSKIN. Yes.
INVESTIGATOR. Tell us about your crimes.
ZUSKIN. I was absorbed in my work as an actor.[1]

JUNE 11–12, 1952
TRIAL
TESTIMONY BY BENJAMIN ZUSKIN

CHAIRMAN. What is your connection to the Jewish School of Acting?
ZUSKIN. I was a teacher there.[2]

JANUARY 11, 1949
PRELIMINARY INVESTIGATION
INTERROGATION OF BENJAMIN ZUSKIN

INVESTIGATOR. Do you plead guilty to conducting anti-Soviet nation-
    alistic activity?
ZUSKIN. Yes. I held sentiments against Soviet power and was in con-
    tact with the nationalistic underground.[3]

JUNE 11–12, 1952
TRIAL
TESTIMONY BY BENJAMIN ZUSKIN

CHAIRMAN. You stated that . . . you embarked on a hostile and anti-
Soviet path.
ZUSKIN. I categorically deny that.[4]

DECEMBER 24, 1949
PRELIMINARY INVESTIGATION
INTERROGATION OF BENJAMIN ZUSKIN

INVESTIGATOR. You were a member of the Jewish Anti-Fascist
Committee.
ZUSKIN. It is true.[5]

JUNE 11–12, 1952
TRIAL
TESTIMONY BY BENJAMIN ZUSKIN

ZUSKIN. I worked in the theater, the cinema, and even at the club of
the Ministry of State Security, and I produced the performance
given by the border guards' ensemble. There you have it, my
entire life.[6]

I'd like to describe . . . things that are not found in the forty-
two volumes of the Investigation File.[7]
CHAIRMAN. You yourself wrote articles? What was nationalistic and
slanderous in these articles?
ZUSKIN. Absolutely nothing . . . How could I not write when people
were weeping with joy that they had been awarded.[8]

1. Zuskin, 1938.

2. Zuskin as the Sorceress
in *The Sorceress*, 1922.

3. Leybe and Chaya Zuskin, 1945.

4. Zuskin, 1908.

5. Zuskin, 1921.

6. Zuskin (left) and Solomon Mikhoels, 1924. Mikhoels's likeness
reproduced with permission by Mikhoels's daughters, Natalia Vovsi-
Mikhoels and Nina Mikhoels.

7. Zuskin as Prince von Flasco Drigo in *Three Jewish Raisins,* 1924.

8. Zuskin as Soloveychik the Shadkhen in *Two Hundred Thousand,* 1923.

9. Zuskin as Second Badkhen (left) and Solomon Mikhoels as First Badkhen in *By Night at the Old Marketplace*, 1926. Mikhoels's likeness reproduced with permission by Mikhoels's daughters, Natalia Vovsi-Mikhoels and Nina Mikhoels.

10. Zuskin as Sholem the Shadkhen in *The Divorce Paper*, 1923.

11. Zuskin and Eda Berkovskaya, 1934.

12. Eda Berkovskaya in *The Tenth Commandment*, 1926.

13. Zuskin as Senderl (left) and Solomon Mikhoels as Benjamin, *The Travels of Benjamin the Third*, 1927. Mikhoels's likeness reproduced with permission by Mikhoels's daughters, Natalia Vovsi-Mikhoels and Nina Mikhoels.

14. Zuskin as Friedl in
The Tenth Commandment,
1926.

15. Zuskin, 1928.

16. Zuskin as Senderl in *The Travels of Benjamin the Third*, Moscow, 1927.

17. Zuskin as Naftole Hoz in *Court Is in Session*, 1929.

18. Zuskin as Solomon Maimon in *Solomon Maimon*, 1940.

19. Zuskin as Uncle Misha in *Spets*, 1932.

20. Zuskin (left) and Solomon Mikhoels, 1930. Mikhoels's likeness reproduced with permission by Mikhoels's daughters, Natalia Vovsi-Mikhoels and Nina Mikhoels.

21. Zuskin as Yosl Bobtzes in *The Deaf Man*, 1930.

22. Zuskin as Arieh in the film, *Border*, 1933.

23. Eda Berkovskaya as Agnes in *The Millionaire, the Dentist, and the Pauper*, 1934.

24. Zuskin as Anatole in *The Millionaire, the Dentist, and the Pauper*, 1934.

25. Solomon Mikhoels as King Lear in *King Lear*, 1935. Mikhoels's likeness reproduced with permission by Mikhoels's daughters, Natalia Vovsi-Mikhoels and Nina Mikhoels.

26. Eda Berkovskaya and Zuskin, 1938.

27. Zuskin as the Fool in *King Lear*, 1935.

28. Zuskin as Pinia
in the scene: "Pinia
Kopman—King
of Shleykes!" in
the film *Seekers of
Happiness*, 1935.

29. Zuskin as Hotsmakh in *The Wandering Stars*, 1940.

30. Zuskin as Kabtsenzon in
The Capricious Bride, 1944.

31. Zuskin as Liakhovich in *The Tumultuous Forest*, 1947.

32. Eda Berkovskaya, 1941.

33. Zuskin, 1941.

34. Zuskin as Reb Yekl in
Freylekhs, 1945.

35. Dr. Tamara Platt (born Zuskin), 1987. Tamara's likeness reproduced with her permission.

36. Author in Zuskin's former dressing room in GOSET, 1999.

37. Eda Berkovskaya as Marketplace Dancer in *The Sorceress* (new adaptation), 1948.

38. Memorial to the JAC members executed Aug. 12, 1952. Established in Jerusalem, Israel, in 1978. Photograph by author.

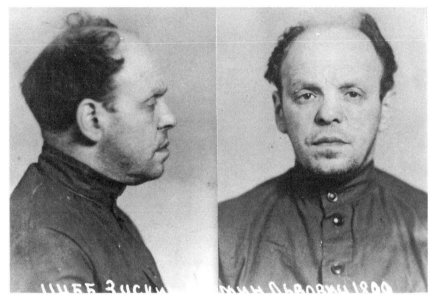

39. Zuskin in jail, 1948, *Stalin's Secret Pogrom*, eds. Rubenstein and Naumov, Yale University Press, 2000, photo gallery after page 64. Courtesy of Yale University Press.

40. Zuskin as Reb Yekl in the final scene: "Blow out the candles!/Blot out the sorrow!" in *Freylekhs*, 1945.

8

Act Four
(1939–1947)

Prize Laureate

In honor of the GOSET's twentieth anniversary, telegrams, letters, and phone calls arrived at the theater from all over the Soviet Union, and congratulations were published in the press and broadcast on the radio— countless good wishes.

On March 31, 1939, a decree was issued by the Soviet government awarding prestigious titles, orders, and decorations to many on the theater's staff. Solomon Mikhoels was awarded the title: "People's Artist of the Soviet Union," and Order of Lenin; Zuskin and Pulver, the musical director of the theater and the in-house conductor, were each awarded the title "People's Artist of the Russian Soviet Federal Socialistic Republic" and Order of the Red Banner. Several of the actors were awarded the title of "Distinguished Artists of the Russian Soviet Federal Socialistic Republic" and medals.

The festive evening was held in the GOSET building. Actors from the finest theaters in Moscow and in other cities participated. The evening was organized as a theatrical event and ended with a huge ball.

The newly decorated honorees were invited to the Kremlin, where Mikhail Kalinin, president of the Supreme Council of the Soviet Union, awarded certificates, decorations, or medals. At the reception held after the ceremony, Kalinin and his assistants noted the achievements of the theater as part of Soviet art. About the unique nature of the theater as representing the culture of a specific nationality—there was not a word.

The actors and actresses left the Kremlin, excited by the awards, and Zuskin was also smiling, exchanging jokes with his friends. Suddenly the doubts that had gnawed at him awoke, and in a sharp flash the realization that there was no longer a need for the theater flickered in his mind.

Teacher (End)

If there was no need for the theater, then why cultivate the next generation?

Although he, Zuskin, was a truthful person, he was forced to deceive these boys and girls who planned to study theatrical art. Yes, they were full of hope, and he was promising them a future that was connected to the Jewish art, but what kind of future did the theater have, and did they need him? Especially those for whom the connection to Jewish values or the Yiddish language was not inherent as it had been for his own generation?

Zuskin had just returned to work at the school after the vacation, and he already submitted his letter of resignation. Mikhoels and Belenky were not even willing to hear of it, especially not now in 1939, the last year of studies for Zuskin's class.

Zuskin was forced to continue teaching but made his consent conditional upon terminating his employment the moment that his class graduated. As we have already seen in Act Three of this book, he held *An Evening of Peretz* with his students, and brilliantly so.

Despite the success of the final production, Zuskin did not give up the idea of leaving teaching. He only agreed to serve as a member of the admissions committee for the incoming class. He dreamed of seeking out talents but was convinced that he would have to plow his way through a thicket of "assimilated ways." To his total surprise, the dream was realized.

And even more surprising was that the dream was realized thanks to the forces of evil.

In the Non-Aggression Treaty between Germany and the Soviet Union signed on August 23, 1939, the map of Eastern Europe was determined anew, and in 1939–1940 the Baltic States were added to the Soviet Union as well as the western provinces of the Ukraine and Belorussia. The Jewish youth in these states and provinces preserved perfectly the spirit of Jewishness that Zuskin so admired. Young people of a species that has already been forgotten appeared before the admissions committee.

One young man with a mane of wavy hair and dreamy eyes, at the emotional Mikhoels's request, recites Tchernikhovsky in . . . Hebrew, which is forbidden in the Soviet Union. The committee members eagerly watch whatever this young man and the one after him perform.

Now it is the turn of a young girl of sixteen. She is tall but looks like a girl who has not yet matured. She begins shyly with a story that she has prepared, in a low voice. Slowly her voice gathers strength and she is set free of her bashfulness. She is truly amazing! Willowy, beautiful, talented! She undoubtedly has that Jewish spark that Zuskin the teacher dreamed of finding in his students for years, and was disappointed of.

To give up such students?! No, he had not left his senses that completely.

On the first day of class, Zuskin had barely appeared at the door, and the students whispered, "Zuskin!" "Zuskin?" wondered the student Ethel Kovenskaya, the young girl who had astounded Zuskin at the audition. "I saw him for the first time in the role of Senderl. He was poorly dressed, miserable. And suddenly a man comes into the classroom, handsome, athletic, and then I realized the power of magic in the shift from the stage to life,"[1] Ethel Kovenskaya describes many years later. Ethel Kovenskaya, Israel Rubinchik (the one who recited from Tchernichovsky), and Israel Becker (who was auditioned after him), toward the end of their life, in Israel where in time they were to act, would describe first and foremost not themselves but Solomon Mikhoels and Benjamin Zuskin.

Zuskin was positive that in order for the teaching to be productive, he must know the people he is about to teach very well. And in order for the teacher to know his pupils, they must express themselves. Zuskin invented a most original means of expression. Rubinchik tells about it: "Zuskin told us, The first year you will not speak but tell something with movement . . . Only at the end of the year we were allowed to say, 'snow' and 'flowers.'"[2] How developed one's imagination must be to choose these precise words in order to break the conspiracy of silence that had lasted so many months.

Although the students were far from idle, they enjoyed the rare times when their teacher came late, because then, he would impersonate the people who delayed him or tell fascinating stories about them.

The students were apprehensive, and not without reason, that they, too, were likely to become a subject for imitation. This teacher not only teased them but also taught them to "steal," that is, to observe and understand how an actor approaches his role, and why.

On April 12, 1941, the teacher Benjamin Zuskin was given the title "docent."[3] The title was awarded for the success of *An Evening of Peretz* and the high standard of his teaching.

In June 1941 the first year ended for the graduating class of 1940–1944 so dearly loved by Zuskin. Several days passed, and the German army overran the borders of the Soviet Union.

The acting school, together with the theater, was moved far away from the front line, to the city of Tashkent, the capital of Uzbek Soviet Republic. There the second school year began in classrooms that were not heated, with a shortage of male teachers and students since some were drafted into the army, the students were hungry most of the time, some had no connection with their families, and occasionally the entire class was sent to kolkhozes or factories to replace the workers who were on the front fighting. It is impossible to disregard all of this, or otherwise one could not appreciate the efforts of the students and of the teachers, Zuskin among them.

Zuskin notified the class that this second year they were already permitted to speak. With this, before a student was going to express himself "in his own language," he must be "multi-lingual," that is, he must test himself in all styles. Thus, "he gave everyone a role that was contrary to his real character,"[4] recalls Rubinchik. Zuskin, despite the fact that he was gentle and polite, knew how to get what he wanted; for him there was no room for compromise in art. The curriculum in the third year was made up of working on segments from plays.

Would Zuskin's method of teaching leave an imprint on his students when they became actors? Rubinchik recounts: "In all my roles, I always had the thought, What key would Zuskin have found for doing this role? Zuskin was an extraordinary teacher. He was a gift of God. He taught us like Leonardo da Vinci taught his students, like Michelangelo would teach."[5] In this context I would like to quote here the words of Giorgio Vasari, sixteenth-century Italian art scholar: "Sometimes in moments of benevolence and nobility, the heavens grant one person a gift of great grace and with it, tremendous talents . . . The great Renaissance artists helped their students greatly and taught them as though they were not their students but rather their children."[6] The analogy with Zuskin seems perfect.

In 1943 the acting school returned to Moscow where the last year of the class was held. The class prepared *The Bloody Hoax* (*Der blutiker shpas*) based on a work by Sholem Aleichem as a graduation production. The plot takes place in Russia and it is about a Jew and a gentile, two friends in the gymnasium who decide to switch diplomas and identities: the Jew will appear as the gentile with his diploma which has fairly average grades, and the gentile will appear as the Jew who excelled in studies. During the performance, the gentile is convinced how hard it is to be a Jew. The expression "It's hard to be a Jew" (*Shver tsu zayn a yid*) would later become the name of this play in many other Jewish theaters all over the world.

The play turned out to be a very impressive performance, in terms of both directing and acting. Immediately after it was staged at the school, they held it at the GOSET theater, and it steadily reaped success. In the Moscow theater community a rumor circulated that Zuskin had directed an interesting play; among the GOSET audience one could meet renowned Russian artists who came to watch the play.

And so, the class of 1940–1944 had ended. Zuskin found it hard to part with his class. He knew that he would never have such students again.

He was convinced of that already in Tashkent. According to Zuskin, the acting school started to be less strict about requiring students to be devoted to the profession that they have chosen, and to Jewish culture and theater. Zuskin turned to Belenky and Mikhoels and renewed his request to be released from teaching. Mikhoels reacted angrily, "What right do you have to flee like a rat from a sinking ship?" There was no escape. Zuskin remained on the "sinking ship."

In the new class that began in 1944, the curriculum changed beyond recognition. The subjects were still diverse, and the teachers excellent, but they cut the number of hours allocated to Jewish subjects. Zuskin used the hours given to him for acting to instill in his students an appreciation for Jewish classical works.

Arn Friedman

Now I am returning to 1939, the year that marked the twentieth anniversary of the GOSET. In November 1939, the theater came out with a new production, the first after its anniversary celebrations, *The Banquet* (*Der moltsayt*) by Perets Markish, which was dedicated to the struggle against anti-Soviet gangs in the Ukraine during the civil war that broke out after the October Revolution in 1917.

Zuskin did not act in this play but Eda had a fairly large role, as Blumke the Red, a dreamy girl who carries out a daring act of revenge—at a banquet where members of the gang are getting drunk, she dances, and when the modest dance turns into an impassioned one she murders the head of the gang, "like biblical Yael who killed Sisera."[7] Markish, too, was happy with the interpretation that Eda gave the role of Blumke.

In parallel to *The Banquet*, at the theater they were preparing the new play, *Arn Friedman* by Shmuel Halkin, and Zuskin was given the leading role, Arn.

In the play the characters operate in a kolkhoz in the Crimean peninsula. Arn is a retired teacher who is enthused about his new life in the kolkhoz, in contrast to his son Lev who yearns for the small town they left. The play also has a confrontation between Arn and his daughter-in-law's father, who had been a shopkeeper and remains an individualist. At the end of the play, Arn is reconciled with his son Lev and blesses him as he is recruited into the Red Army.

Nathan Altman's stage set was impressive, and outstanding actors took part in the production. Nevertheless, it was so gloomy that Zuskin was afraid of drowning in its water. And yet he managed to float and to resurface above the water, to become a character who seemed to have walked off a propaganda poster into a "character full of life and convincing as both Soviet and Jewish."[8] Zuskin succeeded in combining the un-combinable.

Vulnerable Soul

One morning in December 1939 a disagreement broke out between Mikhoels and Zuskin. At first the dispute was conducted peaceably, because it revolved around a marginal issue. But gradually the dispute spread to other subjects and to the astonishment of Mikhoels and Zuskin, their voices became louder and more strident. Zuskin poured out his heart with feelings he had so far kept hidden, even though they were directed at Vovsi rather than at Mikhoels. Mikhoels was aware of Zuskin's powers of observation and understood that in some of the matters, he was right, but to admit it, and aloud yet?

About what was Zuskin arguing?

About Mikhoels. About the fact that he was too busy with matters outside the theater; about the repertory; about the distribution of roles in the productions, and so forth.

About himself. Now Mikhoels was not undertaking any new stage roles, and Zusa was the number one actor in the theater. Despite this he continued to play himself down, to stay in the shadows.

About Eda. She assumed that they rarely gave her dramatic roles and skipped over her when handing out awards because if they treated her according to her true worth, it would be interpreted as based on her special status as Zusa's wife.

Zuskin, who was sensitive, felt on the one hand that he had not stood up for himself enough and on the other, he blamed himself for behaving seemingly rudely toward Mikhoels.

The problems connected with Mikhoels would leave Zuskin's heart bitter and would surface more than ten years later, in the summer of 1952 during the trial: "Since 1939, I have not spoken with Mikhoels, I mean with Vovsi. I spoke with Mikhoels only because I was involved in the theater."[9] How could that be?

I am trying to visualize my father in the prison. He is shocked when he awakes between its walls from his deep sleep at the hospital. Under such conditions what else could my father have said about the relationship between him and Mikhoels, or Vovsi?

It is hard to decipher the relations that were formed between them over time in real life—even in periods of external pressure and fears— by means of statements that were made in the interrogation and trial, that is, in circumstances that cannot be called life and certainly not real life.

What a pity that excerpts from the bitter statements made by Zuskin against the late Mikhoels have been published with no explanation at all by those who wrote about the events in question—by everybody but one: "Mikhoels did not dare spell out his worries, not even to Benjamin Zuskin, his closest friend. Zuskin was more than a friend . . . He became nervous, irritable, suffered from insomnia . . . Zuskin, an actor divinely graced . . . a man who is a 'vulnerable soul.'"[10]

Stage Director (Continuation)

In 1940, the Nemirovich-Danchenko Musical Theater of Moscow contacted Zuskin with an offer, that he help its director Pavel Markov direct the opera *The Family (Sem'ia)*. The opera's plot revolves around the plot of the film *Seekers of Happiness*. The creators of the opera were not knowledgeable enough about the Jewish way of life, particularly in Birobidzhan, but they were familiar with Zuskin and loved his acting in the film, and they also found out that during the filming, he was a kind of "consultant on ethnic issues" to the other actors. "He generously shared with us his experience as a brilliant actor and his vast knowledge of Jewish life and culture, and his detailed and carefully reasoned suggestions, his insisting some fusion of lyricism and humor, were accepted by the actors willingly and gratefully,"[11] recounted Pavel Markov twenty years later.

In 1959, when my father was no longer alive, at the Actors House in Moscow, at a special evening to mark his sixtieth birthday, Markov was the main speaker. Later his moving speech was published as part of an article, which I use as a source for quotes scattered throughout this book.

Solomon Maimon

One summer day in 1940 Zuskin borrowed from the theater critic Joshua Liubomirsky the book *About the Life of Solomon Maimon*, which was written by Maimon himself. He explained that in GOSET they planned to put on the play by Mark Daniel, *Solomon Maimon*, and that he, Zuskin, was offered the role of Maimon. "I said to Mikhoels, The role suits you, after all, you studied the history of philosophy. Philosophy and the play are in different realms, Mikhoels answered."[12] And so, Zuskin started to study Maimon's book.

He was happy to discover that there were reference points that connected him to the character of the philosopher. Both spent their childhood in Lithuania and that is where their wishes came to fruition—Zuskin for the theater arts and Solomon Maimon for the science of philosophy. Zuskin was also excited by the fact that Maimon, a small shtetl man, succeeded, without formal education, to capture the peak of philosophical thought that was close to the doctrine of Immanuel Kant, and even to criticize the hypotheses of that eminent philosopher. After all, Zuskin, too, had not acquired his education in the art of acting in an organized manner.

The play indeed does deal less with the philosophy of Solomon Maimon (1753–1800) and more with the life of this philosopher. His life in the period of time described in the play is stormy and dramatic, and there are many transitions from one situation to another: In the shtetl—from a quiet family life to a temperamental outburst against a person courting his wife; from the shtetl to Koenigsberg, the city of Kant and the center of philosophical thought in those times; from Koenigsberg to Berlin; and from intellectual society to a life of wandering because of his unconventional ideas. Zuskin-Maimon makes a brilliant graduated transition from the fear and impotence that engulf him when he encounters the Berlin rabble to more complex stirrings of the heart toward these unfortunates, and back to the salons of Berlin where he is sarcastically mocking Moses Mendelssohn, the founder of the Enlightenment movement who had recently been the subject of his esteem.

Mikhoels thought that one cannot understand the fine points of philosophy by hearing alone, and he found it appropriate to present the Jewish philosopher to the Jews in the audience so that they would get to know him and to arouse their sympathy for him. Mikhoels made the right gamble. "The actor succeeds in turning the invisible process of thinking to a condition where one can see it and sense it."[13] Thus, philosophy and the play are in realms that are not so different from each other after all.

Old Bashkir

I have already mentioned that in Moscow I lived not far away from the cinema house that showed old films. Sometime in the late fifties they screened the film *Salavat Yulaev* for a week. The film was named for the man who was a hero in the eighteenth century and also the poet of the Bashkirian people that inhabits a region located in the Ural Mountains. The film, which depicts the life of the hero and the struggle of the Bashkirian people for liberation from the yoke of the Russian Tsar, first appeared in the movie theaters in 1940.

In this film, Zuskin plays a minor role, so minor that the name of Zuskin does not appear on the cast list but rather under the title: "Also appearing . . ." without noting which role each of them played. Only few know that Zuskin was in this film, and of those who know, not many would remember.

The film is an action movie studded with ethnic characterizations of the Bashkirian people. Salavat Yulaev wears a cap festooned with a fox-tail that waves in the wind, and mounted on a horse, moves across the screen striking left and right with his sword, triumphing over the oppressors and rescuing the oppressed. The film also has love and a tale of friendship. Could it succeed otherwise?

The tension in the film comes to a climax when soldiers in the Russian Tsarist army enter the village where Salavat lives. Salavat is taken captive and they move with him from house to house so that the inhabitants will either confirm or refute his identity. Loyal to Salavat, the inhabitants pretend that they are seeing the man for the first time in their lives.

When it is the turn of Old Bashkir, played by Zuskin, the residents of the village, the soldiers, and the audience are certain that the old man will turn over the hero because his son was killed on account of Salavat, albeit inadvertently. "You," the officer turns to the old man, "Look! Is this Salavat?" Pause. The shout of the young viewers in the cinema, "Don't give him away!" splits the tense silence.

Zuskin-Bashkir makes a clear gesture as if to say that he can be trusted unconditionally for those things that he is about to say; he looks at Salavat with a long studied gaze and then in a voice that seems filled with malicious joy, in his stumbling Russian he says slowly, "I see Salavat—I choke Salavat with my own hands." Again a pause. The tension in the old man's body and his gaze relax, and he says quietly and confidently: "This man is not Salavat." The audience breathes a sigh of relief. Salavat is released from captivity, and Zuskin from the film. Other assorted events take place in the film before its happy end, as is the fashion with action films.

In this minor role, Zuskin made use of all of his nuances as an actor. The role also served as proof of his opinion that an actor who knows how to apply correctly and in the proper measure the features of his own nationality is also capable of applying those of any other nationality. With this, he does not overdo the ethnic features. The great Russian stage director Stanislavsky was right: There are no small parts, only small actors.

Hotsmakh

Toward the end of the 1940s, I had already begun to see my father on stage and although even then my impressions were still not sufficiently mature, I think that I can report them, and also write about the thoughts they aroused in me later.

Which of my father's roles that I had seen was my favorite? I reserve a special place in my heart for *Freylekhs*, which was so colorful, so full of deep meaning; I related to it in part in the Prologue and I will return to it again.

But even more, I loved another play, something that made me accuse myself of bias, because my preference stemmed from personal reasons. I felt better only when I read that "another GOSET performance, less known but not less dazzling, is included in the miracles of the 1940s."[14]

My father also had a special relationship with this play: "In my roles I try to find features that are close to my heart . . . like, for example, in the play *The Wandering Stars*."[15]

The Wandering Stars (Di blondzhende shtern) is a novel by Sholem Aleichem that tells the story of Jewish actors in the period between the end of the nineteenth century and the beginning of the twentieth. The novel was adapted to a play by Yekhezkel Dobrushin, and the play that was staged in May 1941 was directed by Solomon Mikhoels, costumes and stage set by Alexander Tyshler, and composer Lev Pulver. The production ran until the end of Father's career, in other words, for a long time—perhaps so that I would grow up and see it and remember it? For me Father's role in the production *Freylekhs* is a summing-up of his being an actor, while the production *The Wandering Stars* contains an expression of his personality.

In this play, "when Zuskin's moment came, there was a silence in the hall, and everyone's breath was held."[16] These are the words of a critic. "Zuskin's moment" lasted eighteen minutes. It was a monologue that my father's character Hotsmakh delivered in the middle of a neglected storehouse used as a theater in which he tells the story of his life.

Zuskin's Hotsmakh tells of himself as young gofer in the theater, who does not refuse any errand including shining the shoes of the owners or the leading actors or cleaning out the stable. In Zuskin's mouth, these stories sound like echoes of what he underwent in his youth when he was in charge of whatever was needed—just to be in the theater environment and to breathe its air.

Hotsmakh gradually opens the fetters of his heart and with increasing fervor he jumps from role to role, reenacting all of those he had played on the stage. Now here he is, his eyes bound with a scarf, playing "Blind Man's Bluff" and singing, in his own voice and in the voice of a child, a ditty that has been kept in my memory from then until now:

Hotsmakh is blindfolded
All the kids have bolted,
Where are you, dears?
All of us, we're here!

Hotsmakh is eager to tell of an incident when they asked him to appear on stage instead of the actor in the role of the lover, who had suddenly died. Then, Hotsmakh has barely mounted the stage, and the audience begins to roll with laughter. The more serious the hero becomes, the louder the audience laughs. At the end of the performance, he receives blows at the hands of the theater owner: Villain! Why didn't you tell us that you are a comic actor!

Comic actor? Hotsmakh confesses that at the time he didn't even know what the word meant. But from that moment, he began to play such roles! "You hear me boy, you have just mounted the stage, immediately all of your sorrow and suffering dissipate like smoke and wind . . . On the stage, I am a completely different person,"[17] Hotsmakh says, in a voice filled with emotion, turning to a young boy Leybl who is listening to him most attentively.

As though bewitched, Leybl listens to Hotsmakh, and the audience to Zuskin. The audience understands that Zuskin is also telling about himself, and that before them is a work of art where, as in life, pain and humor are interwoven. At once, Hotsmakh forgets the bewitched boy and tells poignantly of his worry for his mother and his sister.

And then instantly he replaces the sadness with ricochets of humor; he turns around to Leybl in movement and song, "Come, come, come to me," the song of the Sorceress, who stars in the early career of Hotsmakh himself, of Zuskin, and of every Jewish actor worthy of his name. "How was it possible not to come, not to fall in love with this magical theater when the seducer is Hotsmakh-Zuskin!"[18] How can one free oneself of this enchantment?

Hotsmakh persuades the boy Leybl to steal money from his parents and flee with him to another country. "I interpreted Hotsmakh's character as someone who detects in the boy the qualities of a great actor and not as someone who is exploiting him,"[19] explains Zuskin.

With the money that Leybl steals from his parents, Hotsmakh sets up his own theater, makes Leybl the main actor, Leo Rafalesko, and appoints himself manager-director, Bernhard Holtsmann. As full of splendor and majesty as he becomes, he actually turns into Leo's shadow.

That is how the plot develops in the novel and in the play. "But, in the stage play the stars changed their course. Leo Rafalesko was astonished to see the person who used to be his fool, Hotsmakh-Zuskin, acting with total self-abnegation."[20] At the beginning of his monologue, as he speaks, Hotsmakh moves benches on the stage and arranges them in lines, like chairs in the theater. At the climax of the monologue, he sways on the narrow benches and these movements are truly miracles of acrobatics, and nonetheless, seem to be an organic part of him. Leybl is enchanted. He fixes his gaze on Hotsmakh and as though hypnotized, walks toward him, unwittingly, he skips over the benches, trips on one, and falls.

In the mind of theater critic Inna Vishnievskaya, who was no less impressed by Hotsmakh's monologue than young Leybl was, the benches awaken associations with the French play *The Chairs* (*Les chaises*) by Eugène Ionesco, one of the foremost figures of the theater of the absurd. "Much time will pass before they stage Ionesco's *The Chairs*, but in GOSET, Zuskin's chairs-benches have already taken on life, and now they have already told of fate and the fates."[21] In the play by Eugène Ionesco, an old man and an old woman arrange an endless number of chairs for guests who are supposed to come, although the two of them understand, as Zuskin does now, that the audience who is willing to listen to any message is rapidly vanishing. Once more here is an inanimate object—this time, a bench or chair—not in reality, only in a stage role, but in a role that more than any other reflects his personality.

The show keeps going. Leo Rafalesco and Bernhard Holtsmann travel to London and there Leo enjoys rapid success, while Hotsmakh-Holtsmann suffers a dismal failure, his love for and devotion to the theater shattering in face of his contacts with businessmen. Leybl travels to New York—without Hotsmakh. Hotsmakh is beset by his childhood disease, tuberculosis. Everyone leaves him, even his beloved protégé Leybl. Sick and alone, he must take care of his elderly mother and his young sister Zlatke who also loves Leybl, and who has also been abandoned by him.

As fate would have it, during the days when something especially difficult was gnawing away at my father's heart, it was precisely then that the theater staged *The Wandering Stars*.

One morning—already after the murder of Mikhoels—I saw my father pacing the room and memorizing the words of Hotsmakh's role. Suddenly, in a gesture revealing a hopeless anguish, Father actually threw himself at me, hugged me, pressed me to his heart, and together with me, continued to pace the room and to memorize the words of the role.

That evening I saw the performance. When Hotsmakh, gripped by pain, embraces his sister Zlatke, I felt something pulsating in me: in those days, despite my parents' closing themselves off, I knew that my father was despondent, but the depth of his despair had been revealed to me only at that moment.

It is interesting that the actress who played Zlatke, and naturally knew this scene inside out, was gripped that evening by a tangible fear for her partner, my father.

In principle, if my father imprinted his role with traits and characteristics of various people or feelings that were his own, whatever the role, the result was never a patchwork cloth but rather a complete fabric. It was only that this "complete fabric" was more painful when the pain in my father's soul was too difficult to bear.

But even feelings must have theatrical expression, and here again an inanimate object came to the rescue. When Hotsmakh lies on the sofa, ill and abandoned, his face is covered by a black scarf, and when he bestirs himself for a moment from the despondency, and hope ignites in his heart, the scarf is waved on high triumphantly. And then Hotsmakh is returned to reality, and in his heart is the realization that he will never mount the stage again, and with the words, "The doctors say that I need rest, air, and the sea . . . For what . . . without the theater?"[22] he winds the scarf around his neck—as though it were a noose.

For my father, these words of Hotsmakh were like the motif of the role and—I think—of his own life.

And yet the role has not yet come to an end. There is still room for laughter and dancing. He begins with the eternal song of the Sorceress, "Come, come, come to me," and this song sounds like sorcery. The song ends. Hotsmakh is gathered to his fathers, but the sorcery remains and envelops us.

Prophet

Sorcery. It does not seem a coincidence to me that my father became an acclaimed actor because of his role as the Sorceress. My father had a kind of sorcery-lore that helped him penetrate the past, feel the present with all his might, and guess-predict the future.

When it occurred to me that my father knew how to convey messages from the past using expressions of the present, I remembered an old television transmission where a famous Soviet musician was stating decisively that in the modern age, one can listen to Bach's music and understand it only if it is played at an accelerated tempo in comparison with the time when the composer lived. It is clear that the speed of the tempo is relevant to the music. In the theater, Zuskin adopted other precise techniques with which his audience could absorb with their senses the echoes of the past.

And of the future, too. "Zuskin was one of the first to hear the distant rumblings beneath the surface that announce the coming catastrophe . . . the omens portending evil in days that appear serene and calm."[23]

Many people take notice of Zuskin's intuition. As for Zuskin himself, he thought that it served him only as starting point for his work on a role or for his considerations in finding his way in life. Even so, if intuition is the ability to instantly penetrate the essence of things, then it is a unique quality from which sorcery, vision, and prophecy stem.

These verses from the Bible come to my mind: "A band of prophets coming down from the high place with a psaltery, and a timbrel, and a pipe, and a harp, before them; and they will be prophesying" (1 Sam. 10:5) . . . "Then the people said one to another: 'What is this that is come unto the son of Kish? Is Saul also among the prophets?'" (1 Sam. 10:11).

Would it be a vain thought that the actor is a prophet?

Man and War (Beginning)

Like every summer, Zusa and Eda and the GOSET people went on tour.

On Sunday, June 22, 1941, the day that the German army invaded the Soviet Union, they were in the city of Kharkov in the Ukraine. Mikhoels and the administrative staff of the theater began to race between the local authorities in Kharkov to find out what to do. The other GOSET members waited, panic-stricken, in their hotel rooms until Mikhoels returned and told them that the next day they would be returning to Moscow.

And in Moscow that same day that the Nazis invaded, Tamara, train ticket in her pocket, was packing her suitcases. Lithuania, as one of the three Baltic States, was annexed to the Soviet Union following the Non-Aggression Treaty signed between the Soviet Union and Germany, and so from 1940 it became an integral part of the Soviet Union. Thus, Tamara's mother Rachel became a regular Soviet citizen. Now Tamara was studying in medical school. Just the day before, she had finished her exams and was planning to travel to Lithuania to spend her summer vacation with her mother. Suddenly she heard the radio announcement that war had broken out and the Nazis had overrun the western regions of the Soviet Union, including Lithuania. In any event, she went to the train station with the hope that her mother and her mother's family had managed to escape.

When the GOSET returned from Kharkov to Moscow, Zuskin found her at the train station, sitting and waiting.

One month later, German planes bombed Moscow. Activity in all institutions continued, although most of the men were drafted into the army. The bombings took place at night, and when the women, children, the elderly, and the weak were sent to bomb shelters, the men who remained went up to the roofs every night to prevent the pieces of burning shells from starting a fire. Mikhoels and Zuskin volunteered to serve as fire fighters in the building where we lived.

They were equipped with hats, aprons, and fire-proof gloves. They undertook the assignment with a full sense of responsibility, and in the lulls between the bombings, they sat at the entrance to the roof, and the neighbors joined them. So they improvised some type of amusing performances to shake off their fears and to distract their neighbors from worrying.

It should be said that all of this took place in the evenings when they did not appear in the theater. The theater performances continued despite the bombings, and the hall was filled to capacity, because people came from all over to any place where one could ignore the war. In September *The Wandering Stars* was even staged for the first time in Moscow. It premiered in May in Leningrad.

In the beginning of August 1941, a government order was published under which all children up until the age of fourteen had to be evacuated from Moscow to safe areas. They were sent either to relatives, if there were any, or to dormitories. Some of my father's relatives continued to live in Penza, which is far away from the frontline of battle. My father brought me to his cousin Bertha and returned to Moscow. Almost as soon as I was taken to Penza, I fell ill and Father came to Penza to see me and to speak with the doctors.

On the night that he came to Penza, I was sleeping, and through my sleep, I made out the features of his face in the red-tinged blur of the nightlight, and heard his voice. He was stammering! I didn't know at the time that in moments of great emotion, his childhood ailment returned to him. Later, many witnesses told me that occasionally this affliction returned to him in daily life but never once on stage.

Next day, Bertha prepared a special welcome for my father, not without Lithuanian-Jewish delicacies that were Father's favorites: teigekhts—a pudding made of grated potatoes, and teiglekh—a mixture made of walnuts and dough balls in honey. The names of these two dishes are so similar that I kept confusing them.

Since then, whenever someone begins to speak about my father's difficulties in life or his stammering, I see in my mind's eye the room lit up by the red haze of the nightlight, and in my mind, I try not to mix up teigekhts and teiglekh.

Anti-Fascist (Beginning)

Zuskin returned to Moscow from Penza. The next day there was no activity at the theater—a vacation day. But Zuskin went there to work on refreshing one of his roles. When he finished, he met Mikhoels and the poet Samuel Marshak in the corridor. "Here is someone who can type for us," Mikhoels said happily. The three of them went into the office. Zuskin typed out the text that he didn't really look at but understood was some kind of anti-Fascist proclamation. Mikhoels invited him to attend with him an anti-Fascist rally.

Again, there was an inanimate object at a crossroads in my father's life. Again, it was a typewriter. And this time it was a crossroads from which there was no return.

Zuskin arrived at the anti-Fascist rally, listened to Mikhoels's speech, and realized these were the words that he had typed. He identified with every word in Mikhoels's speech and with the other speakers. And it was clear that they had not come to merely another meeting but to an anti-Fascist rally, and that whatever was said there came straight from the heart and penetrated hearts. Since the speeches were transmitted by radio to the entire world, the rally received its name—The Radio Rally.

In all the speeches the "central subject is Jewish solidarity, and the expression 'Fellow Jews' is repeated again and again. Ideas, emotions, and expressions which had been taboo in the Soviet Union for many years suddenly received the blessing of the regime."[24] Suddenly it was permissible to call Jews across the seas "brothers" and even to ask for their support; it was permissible to mention the tradition of the Jewish people and its ancient history; it was permissible to tell of the suffering of Jews who were sent to ghettoes.

At the August 24 Radio Rally, they had not yet announced the establishment of a Jewish Anti-Fascist Committee and no one knew yet that Mikhoels would be appointed as its chairman and sent to America in this role. Zuskin could not have guessed that his presence at the rally would be noticed, and that he would be appointed a Committee member. He could not even fathom that he, with his own hands—not by pen but by typewriter—had in effect signed his own death sentence.

Is it possible that this sentence might have been signed much earlier, when after he finished tapping out something on a typewriter (again a typewriter!) he flew through the air, riding on the Sorceress's broom? Or perhaps even earlier, way back then in the small city of Ponievezh, when Chaya Zuskin gave birth to her third son, Benjamin?

Resident of Tashkent

On October 16, 1941, the war took an unfavorable turn for the Soviet Union and rumors began to fly that the Germans were about to overrun Moscow. The authorities immediately began to evacuate its institutions to cities in the rear lines. The GOSET was sent to Tashkent, the capital of the Soviet Republic of Uzbekistan. Mikhoels made a detour from the road to Tashkent and went to Kuybyshev where the government institutions had moved. He was supposed to arrange the theater's documents and fulfill his public obligations. My father traveled with the theater but also detoured from the route to pick me up from Penza.

When the GOSET arrived in Tashkent, it became clear that nothing had been done to prepare for its arrival, and the theater was sent to Samarkand where it remained for five weeks.

We returned to Tashkent and lived there for two years. In the first two weeks we lived in a hotel where we shared a double room with theater artist Alexander Tyshler and his wife. Afterward we were housed in the apartment of an Uzbek family whose husband and sons were off fighting on the front and only the wife and daughter remained at home.

The theater building was located not far from the house where we lived, but the acting school was relatively far from it, and to get there took a lot of time not because of the road's length but rather because of the marketplace that the road passed through. The marketplace was bustling with people: Uzbeks wrapped in colorful cloaks were positioned near the stands tempting the passersby to buy no less colorful Asiatic fruits. Temporary residents who were on an enforced stay there ran about, to exchange for food the vestiges of their former ostensibly more elegant life which they brought with them from their now-occupied or bombed-out cities.

Public transportation . . . actually there almost wasn't any. Zuskin suffered from flatfoot and despite the overload of work, he had to organize his day so that he could rest with his feet up before the evening performance.

At the school he did not give up teaching, and at the theater he was called upon to exert his mental forces even more because Mikhoels's many activities did not allow Zuskin any rest. Mikhoels traveled frequently from Tashkent to Kuybyshev. Zuskin assumed that Mikhoels had important matters there.

That was correct. Mikhoels was busy with deliberations related to setting up the Jewish Anti-Fascist Committee that he, Mikhoels, was to head. The establishment of the Committee would be announced the moment the government offices in Kuybyshev were organized. Besides, Mikhoels was consulting for the direction of an opera in the Theater of Opera and Ballet of the Uzbek Republic, directing a production in the Uzbek Theater of Drama, and his fingerprints were detectable on whatever was happening in Tashkent in the various cultural organizations.

Zuskin didn't articulate even to himself his feelings that Mikhoels was abandoning his theater. Mikhoels for his part presented his activities "among the anti-Fascists and the Uzbeks" as a contribution to the struggle against Fascism and a payment for the fine reception that the GOSET was given in the city.

In May 1942, the second anti-Fascist rally was held in Moscow, and many public personages participated. Then it was announced that in April of that year the Jewish Anti-Fascist Committee had been formally established.

A year passed, and the regime sent Mikhoels and his deputy on the Committee, Yiddish poet Yitsik Fefer, to the U.S., Canada, Mexico, and England. The purpose of this mission was to capture the attention of the public in those countries, to marshal its support for the Soviet citizens who were fighting Nazis, and to recruit Jewish capital for these aims.

The evening before the trip Mikhoels asked Zuskin to serve as his replacement at the theater while he was away. Zuskin refused the offer—his field of activity was not leadership. However, in effect Zuskin took upon himself the responsibility for the theater although he was not officially appointed.

He was responsible for performances and rehearsals, assigning replacement actors for those who had been drafted into the army, soothing actresses who were waiting longingly for letters from the front, imposing discipline and order so that even in the new situation, which was in no way simple, the reputation of the theater and the acting school would not be destroyed. All of these duties were added to his ongoing activity as an actor, director, and teacher. During this time, he even suffered fainting spells. But he made no concessions for himself and expressed his dissatisfaction only to Eda, if at all.

In the beginning of 1942, the GOSET staged its first performance in Tashkent, *Khamza*, which was translated into Yiddish from Uzbek. The play describes the biography of Khamza Niyazi, an Uzbek poet, playwright, and composer who lived in the years 1889–1929. Since Khamza was the founder of the Uzbek national theater, there are similarities and common denominators between the Uzbek theater and the Jewish theater: both applied the rule "remove the old to make room for the new," namely, giving up the old-fashioned culture for the Soviet culture. Nonetheless, both theaters preserved, albeit in moderation, loyalty to the national tradition and culture. The authorities presented this phenomenon as a role model for others.

I have sentiments about the play *Khamza*. My father did not act in it but "loyalty to the national tradition" was demonstrated by my mother who danced an Uzbek folk dance with a pitcher on her head.

The second performance in Tashkent was *An Eye for an Eye* (*An oyg far an oyg*), a play by Perets Markish, and it was first staged in the fall of 1942. The subject was the current war besetting a small town in Poland occupied by the Nazis, and the Jews who live in the town ghetto. In the play the occupiers do not distinguish between Jews and non-Jews: in the first act, they execute a group of Poles and destroy the statue of the Polish national poet Adam Mickiewicz. Only afterward do they find time to harass the Jews. The Jewish youth, for whom the Nazis are the enemy of all freedom lovers and not only the persecutors of the Jewish people, join the Polish partisans.

The plot of the play is in accord with the atmosphere prevailing in the corridors of the Soviet authorities: one is permitted to express national feelings but it is not recommended, to put it mildly, to highlight the uniqueness of a particular nationality. Such an emphasis impinges upon the idea of equality among nations and must lead to bourgeois nationalism, heaven forbid.

The "bourgeois nationalist" Markish, indeed adapted his play to the "prevailing atmosphere." With this, although Jews go to fight the Nazis alongside non-Jews, their farewell blessing consists of the words said to their teacher Moses at Mount Sinai: "But if any harm follow, then thou shalt give life for life, eye for eye" (Ex. 21: 23–24). It was not by chance that Markish chose the name *An Eye for an Eye* as the title for his play.

Zuskin plays the role of an "ostensible victim"—the elderly Doctor Sephard who was a devotee of the German Enlightenment movement and therefore initially does not believe in the brutality of the Germans.

Zuskin and the other actors, along with their work in the theater, appeared as volunteers at a variety of artistic events, in hospitals for wounded or disabled servicemen, in hostels for refugees, in orphanages, and dormitories. They also appeared in concert halls where tickets were sold and the revenues devoted to those institutions. Since Yiddish was not the language of the general public, the GOSET actors appeared in song or dance or in humoristic pantomimes.

The audience delighted in *The Old Tailor*, Zuskin's eternal one-man show, or the boastful-sad song of Hotsmakh from the play *The Wandering Stars*, and his distress was set aside.

Zuskin loved to be among young people. In Tashkent, GOSET shared his building with the Conservatory. Once during a meal in the shared dining room, a girl, one of the student-vocalists, identified Zuskin as the actor who played Pinia in *Seekers of Happiness*. A conversation developed between them, and other students joined in with her. Future musicians and singers became friends with Zuskin. He asked them about their plans and spoke fervently about diverse artistic topics. Being among people offered him relief.

Enchanted

Although all around war was raging and bringing in its wake tragedy and heavy casualties, people tried not to sink into despair, to lose their ability to laugh. And who could help with this if not Sholem Aleichem, with his "laughter through tears," which has stood the test of time? In 1943 Zuskin directed Sholem Aleichem's story *The Enchanted Tailor* (*Der farkishefter shnayder*), which was adapted for the stage by Dobrushin. Zuskin also acted in this play, taking the lead role.

Against the background of a familiar landscape highlighted by time-less music, Shimen-Ele the tailor strides in the footsteps of an unfading hope. Shimen-Ele is poor, but of course, his spirit is not weak, in any way; he tells jokes, fends off the aggressiveness of his "better half" with speech that professes to rely on Jewish sources, and although he is completely disconnected from reality, he dreams up a business venture that promises a healthy profit.

Shimen-Ele hears from his neighbor that in the nearby village, they are selling a she-goat, cheap. He goes to that village, buys the she-goat, and on the way home, stops at a tavern. There they ply him with drinks until he is thoroughly drunk and then switch his she-goat for a billy goat. At home, his "better half" curses him as a "good-for-nothing." He doesn't even know how to tell a she-goat from a billy goat! And for her part, she cannot even begin to conceive that someone switched her husband's bargain on him.

So the poor entrepreneur's feet carry him back to the village, and again he stops at the tavern, and again they switch the he-goat for a she-goat and afterward the she-goat for a he-goat and back home he returns.

There are not many characters in this play. Truth be told, that is also one of the reasons that they decided to stage it, since some of the male actors had been drafted into the army. Zuskin, as a director working with an individual actor or with small groups of actors, worked according to his favorite method—a combination of teaching and directing. Nevertheless, he envisaged the entire picture of the onstage performance clearer than ever before. What guided him here was the dogged movement of Shimen-Ele forward, to happiness.

Zuskin the actor was still captivated by the charm of his Senderl, and he gave his hero a distinctive comical gait that was not sparing with the grotesque. Zuskin the director was still under the spell of theatrical techniques from Granovsky's era, and he structured his movement so that Shimen-Ele's profile was always facing the audience. In one hand was a sack, instead of Senderl's bag, in the other a rope to tie up the she-goat, or the he-goat, as was the case. Most of the scenes were staged according to this guiding principle.

It is clear that in the 1930s and 1940s, styles on stage had changed as compared with the 1920s, but the comic situations in *The Enchanted Tailor* allowed some joking around, especially considering the authorities' ambition to allow performances that were capable of helping people forget the war and its repercussions upon the citizenry.

The audience was enchanted. They rolled with laughter and yet felt a twinge of helplessness in their hearts. This phenomenon recurred every time with the characters Zuskin played. "Every one of his heroes has the fortitude to suffer, to maintain self-discipline and restraint, to weep, and to gather up the burnt ashes of his people."[25] All of his heroes ultimately are left with the he-goat.

Man and War (End)

On October 4, 1943, the GOSET returned to Moscow. The war had not yet come to an end but now it was far from the capital. People had to return to daily life. Mikhoels had not yet returned to Moscow. That was to happen in December. All the same, in the theater and the school of acting, they restored order. In the Zuskin home, they opened the windows, washed, cleaned, and put everything in its place. And what about their relatives?

Tamara was still at the front. At the beginning of the war, she had enlisted in the army, as did most of the medical students, and worked as a nurse in a field hospital. At the front she met an officer named Samek Greenstein, a Jewish refugee from Poland. They decided to get married, and Tamara went with him for a while to Tashkent so that he could meet her father. After the short stay in Tashkent and afterward in Moscow, Tamara returned to the front. She would operate on the wounded under fire, and together with the first Soviet Army troops, would enter Berlin. At crucial intersections in the war, she would meet up again with Samek her fiancé, they would marry, and after the war, would remain in Poland, her husband's homeland. In the late 1950s, after Samek was killed in an air accident, she would immigrate to Israel, establish a new family, and work as a doctor for thirty years (she died in 2014).

Rachel, Tamara's mother, her husband, and two of their three children were murdered in the Kovno Ghetto; only the elder, Bela, survived.

My mother's brother Max (Mordechai) Berkovsky and his wife Rosa had perished in the ghetto in Minsk. Max was one of the first to be murdered, while Rosa, a well-known dentist, officially treated the teeth of German soldiers and officers, and unofficially, of the ghetto residents and the partisans in the forests surrounding the city. (One can never guess what strength may be hidden in a "pampered lady"!). Their daughter with her husband and baby escaped from Minsk at the last minute before the Nazi's invasion, and their son was burned to death in a tank on the battlefield.

Anti-Fascist (Continuation)

On April 2, 1944, Zuskin participated in an anti-Fascist Jewish rally in Moscow, the third of its kind. Ever since the first rally in August 1941, which he joined by chance—and the reader will remember that a typewriter was involved—Zuskin had not taken part in any anti-Fascist activity.

During the break, Shakhno Epshteyn, the Committee's secretary, invited him to the Committee plenum that was scheduled to convene a week later. Zuskin promised nothing because he didn't remember the schedule of his own performances, but Epshteyn didn't let up because the presence of all Committee members was required.

Only then did Zuskin find out that he was a member of the Committee, even a member of long-standing, because, as it turns out, he was made a member on the very day the Committee was established in the spring of 1942. "In Tashkent . . . I lived until October 1943. No one informed me that I was assigned to the Committee, and no one sent me any material,"[26] he says at the trial years later.

Zuskin arrived at the building of the Jewish Anti-Fascist Committee for the convening of its plenum, and there he learned that there was a decision to set up a chairmanship for the Committee, that they named the "Committee Presidium." From the podium of the plenum they read out the list of people recommended by the top authorities for the presidium. Zuskin was surprised to hear his name, and he asked Epshteyn how they could elect him; after all, he was over his head in work. Epshteyn answered that as a popular actor known by all, Zuskin was obligated to be a member of the presidium and that he wouldn't have to work—there would be others to do the work.

And in fact, Zuskin was not to be very active in the presidium. Epshteyn was right about that. But neither of them was aware that membership in the presidium of the Jewish Anti-Fascist Committee would exact from Zuskin not his time but his life.

In his heart of hearts Zuskin blamed his skill on the typewriter. Eda was also unhappy about the role imposed on Zuskin. For her, Zusa was first and foremost an actor, and she was afraid of an attack of emotional tension as happened in Tashkent when he was involved in other affairs in parallel with his artistic endeavors.

As Zuskin foresaw—that is what happened. He was absent from most meetings of the presidium because of his participation in theater performances. Therefore, he was not a partner to the stormy debates in the presidium and in the Committee itself. The debates did revolve around the question of whether the Committee was supposed to deal only with propaganda addressed to the West or with the problems of the Jews domestically.

These debates intensified after World War II, and in the meantime, there was elation in the Committee. The success of Mikhoels and Fefer in England, America, Canada, and Mexico was beyond all expectations of their most committed admirers and of the Soviet authorities as well. "The Soviet leadership intended to use the JAC [Jewish Anti-Fascist Committee] as a master key to American wealth"[27] but Mikhoels's profound faith in the justice of the struggle against the Nazis, the gnawing pain in his heart because of the suffering of his people under the Nazi yoke, his sincere desire to secure the moral and financial support of the West, his talents as an actor and speaker who knew how to sense his crowd—all of these had a magnetic power, and did lead to unpredictably huge contributions.

By the end of and after World War II, because of the Cold War between the Soviet Union and the West, the necessity to maintain international ties decreased, but the problems of the Jews within the Soviet Union increased. Jews who had managed to flee the Nazis or survived in the ghettos and battlefront began to return to their homelands. They found their homes destroyed or occupied by others. To their surprise, the local authorities were in no hurry to solve their housing and other problems. To whom could they turn? In every Western country, there were Jewish communities. In Russia, too, before the Revolution there was such an arrangement.

There were no Jewish communities in Soviet Russia, but there was a Jewish Anti-Fascist Committee. The Jews in distress did not investigate what was above their heads and did not consider the fact that no one had authorized the Committee to handle their problems. With no other organization in sight, they accorded the Committee the status of the community leadership, and this was taken for granted by them. There were also those who didn't know anything about the existence of the Committee, what they did know, was just one name, and they either wrote, "To Comrade Solomon Mikhoels, Leader of the Jewish People, the Kremlin, Moscow," or they came, and mostly not to the official Committee reception room but to Mikhoels at the theater, where they sat on line waiting for Mikhoels as though for a dentist. Zuskin started to express his strenuous objection to

Mikhoels about his receiving the public at the theater. For him, after all, the theater was a sanctuary. Finally Mikhoels avoided receiving the public in the theater.

My father was forced into public activity, not only in the Jewish Anti-Fascist Committee and its presidium. Immediately at the end of the war, Mikhoels and Zuskin were elected as delegates to the local government in Moscow—Mikhoels in the city municipality and Zuskin in one of the city districts there. Zuskin behaved at the council as he behaved at the Committee: he preferred tangible things over dealing with bureaucracy. I remember how Father tried to fulfill the requests of those who had elected him, although he was either absent from the tedious council meetings because of performances or travels with the theater, or else he sat in the back row and played chess.

Molkho

In 1944 the GOSET was permitted to put on the play by David Bergelson, *Prince Reuveni* (*Prints Reubeyni*).[28] The plot takes place in the sixteenth century. The main protagonist, David Reuveni, is a Jew from Portugal, and by his own declaration, a descendant of one of the lost tribes. He is known in Jewish history as a false messiah. In the Christian royal courts of Europe he is received with the honor granted one who was of the status of kings, although ultimately, they turn their back on him, and he is arrested and dies in prison.

Mikhoels directs the performance and plans to take the role of David Reuveni. The role of his comrade in arms Shlomo Molkho, a converso who reverts to being a Jew and is devoted to Reuveni with all his might while more anchored in reality than him, would be played by Zuskin.

Zuskin is fascinated by Molkho's personality. And even more, he is enthralled by the opportunity to wander about in the history of his people, to stop "marching in place" in the theater, and to act with Eda, for the first time in their lives, in the role of a pair of lovers.

There was never a premiere of the play *The Prince Reuveni*. The authorities prohibited its staging even though the production was all prepared and ready. From the viewpoint of the GOSET and its actors, this was not just one play less—it was one world less: a world of spirituality, of reviving forgotten experiences, of a link between times and eras.

For Mikhoels it was a lost opportunity to express his worldview. "Reuveni is an allegorical representation of Mikhoels . . . Like Reuveni, Mikhoels had suddenly appeared in the Western world as an emissary from a forgotten Jewish community in the East, seeking Western support against a common enemy."[29] Like Reuveni, Mikhoels felt that if he had been sentenced to lead this "lost tribe," there was no other way but to flirt with the "royal court," and not in a foreign country but in the very country where he lived and operated. "I am a bogus prince and a false prophet, because with these wolves, I am unable to speak otherwise. Yes, they are wolves pursuing my herd,"[30] wrote Mikhoels in a personal letter to his wife. Is there anything to add here?

I felt truly grieved that they were not permitted to put on the play. By then I was already able to value Father's acting the same personage, Molkho, in different guises: in the guise of a devoted friend, of a Spanish-Portuguese aristocrat and statesman, of an adventurer, converso, and of a Jew who is burned at the stake by the Inquisition.

Most painfully, the last of these guises is similar to what befell Father in real life.

There were many other roles offered to my father or that he yearned to perform and in the end did not.

In the mid-1930s the idea arose to stage *Sunset* (*Zakat*) by Isaac Babel. My father was assigned the role of Benia Krik, who is a kind of "noble-minded bandit," and Mikhoels the role of Mendel Krik, Benia's father. But after some time Babel was arrested and that idea came to naught. The roles of "noble-minded bandits" and "tricksters" never brought any luck to either Zuskin in particular or to the theater. On that same path to annihilation marched Isaac Babel with Benia Krik in *Sunset*, Moyshe Kulbak with Chaim Boytre in *Boytre the Bandit*, and Benjamin Zuskin with Hershele Ostropoler in the play *Hershele Ostropoler*, which he directed.

When *King Lear* was such a success, Zuskin felt the yearning for a world classic, and since he never really said goodbye to Senderl, he was filled with a longing to play Sancho Panza in *Don Quixote* by Miguel Cervantes. But at the theater they had started preparations to put on *The

Little Tragedies (*Malen'kiye Tragedii*), a collection of short one-act plays written by Alexander Pushkin, including the short tragedy entitled *Mozart and Salieri*, with Zuskin as Mozart. That was long before the following was written about Zuskin: "He was blessed with a sense of rhythm and musicality and an agility that cannot be taught . . . he is—Mozart."[31] I never managed to find out why the play was not staged.

How many monologues from the Russian classics raced about in my father's head! It may be that in 1938 he wanted to leave the GOSET not only because the GOSET had no more challenges to offer, but also because of the urge to liberate the characters from their hold on his imagination. For example, the role of Tsar Fyodor. In the Art Theater of Moscow he had been played by Khmelev, one of the actors Zuskin admired. Yet at the same time, he couldn't restrain himself and when he was alone, he attempted to act the role of Fyodor, as pure-souled as Senderl and as eager to try out the throne for himself as the Fool of *King Lear*. In the style of acting and also in reality, the two had much in common, Khmelev and Zuskin. It was only that Khmelev had better fortune than my father: he died on stage, while delivering the monologue of Tsar Fyodor.

And what Jewish roles did Zuskin dreamed of enacting? After Solomon Maimon, he dreamed of playing the role of Barukh Spinosa— Mikhoels had decided to stage a play about this philosopher. However, this vision, too, never materialized. In 1945 Zuskin was offered the role of Mendel Beilis in the film on the Beilis trial. Zuskin was very excited and overjoyed. To his regret the supreme authorities found that the time was not propitious for historical films. Is it true that this was not the right time, the period after World War II—when the magnitude of the Holocaust became known—to deal with Jewish history?

Kabtsenzon

In Tashkent before Mikhoels went to America it was decided to add to the theater's repertory the vaudeville *The Capricious Bride* (*Di kaprizne kale*) based on the work by Abraham Goldfaden.

The play with its day-to-day values fit in well with the exigencies of the hour. After all, "the regime satisfied the people's demand for relaxation,

stability, and conservatism."[32] Theatrical forces were meant to emphasize these values—to "wow" Moscow where theater was already back in
operation.

They invited a guest director, A. Kaplan, but the music, stage set, and
costumes were designed by the GOSET artists: the composer Lev Pulver
and the stage and costume designer Alexander Tyshler. The first performance of *The Capricious Bride* opened in 1944, with Mikhoels's return
but before the end of the war.

The twists of the plot revolve around a young woman suffering from
over-education. At first she dreams of building her life according to the
books she reads, but ultimately, she falls in love and gets married, like
everyone else. The essence of the story of the bride, presented in the prologue, recalls commedia dell'arte: on the downstage the bride and groom
and between them Kabtsenzon are as immobile as statues, and the bride is
holding a book that she seems to be reading. Kabtsenzon awakens first of
the three; he awakens the other statues with a magic wand. According to
the definition of the role, Kabtsenzon is the groom's messenger. Actually,
Kabtsenzon is the comedian-jester who drives the performance.

Zuskin is Kabtsenzon, of course. Ethel Kovenskaya is the bride. Years
later she would recall: "My heroine, in waking to life, must make some
special movement with her body, while spreading her arms wide. I was
young and inexperienced and I didn't succeed. Suddenly my teacher
Zuskin comes over to me and whispers in my ear, Imagine that you are
embracing the world and everything in it. And I did! Instantly!"[33] The
forty-five-year old "boy" Zuskin, like the magician in the circus, gives a tap
with his magic wand and motivates everyone to play the game.

In this game Zuskin-Kabtsenzon seems like "a rubber doll, a man
without any bones,"[34] and with his virtuoso movements he expresses his
humor, since "for Zuskin, humor is a way of seeing the world."[35] At times,
his humor is hidden under the mask of seriousness, for instance, when he
and his lady-partner are dancing can-can and singing a song whose words
seem to be "the pinnacle of cleverness": "Without you I am as poor/ As a
handle with no door."

Zuskin dances like a child but in his approach to the role, newly
achieved signs of maturity are apparent. And yet: "The role reminds me of

some of my previous works,"[36] says Zuskin who was not completely satisfied. He was seeking roles with understanding and depth, and this light comedy was not enough to challenge him.

Reb Yekl

Mikhoels, too, no less than Zuskin, was interested in understanding and depth. In his heart he longed for something that would join the pain to happiness. In February 1943, when the Nazi army was defeated at Stalingrad, Mikhoels made himself a resolve to stage a folksy spectacular that would be a kind of Kaddish[37] to the memory of the victims and where there would be a wedding, a kind of promise to future generations. And the wedding would be a traditional wedding, because where the loss is so profound, the nation must return to its roots. Mikhoels sketched a guideline for the play to be implemented by other artists: the playwright Zalmen Shneer (Okun'), the composer Lev Pulver, the stage set and costume designer Alexander Tyshler, and the choreographer Emile Mei.

Later in 1943 Mikhoels was sent to America, and the work of producing *Freylekhs* fell to Zuskin.

In the premiere that took place in Tashkent on July 15, 1943, and in additional performances, in Tashkent and afterward in Moscow, the theater was full to bursting with spectators. Except that Zuskin felt that something was lacking in the performance. Perhaps, even with good news from the battleground, it was too early for a mental relaxation.

When Mikhoels returned and revamped the production, it would be clear to all that in Zuskin's version of direction there were achievements and inventions that made a valuable contribution to its success.

And its success, in addition to other of Zuskin's achievements in Tashkent, made a valuable contribution to his having been awarded the title: "People's Artist of the Uzbek Soviet Socialistic Republic."

Mikhoels began the job of revamping with the play itself. He wanted to focus the fundamental thinking: the life of the nation does not stop after its sons and daughters "have died, been killed, murdered, slaughtered, burned, drowned, and strangled."[38] What did Mikhoels mean exactly?

Was he looking at catastrophes of the war that had just ended or at the catastrophes that might still occur? It is difficult to say.

Actually, *Freylekhs* sums up both the way of Benjamin Zuskin the actor and also that of the GOSET, and so, I have designated it to be a kind of framework for whatever I relate in this book: Therefore, segments of this play open the book in the Prologue and close it in the Epilogue. In this sub-section, I present a full description of the production.

Every traditional occasion has its own particular customs. At a traditional Jewish wedding, a badkhen would lead the festivities. But the wedding in *Freylekhs* has a double meaning. How can you show this? It is not difficult at all. After all, we are not a theater for nothing!

Players, play! Actors, act! Let us recall bygone days! Let us remember the early years, years of unreservedly theatrical theater, metamorphoses of characters, masks, carnivals . . . the "alter ego." The badkhen must split into two. Yes, he has two faces: Reb Yekl and also Reb Ber.[39]

Benjamin Zuskin as Reb Yekl, the First Badkhen who calls, "Let us collect all the sadness in the world and out of it create love," embodies the spirit of joy while part of him appears as the spirit of sadness.

The other face is Reb Ber as the Second Badkhen, the traditional entertainer who is interested in making a living, who knows how to tell a vulgar joke, to take a drink. He is portrayed by Mikhail Shteyman.

The connection between both faces of the badkhen is like the connection between the experiences of the soul and the experiences of daily life, and it is this that infuses the production with its double meaning, similar to the meaning of life.

The two badkhens are dressed in the same style: a black *kapote*; a waistcoat with fringes that remind one of *tsitsit*;[40] black pants snug at the knees and long white socks; a black *kippah* (skullcap). With this, each one of them has a characteristic color: Reb Yekl's waistcoat is half-white half-red, Reb Ber's half-white half-blue; a handkerchief in the hand of each one of them is white with Hebrew letters in red (Reb Yekl) or blue (Reb Ber). The badkhens' assistants, three for each, are dressed similarly.

The costume and stage designer Alexander Tyshler was daring in departing from convention in two matters: despite the anti-religious Soviet environment, he clothed the badkhens and assistants in religious Jewish clothing, and in defiance of the rigid dress code practiced by pious Jews, he stylized their costumes theatrically. In addition, Tyshler wrote on the stage set itself the part of the verse pronounced at Jewish weddings, "The sound of joy and the sound of gladness, the voice of the groom and the voice of the bride." To write Hebrew, a forbidden language, in a Soviet theater? Informers had not paid attention to these writings: After all, the letters in Yiddish and in Hebrew are the same.

Freylekhs is not only a production devoted to the nation but is also a mirror of the nation.

In the first act, the relatives of the groom and bride cross the stage together with the wedding guests. They pass through slowly, in a celebratory, dignified way. They cross from one side to the other, their profiles to the audience, and in the language of the GOSET, this signifies that the nation is eternally on the move.

In the second act, every man and woman tells something about himself or herself using dance.

The production's success was achieved in large measure also thanks to the outstanding choreographer Emile Mei. By the way, Eda Berkovskaya, my mother, was his assistant.

The dances are followed with Reb Yekl's narrative and Reb Ber's kitschy comments.

Zuskin never related to himself as though he were a soloist. He felt that he was part of the theater, and so—it seems to me—he would have enjoyed the fact that I mention, even though perfunctorily, his colleagues and friends on stage.

My memory has retained sharp images. Yefim Zhabotinksy in the role of an older and gloomy wedding guest who had been a soldier in the Tsar's army. Ethel Kovenskaya in the role of a matron showing off her wardrobe and making the spectator forget that she has only a small role. The size of the role is also forgotten when one sees a poor aunt played highhandedly by Lelia Romm. Whom else do I remember? A heartwarming couple: Esther Roytman in the role of an old woman and Lyova Traktovenko as her elderly husband; Chaim Spivak slowly following the weepy Rachel Skidelskaya's heroine who justifies her presence at the joyous occasion by the excuse that there it is "happier to cry." I remember how beautiful was "the bride" Frieda Friedman; how "the groom"—alternately Zalman Kaminsky or Emile Horowitz—sang; how I understood that Tevye Khazak, "the groom's father," robust in body and expression, was only pretending to be frightening and that Hirsh Lukovsky, "the bashful father of the bride," was only pretending to be bashful; how I enjoyed Adele Mazur "the grandmother" who barely can get out of her wheelchair and then suddenly begins to dance as light-footedly as a young girl; she is also the one who settles disputes between Khana Blinchevskaya—"mother of the bride," and Yustina Minkova—"mother of the groom"; how impressive was Dancing Violin as enacted by Etia Tayblina.

Finally, they are escorting the bride to the wedding canopy.

Zuskin-Reb Yekl stands on the downstage and observes the eager crowd, "as though he is detaching himself from the preparations for the wedding and soaring over wide open spaces."[41] What does he see, or hear, or forecast? "An actor, like an accurate seismograph, is the first to pick up the coming thunder, the rumble of shocks in society, of social changes or of eruptions in historical processes."[42] If during the period of *King Lear* in 1935, Zuskin sensed "the coming thunder," then surely now, ten years later, it was not difficult to detect it in even greater measure.

He stands on the edge of the stage near the orchestra pit. But, no. In truth, like the Fool, he is standing at the edge of the abyss.

Reb Yekl triumphs. He triumphs because, like Sholem Aleichem, he understands: "As long as people are crying, you can mistreat them; there is still something left to take away from them. But when the mistreated laugh, you can't frighten them with anything; it's as though they are protected by being detached from the material world—everything tangible has been taken away from them, and they are left only with the spirit."[43] A spirit of joy, and a touch—a spirit of sorrow.

On June 5, 1946, Mikhoels, Zuskin, and Tyshler received the Stalin Prize for their work in creating *Freylekhs*.

About a year and half later, the prize-laureate Mikhoels was to be murdered and not long afterward, the prize-laureate Zuskin would also disappear.

Stage Director (End)

In 1944, Zuskin was offered the job of directing variety shows. He accepted willingly. He was captivated by the opportunity to try a new field of endeavor, and to find an outlet in the current atmosphere at the theater: except for *Freylekhs*, there were almost no interesting plays.

Zuskin began to stage the performances of Arkady Raykin, artistic director and actor of the "Theater of Miniatures" (short entertainment sketches), who would in time become the top-rated stand-up comedian in the Soviet Union.

A mutual affection sprang up immediately between Zuskin and Raykin. Zuskin understood at once that Raykin's heroes were extremely funny and yet evoked profound sadness. Raykin, on his part, for the first time in his life, was meeting a director whose advice was a combination of humor and lyricism.

I cannot allow myself to skip silently over Raykin's appearance in Moscow in 1969, at an evening dedicated to the seventieth anniversary of my late father's date of birth. In contrast to the other participants that evening, Raykin did not speak and did not share his memories with the audience. He delivered a monologue where an elderly Jew tells of the visits he and his wife made to their children who live in various cities far from their parents. With each child, the two old people repeat the same cycle of unending activity: "Sarah launders and I wring out." How similar this is to my father's beloved Senderl who returns to the cycle of life in the shtetl Tuneyadevke, and how it reminds me of my father himself who keeps returning to the cycle of fate of his people. For me, this performance by Raykin was akin to establishing a real memorial to my father.

I clearly remember Rugena Sicora, a young singer full of charm and talent. My father directed the theatrical side of her performance. Once at the end of a rehearsal that was held in our home, Father said to Rugena that everything was going well and in the very near future, she would be flooded with offers to appear. "No," replied Sicora, "it will not go so smoothly for me because I am not a Russian. I came here from Czechoslovakia. I'm a Czech." "What?" My father asked in astonishment. "Being a Czech is also bad?"

Another singer was Tamara Avetisian. Her performance was composed of different folk songs, including songs in Yiddish although she was not Jewish but Armenian. Here is Avetisian's story:

> Zuskin directed three songs that I sang . . . He never approached the song directly but always explained phenomena described in it.
>
> About the Jewish mother depicted in one of the songs, he explained that a woman in the Jewish shtetl always bore the burden and so she held her head up not straight but at an angle . . .
>
> After I worked with Zuskin, no director was capable of impressing me . . . Zuskin also educated me in good taste: you must not exaggerate the intonations . . . not make a Jewish song too Jewish . . . Zuskin believed that a singer needs talent, intuition, control of his art, and as varied and broad a knowledge of culture as possible. Working with him was for me a kind of university of the highest order.[44]

With entertainment shows, or as they were called, "small stage performances" in which "one may sometimes see great art,"[45] Zuskin actually fell in love.

Doctor Fishman

While in Moscow rehearsals were underway for *Freylekhs* in its latest version, in Kiev the director Mark Donskoi was beginning to work on the film *Unvanquished* (*Nepokorennyie*) in Russian, based on the book by Boris Gorbatov, which the author himself and director Donskoi adapted for film.

The performance in Moscow and the film in Kiev were both works intended to serve as a memory of those who perished in World War II and to highlight those who could not be vanquished.

At the center of the film are two men in their sixties, a Ukrainian worker named Taras Yatsenko, and a Jewish doctor named Aaron Fishman. "In an artist's life, there are moments that because of their rich value are imprinted in the memory forever. For me, these were the moments when before the camera stood two brilliant actors, Amvrosii Buchma and Benjamin Zuskin,"[46] writes Mark Donskoi.

The plot of *Unvanquished* takes place in a city in the Ukraine during the Nazi occupation. The name of the city and the name of the place where Jews were executed are not mentioned in the film, but it is clear that the city is Kiev and the killing field is Babi-Yar. During Soviet rule, this tragedy was passed over in silence. No artist, except for Mark Donskoi, dealt with this subject.

In summer of 1960, I together with Yuri Perelman, later to be my husband, went to Kiev and visited Babi-Yar. We found the site empty, neglected, frightening. A thought passed through my mind: My father had come here as Doctor Fishman, who was one of the victims in the movie, but in reality my father also was a victim and the fates of Fishman and Zuskin were actually identical.

I watch the recording of *Unvanquished* and I see on the screen, in the scene of the Jews' execution, a dark scarf caught in the branches of a single tree, flapping against the heavens above Babi-Yar filled with corpses. Again, an inanimate object laden with symbolism.

After Zuskin's arrest, they stopped screening the film *Unvanquished*. Here and there it was still mentioned in a random article, although they did not mention that in 1946, at the Venice Film Festival, the film won a gold medal, and they certainly did not mention the Jewish issue or Zuskin. And yet, *Unvanquished* exists and Doctor Fishman, on his way to nowhere, crosses the screen with his eternal medical bag.

And perhaps Zuskin, like Doctor Fishman, is also unvanquished?

Anniversary Honoree

On September 24, 1946, the GOSET audience saw the production *Frey-lekhs*. At the end of the performance, Zuskin stepped out onto the downstage and took his bows as usual. At that moment they announced to the crowd that the day marks the twenty-fifth anniversary of Zuskin as an actor; he had, after all, first appeared on the GOSET stage on September 24, 1921. The audience rose to its feet and applauded in honor of the much-admired actor. The theatergoers scattered, and then onto the stage came the members of the household: actors, orchestra musicians, members of the management and theater clerks, stage hands, students and teachers at the School of Acting. Everyone came, no one was absent, and they congratulated Zuskin.

Zusa and Eda returned home excited. Their apartment was filled with bouquets and baskets of flowers. In one of the baskets under the flowers, Zusa and Eda found a small package. Some ten years later Mother would tell me that they took off the wrapping, opened the wallet, and read the words—"Zuska, my place in the theater will be yours"—written on a scrap of paper hidden in one of the wallet's pockets.

Whether Mikhoels's heart had already foretold then in 1946 of his coming demise, which was implemented in 1948, or whether he sensed that the horizons of the theater had become too narrow for him, he certainly knew that he had no successor who could lead the theater besides Zusa.

According to Tala, Mikhoels's elder daughter, after his return from America, her father and his wife Asia "were almost never at home; all kinds of invitations, both personal and formal, continued to arrive throughout the last four years of his life . . . Repertory problems . . . irregularities in the theater's budget, streams of guests to the house and the theater."[47] Mikhoels found himself at a dead end.

All of this was not to the actors' liking, but they were silent. "Mikhoels, it's time to go back, the stage is waiting for you," my father tried to convince him. "Solomon Mikhaylovich, you are an actor, and what an actor! Why are you causing such a fuss around you?" My mother joined forces with my father. But the situation that had been created now was inescapable.

It was decided to organize a festive event to mark Zuskin's twenty-fifth anniversary in the theater. Since the theater had just returned to its routine after a tour accompanied by actors' vacations, the date was set for March 1947.

At the theater they prepared for the evening with great dedication. Mikhoels would open the evening—with words about Zuskin's creative work. Zuskin would appear in excerpts from a few shows, including *The Travels of Benjamin the Third*, most important of all—in scenes where Benjamin and Senderl are going to sleep, and when they awaken. Mikhoels was excited. He would mount the stage as an actor! He would go back to being what he had once been!

As soon as it became public knowledge that there was going to be an evening in honor of Zuskin, the demand for tickets exceeded all estimates. It was then decided to hold the festive evening twice, on March 24, 1947, and on March 31. There were five hundred seats in the GOSET theater. They printed up one thousand tickets. And then, that too was not enough, so for important people, they brought chairs and placed them alongside the fixed seats, and less important people were allowed to stand along the theater walls.

For a long time after this evening we kept receiving phone calls, telegrams, guests. There was an atmosphere of happiness in the house.

On one of those happy days, when I returned home from school, I found my father sitting next to his desk, his head slumped on his arms. I ran to him. He had tears in his eyes. Father said that his brother Yitshak in Canada had informed him of the death of their mother. Chaya Zuskin was for me a "phantom grandmother" in the sense that we had never met. My father had not seen her for twenty-seven years.

He had lived and worked and studied in the Urals without her; he had moved to Moscow, been married twice, and fathered two daughters without her. He had become an eminent actor without her. What was he crying for? That he had lived so far away from his mother? In truth, the separation was his initiative, but who could guess that this separation would be forever? And what had he gained? He had no reason to complain. Yet perhaps, a quiet life would have been better than precarious fame and a future shrouded in fog?

I understood that I should leave Father by himself and I tiptoed out of the room. In a few days Father would regain his composure. Life continued.

The period when Zuskin's anniversary at the theater was celebrated was swathed in a pleasant wrapping: the summer before this season and the summer following, the GOSET went on tour in the capital cities of the Baltic Republics: in 1946, in Riga, capital of Latvia; and in 1947, in Vilna, capital of Lithuania. On both occasions, at the end of the performances, my parents and I had a vacation at the Baltic seashore.

Since Latvia and Lithuania were annexed to the Soviet Union following the Non-Aggression Pact between it and Nazi Germany only in 1940, the Jews of Riga and Vilna were known for their sense of affiliation with the Jewish people, and the Nazi occupation only reinforced these feelings. The atmosphere in the local Jewish society was a pleasant surprise for my father.

The vacation at the shore of Riga's Bay on the Baltic Sea, after the theater tour in Riga was over, enabled my father, for the first time since the war, to truly rest and relax.

The following summer, in 1947, the theater appeared in Vilna and again my parents took me along on the trip. Beside a set of performances, Vilna, like Moscow the previous spring, celebrated the twenty-fifth anniversary of Benjamin Zuskin's career in theater. It was flattering, but contacts with local people were less serene. Unlike our acquaintances in Riga, who during the Nazi occupation had managed to escape the Nazis and were not subjected to their crimes, all of those whom we met in Vilna were survivors of the ghetto that had stood within that city. One local Jew who had gone through purgatory in the Vilna Ghetto arranged a tour for the GOSET people through the ghetto, and showed us (I was with them, too) where the Jews had lived, been murdered, and planned the uprising.

Liakhovich

One of GOSET's actresses told me that she once met my father on the street looking unlike his usual self: He was dressed in a long coat of a thick, coarse weave, a kind of garment such as worn by manual laborers, and wearing makeshift thick boots. Zuskin explained that, as she must know, he was busy with rehearsals for the production of *Tumultuous Forest* (*Velder royshn*) and that during the period of rehearsals, without costumes and makeup, the outfit helped him get into the character of Liakhovich the hero. It is possible that in the biography of one actor or another, one can find examples of this kind, but I am not writing about them, rather about my father, the father I was separated from at a very young age. Therefore every crumb of information about him, every characterization that reveals another layer of his personality, even a very small matter, is very precious to me and arouses in me a fierce desire to tell the reader about it.

Although in World War II the Jews suffered more than any other nation, in the Soviet Union after the war, it was not acceptable to emphasize Jewish suffering. "Rather than perform . . . plays by some of the most noted contemporary Jewish writers . . . the theater was forced to . . . perform bland Russian plays by obscure writers instead."[48] And if it happened that among the protagonists in plays translated from Russian, Jewish characters would pop up, their existence would be validated only if they operated alongside non-Jews.

Tumultuous Forest was found to comply with the requirements; it was written in Russian by playwrights Alexei Brat and Grigorii Lin'kov, certainly and fortunately not "obscure" writers, and translated into Yiddish. The play is dedicated to the partisans' struggle against the Nazi occupier. This is the last production that Solomon Mikhoels directed. The composer is Lev Pulver; the designer of costumes and stage set is Robert Falk. The premiere of the play was scheduled for November 7, 1947, the thirtieth anniversary of the October Revolution.

The official reviews praised the GOSET, but the GOSET people were grieving because just now after the war, they were being prevented from creating a truly Jewish production.

At the beginning of the play, in the forefront of the stage, a clearing in the forest is seen, with a man-made mound of earth in the middle and a dried-out tree to the left. A scrap of tallit, caught on a branch, is fluttering in the breeze. Out of the artificial mound a human hand appears. It stretches upward, it falls, then two hands appear, they stretch, they fall, and on the stage a man rises. His clothes are tattered, his hair is tangled, his eyes are burning. From his appearance it is clear that he is trying to remember and understand where he is and how he got there. He looks around and notices the scrap of tallit. His demeanor changes immediately. He remembers and understands everything!

In this way Liakhovich, who is played by Zuskin, introduces himself to the audience: without words it becomes clear that the man-made mound of earth was created by digging a pit, and the Jew has extricated himself from the pit, the only one who survived the valley of slaughter.

Suddenly a German officer enters the clearing; he is in good spirits and not at all frightening. The officer is certain that he is alone in nature, opens the buttons of his uniform, and lays his weapon on the ground. Liakhovich, in the grip of emotional pain, grabs the weapon and murders the foolish officer. Afterward, slowly Liakhovich stretches his body to its full length and with tottering gait, approaches the tree and kisses the hem of the tallit. It would be superfluous to state that the censors, known for their alertness, after several performances banned this silent scene.

Liakhovich joins the partisans and they inform him that as punishment for killing the German officer, the Nazis have executed several innocent residents of the village. This arouses pangs of conscience in Liakhovich who mumbles, "Of people like me, it was said . . ." and with great bitterness, he recites an ancient parable: "If a stone falls on a pot—woe to the pot; and if the pot falls on a stone—woe to the pot. In either case, woe to the pot."[49]

Watchmaker

That same year, 1947, in Moscow at the MosFilm Studios they did the film shoots for *Light over Russia* (*Svet nad Rossiyei*). Zuskin's role there was not large but important to the plot: In the film, comrades Lenin and Stalin invite his protagonist, the Watchmaker, to their offices in the Kremlin and ask him to adjust the chime in the ancient clock in one of the Kremlin towers, so that it will play *The Internationale*.

Zuskin builds the image of the Watchmaker as a small, unassuming man who is enamored of his craft and expert at it, confident of his skill, and the proposal to breathe new life into the Kremlin's ancient clock seems totally natural to him. Therefore he is full of self-importance when he conducts the conversation with his exalted clients.

Toward the afternoon of May 15, 1947, the film director Sergei Yutkevich called Zuskin, and in a happy voice announced that the Film Acceptance Commission decided to approve the film.

Two days later, on May 17, Yutkevich was urgently summoned to the government Ministry of Cinematic Arts where he was informed that the film must be regarded as a political distortion. Yutkevich relates: "'What happened?' I asked. 'The film did not please Comrade Stalin'. 'Do you have a record of his comments?' 'No, he didn't say anything. But the honorable Minister . . . noticed the humphing coming from Comrade Stalin, which indicated his dissatisfaction'. A new page in the management of art,

I thought to myself, using the stenography of humphing . . . 'Your film will never be shown.'"[50] And that is what happened.

In his personal meeting with Zusa and Eda, Yutkevich was candid. He passed on the words of Stalin as he had been told off the record, that beside other things, there is too much of the Watchmaker. "The Supreme Auditor of Art" would yet find an opportunity to get rid of that Watchmaker, and with clockwork efficiency.

In 1957 Mother and I visited the Central Film Archive to watch the films in which Zuskin had participated. They allowed us to watch the films that we requested, but not *Light over Russia*. So, I thought, I will never see the film. Suddenly, in 2010, totally by chance, I found a notice on the Internet that in Moscow the film *Light over Russia* had been taken out of the archive and put out in DVD format. Obviously I now have that film, thanks to the wonders of technology.

Zorekh Zarkhi

Now Zuskin returned to the GOSET's series of workmen and craftsmen that he himself initiated when he played Naftole Hoz in the show *Court Is in Session*. This time he played the role of Zorekh Zarkhi, a retired factory worker, in the play *Holiday Eve* (*Erev yontev*); he also directed the production.

At the beginning of the play Zorekh is busy with a large shiny ball bearing. This ball bearing was brought to my father from some factory, and they even brought him two identical ones. I couldn't understand what an elderly pensioner sitting at home needs with a ball bearing and why my father decorated his desk at our home with the second one. The shoes on the feet of Father's hero are held close to each other, and their toes point outward in an exaggerated and unnatural way. His gait is designed to arouse laughter; his suit is overly meticulous; his moustache and beard are outlandish—all of these undermine the faith I have thus far had in the seriousness that Father relates to each and every role.

I think I understood my father's approach to this role only when I learned that Alfred Hitchcock used to put his personal stamp on every film that he directed: he appeared in every film in a minor role, as though he wished to hint, "Here I am." I understood that Father's "Here I am" in the production *Holiday Eve* was much more complex: he stamped the production both as director and as actor. As a director, Zuskin incorporated some grotesquery here and there (shades of Granovsky!). As an actor, he revealed to the audience his bag of theatrical techniques including irony. As to the ball bearing, isn't it amusing to play with an inanimate object— again, an inanimate object!—on stage which seems to be connected to nothing else that is happening on stage?

As for the production *Holiday Eve*, I cannot help but mention that my mother appeared in the main role. The playwright Moyshe Broderson even made a stipulation when he handed over his play to the GOSET: the role of Nakhama will be played by Eda Berkovskaya.

The play depicts the life of a Jewish family, including their non-Jewish friends, immediately after the war. Each and every one finds his place in the post-war life. Only Nakhama[51] finds no comfort for herself after her husband and children have perished in the ghetto. She lives with the family that is the center of the play, because of a distant kinship and because she has nowhere else to go. Berkovskaya-Nakhama is silent almost until the end of the second act; she rebuffs any attempt to get close to her; just toward the end of the play she begins to awaken to life, cautiously, tentatively. "The character that Eda played behaved exactly like Eda herself, quietly and nobly . . . Eda Berkovskaya has gone from us. She went as she always was. Quiet. Noble."[52] These words were written by the poet Joseph Kerler in his obituary to my mother who died in 1959, and it was clear that Kerler found it hard to draw a line between Eda and Nakhama.

In the last scene, all of the protagonists gather to celebrate the holiday eve, and that is the source of the play's title. They are, of course, marking the anniversary of the October Revolution. Everyone is happy and the old grandfather finally puts down his ball bearing.

If I am honest, I will say that I didn't like the character of Zorekh Zarkhi. It was contrary to what I was used to from the day that I had begun to see my father on stage: his flying, skipping, or suffering. Now I am happy with it: thanks to this role I was able to see my father as an old man and a grandfather.

After all, in real life he never was privileged to be either a grandfather or an old man.

Young. Talented. Cheerful.

Once, in 1946 or 1947, my father was reading the newspaper and blurted out crossly, "Again!" My mother looked at the paper over his shoulder and sighed in full understanding. I also peeked. I read the sentence, "We are again excited at the talent of the young Zuskin, with his characteristic lightness . . ." This was a review that related to a show in which he had appeared the previous day.

My mother did understand what effort was required of Father to achieve this "characteristic lightness." Doubts, hesitations, thoughts, physical training, insomnia—these filled his world and brought "lightness," which made the audience tremble even when he was already middle-aged. Later my mother told me more than once that clichés of this type greatly annoyed him.

"Why doesn't anyone analyze my work seriously," my father marveled. "How long will they go on calling me 'young and talented'?"

Zuskin kept himself away from Party or political missions in contravention of what the authorities expected of people who were prominent in their field of endeavor, and he also did not like to be interviewed. "Today in retrospect, I understand how important to Zuskin was every expression of attention directed to him. They wrote about him, but not a lot, bits and pieces, and in a very superficial way, and he himself was very modest. He underestimated his status as an artist,"[53] recalls the critic Inna Vishnievskaya.

In spite of difficult periods in Father's life, he loved life and life sparkled in him like bubbles in a flute of champagne. As the years passed, the proportions gradually changed between joy and sadness, not because of his age but because of external circumstances. During the last period of his life, the joy totally expired. But until then he never passed up the chance to joke.

Stored in my memory are the moments of sadness experienced by my father, but more frequently I "see" how this man who was in love with life ran to greet me, a joyful smile on his face, his coat wide open, his hat perched on the side of his head, running-dancing as though he forgot that he wasn't on stage.

The writer Vladimir Lidin who lived not far from us frequently strolled with my father and me along Tverskoi Boulevard. Father and Lidin had a lot in common, for instance, they both were book collectors. "Zuskin loved books, read a lot, he lived between the theater and books; the bohemian life typical of many actors was not to his taste."[54] With this, in his memoirs Lidin describes many humorous incidents, such as this one: "One morning I was passing on Tverskoi Boulevard, and I saw Mikhoels and Zuskin sitting on a bench near the house where they lived. Zuskin's face wore the definite expression of a guilty pupil as Mikhoels as a stern teacher reproached him for having got out too early after the flu. This picture was directed at me even though they pretended to ignore me."[55] Here one sees how seriously the two took their fooling around.

According to Lidin, Zuskin was able to find without effort inroads to children's hearts. Once he was present where Zuskin was telling a little girl about a Persian princess who was taken by a Persian cat to a Persian moon. To the girl's question whether this had happened in real life or if he had made it up, Zuskin answered that he didn't know exactly but it didn't matter as long as the story is interesting. "It's the same thing onstage; to make the spectator be interested—they call it super-tasks that an actor sets himself—it is merely alley cats that rummage around in the soul,"[56] says Zuskin to Lidin.

Under my father's influence, I also used to imitate the people around me, teachers and friends. My father knew most of them, and he would help with the impersonation or do it himself. At home or among friends, Father would speak about someone without mentioning his name, just by hinting, or using a nickname known to the initiated only.

Here's an example: Father and I were strolling on the boulevard and coming toward us were my friend and her father. My friend's father was of a type that doesn't dare make himself noticed, who wears dark clothes. This time he was wearing a light grey jacket. My father understood immediately that because of the new outfit, the man was feeling slightly ill at ease and also very pleased; and father gave him the nickname "Grey Jacket."

In the tragic days when Mikhoels's coffin was placed in the theater so that the crowd could pass by and pay respects, my father, shocked and dazed, who understood that his world had collapsed around him, said to me without a trace of mockery, and only by force of habit, "Tell your friend that Grey Jacket can come, as he asked, and stand in the honor guard near the coffin."

At the funeral service for Mikhoels, my father said among other things: "Middle of the night. We are both at Mikhoels's house. Quiet. The clock chimes: two, two-thirty in the morning. We don't want to leave each other."[57]

And when Mikhoels and Zuskin sat with other people, they would begin an amusing duet. One would start humming an old Jewish melody, and the other would join in. In most cases, these were melodies without words, and sometimes they added words that they ad-libbed, even picking up words from a conversation going on in the room. And when my father shifted from song to speech, he would offer refreshments or coffee in the voice of one of his aunts from Ponievezh. Mikhoels, who knew all of Zuskin's relatives from Ponievezh, would join in the game.

I remember how these two eminent personages used to joke around in the company of children my age, on one of my birthdays, when I was seven or eight years old: Suddenly the door opened wide and into the room skipped Mikhoels and Zuskin with acrobatic agility, in winter coats—my birthday is in February—and socks without shoes.

The young members of the theater, especially the women, were afraid of father's teasing. But the one who suffered from Father's joking more than any other actress was my mother. When Mother appeared on the stage in a scene where my father had no role, he would stand behind the curtain—where she could see him—and demonstrate facial expressions of someone she knew. A performance like this was particularly problematic when the person whom my father imitated was her partner on stage. My mother became angry but when Father was no longer with us, Mother recalled these episodes with great affection.

At times Father's barbs were directed at me. If, for example, someone was dining with us who was part of Father's rich "gallery of masks," Father would seat himself at the table between the guest and me and then turn to me, mimicking the face of this guest.

Father had no lack of opportunities for playing his tricks on the GOSET people: on tour or in the theater in Moscow, in the rehearsal halls during the breaks, in makeup rooms. "Ah, those evenings in the GOSET makeup rooms! . . . Mikhoels entered. The two of them exchanged jokes. Zuskin warned Mikhoels about something, Mikhoels . . . frivolously stopped the conversation about their problems."[58] Today it seems to me that I, the daughter of Zuskin, can understand what their problems were at the time. Zuskin apparently was referring to the meeting that awaited Mikhoels at the Jewish Anti-Fascist Committee or the Repertory Committee. And with all of that, they still made jokes!

In my mind's eye I see in the makeup room Yakov Kukles, a trumpet player in the GOSET orchestra. Kukles was particularly thin but for some reason, spoke a lot about food, and when he entered the makeup room, Father became very alert, took on the role of a cordial host, put on an imaginary apron, and began in pantomime to cut and chop, season with sauces, and serve at the table. It was the makeup table, of course. But when they reached the table, the matter of food was forgotten, and they began to play chess, and this time, with the utmost seriousness. My father almost always won; he even won first place among the GOSET people. Although I dearly loved the games and the jokes in Father's makeup room, I was afraid that this would distract him from the character that he was playing and interfere with his concentration. But he thought differently: "On my way to the theater, where I must appear in a show, I try to think only of the role that awaits me. In the intermission, I can speak about matters that are not related to my role on stage, and it doesn't interfere with me."[59]

In early November 1947 the GOSET held rehearsals for a festive event to mark the thirtieth anniversary of the October Revolution. The rehearsal was drawing to a close. Zuskin, who was free in the last sketch, still managed to draw in two or three friends for some stunt, and then Mikhoels announced to everyone that they could go home. Zuskin was asked to stay even though it was already three in the morning.

Zuskin did not yet understand whether he should adopt a serious mood or if Mikhoels wanted to joke, and so he approached Mikhoels with a mischievous grin, but Mikhoels drove the grin off Zuskin's face: "He," Zuskin would testify at the trial, "gestured for me to sit in his chair.

'Soon you will be sitting in this place'. I told him that that was the seat I least wished to occupy. Then Mikhoels took an anonymous letter from his pocket and read it to me . . . 'You kike scum, you have flown so high . . . may your head not go flying off as well'."[60] According to Mikhoels, he had already received a few letters of this kind.

In effect, Mikhoels's warning that his position as director of the theater would pass over to Zuskin is not the first one—remember the gift that Zuskin, on his twenty-fifth anniversary on stage, received from Mikhoels. Nor is this warning the last one.

On January 11, 1948, the administrative director of the theater informed Zuskin of a request by Mikhoels transmitted that morning from Minsk. Zuskin didn't even know that Mikhoels had left; he thought that Mikhoels was absent from the theater because of his public activities in Moscow.

It emerged that already on January 7, Mikhoels had traveled to Minsk, the capital of the Soviet Republic of Belorussia. After all, Mikhoels was a member of the Stalin Prize Committee, and he was sent to Minsk to see a play at the local theater that was a candidate for this prize.

Mikhoels asked Zuskin to make sure that the performance scheduled at the GOSET for that evening, January 11, runs smoothly because some important dignitaries were invited to attend. In addition, Mikhoels asked Zuskin to look at his notes on this production that were in a grey folder in his home, in the top drawer of his desk.

In the top drawer of the desk, in the grey folder, Zuskin found a sealed envelope with his name on it. He opened it, and there was a sheet of paper with Mikhoels's last note.

Two days later, the mischievous grin would be wiped off Zuskin's face forever.

9

Fourth Interlude

DECEMBER 24, 1948
PRELIMINARY INVESTIGATION
INTERROGATION OF BENJAMIN ZUSKIN

ZUSKIN. The tragedy that befell us was unbearable to me.[1]

JUNE 11–12, 1952
TRIAL
TESTIMONY BY BENJAMIN ZUSKIN

ZUSKIN. The coffin with the body [of Mikhoels] arrived at the theater
. . . A great many people came to say goodbye. They buried the
actor Mikhoels and not Vovsi.[2]

FEBRUARY 9, 1952
PRELIMINARY INVESTIGATION
INTERROGATION OF BENJAMIN ZUSKIN

INVESTIGATOR. The Jewish Theater dealt in propaganda.
ZUSKIN. The Anti-Fascist Committee . . . took over the Theater . . .
INVESTIGATOR. . . . . of which you were also one of the directors.
ZUSKIN. I was an actor.[3]

JUNE 11–12, 1952
TRIAL
TESTIMONY BY BENJAMIN ZUSKIN

ZUSKIN. Above all, I direct the Court's attention to the fact that in three and a half years of investigation it has not been determined who Mikhoels was and who Zuskin was. In the investigation materials it says that Mikhoels headed the Jewish Theater, and after his death Zuskin . . .

CHAIRMAN. That is exactly what we are determining here . . . [4] The task of the Court is to verify testimonies of yours.

ZUSKIN. All my testimonies are false.

CHAIRMAN. However, when other defendants unmasked you here . . . you did not state that they were wrong.

ZUSKIN. Believe me, the doctors know the condition I am in. I have days when I am incapable of uttering a single word . . . I would like to give just one piece of information. Granovsky was the artistic director of the Jewish Theater for ten years, whereas Mikhoels was the artistic director for nineteen years. Altogether, for twenty-nine years, but I was the artistic director for only a few months. Who determined what the repertoire would be? . . . I did not, because I was an actor . . .

In addition, I state once again that I was not granted any witness confrontation with anyone.

CHAIRMAN. Witness confrontations are given for clarification and for unmasking people. What would be the point . . . when you confessed to everything yourself?[5]

ZUSKIN. I was prompted to say all that.[6]

MARCH 4, 1952
PRELIMINARY INVESTIGATION
INTERROGATION OF BENJAMIN ZUSKIN

INVESTIGATOR. Do you admit your guilt?

ZUSKIN. Yes. As a member of the Jewish Anti-Fascist Committee, I bear responsibility . . . [7]

JUNE 11–12, 1952
TRIAL
TESTIMONY BY BENJAMIN ZUSKIN

CHAIRMAN. Defendant Zuskin, in what do you plead guilty?[8]

ZUSKIN. I am an actor and am guilty of concentrating all of my activity on my work as an actor.[9]

CHAIRMAN. Do you believe that in the Committee were ardent nationalists?

ZUSKIN. Yes, who turned out after the investigation to be such nationalists.

CHAIRMAN. After the investigation! Did you really not know about this earlier? You said of the theater that it was a hotbed of nationalism.

ZUSKIN. It is correct—again, on the basis of those materials that I read in the case files[10] . . . I do not need life. For me, a stay in prison is more terrible than death. I wanted only one thing—to live until that minute when I would face the Court and tell the whole truth.[11]

I'd like to describe . . . things that are not found in the forty-two volumes of the Investigation File.[12]

Now I would like to speak about Mikhoels's funeral.[13]

10

Act Five
(1948–1952)

Gripped by Anguish

On January 13, 1948, Zuskin was holding a rehearsal at the theater. That day he had come early, before the other directors, and he invited only three or four actors to come in, because it bothered him when those who were not participating in the rehearsal of a specific piece had to wait around in the corridor. That is why, except for the small group that was invited and several administrative workers, the theater was deserted. Zuskin ended the rehearsal of the first scene on the program and left the rehearsal hall for a few minutes. At that moment he heard a phone call in the room of the administrative director. Zuskin thought that the room was empty and that he should answer. He opened the door and saw a person from the administrative staff standing next to the table. He did not look his usual self at all; his face was contorted, terror in his eyes. The receiver was held unsteadily in his trembling hand, and he was shouting in a voice that was not his own: "What?! Are you sure?!"

As a rule a person moves gradually from one stage of life to the next and it is only at a certain moment that those around him notice all of a sudden that the boy is no longer a boy but a young man, or the young man has become an adult. In stark contrast to that rule, I can point precisely to the moment when my childhood ended in one fell swoop: January 13, 1948.

That day I was sitting at the table in our living room and eating lunch before going to school where I attended the second shift. I was eating alone because my mother was waiting in another room for my father who had been delayed at the theater.

The front door slammed and Father came running in, without taking off his hat and without pulling off his galoshes, which was very unusual for him. Even more out of character for him was the fact that he didn't even reply to my playful question, "Where from and where to?" He didn't kiss me, he didn't smile at me, and he only asked me with a somber look, "Is Mother at home?" "She's in there," I pointed toward the small room. Father practically burst into the room, and whispered something to Mother, who let out a chilling scream.

I ran to them in terror, "What happened?" The maid Sonia, frightened, came running in from the kitchen. "Mikhoels . . . was killed . . . in Minsk . . . a truck ran them over . . ." Father answered quietly and slowly, as if he could hardly get the words out. "Them? Who?" "Him and Golubov-Potapov, the theater critic who was traveling with him," Father said in an even smaller voice and asked my mother, "Please help me pack. I am going to Minsk." "What for?" "To find out more details at the scene. I have to hurry. I have less than two hours until the train leaves. At the station a messenger from the theater will be waiting with tickets."

I went to school. That day they didn't let me study very much; I was called outside during every lesson, sometimes even twice in one lesson. I went out to the corridor at the request of one Jewish teacher or another. Their conversations with me were identical: "Where is your father?" "He went away." "Where?" "To Minsk." "When?" "Just now." "You mean, you saw him before you went to school? He was at home?" "Yes." "And you know about . . . Mikhoels?" "Yes." At school I didn't hear the radio of course, and I didn't know if they had already announced the terrible event or if it was the rumor mill which had been at work. But one thing I did understand very clearly: after the teachers heard that another person had been killed together with Mikhoels, they thought it was my father because they couldn't conceive that any other person except my father had accompanied Mikhoels. Their error was not too far from the mark, as it turned out.

When I came back home from school, I found my father at home. A telephone call from the "powers-that-be" announced in no uncertain terms that the trip was not recommended. The next day my father left the house several times, alone or with my mother, called people, or received a countless number of visitors. These visitors did not stay with us long, and they went down, together with my parents, to Tala and Nina or to Asia.

On January 15, the body arrived in Moscow from Minsk by train. My father and mother went to the train station to receive the coffin. After Mikhoels's face, which had been mutilated, was reconstructed in a clinic, the body was brought to the theater. From four in the afternoon until midnight and the next day from morning until the early afternoon, in freezing weather of thirty degrees below zero, a very long line of humanity stretched out, inching its way to the entrance of the GOSET theater. The foyer of the theater where they placed the casket was teeming with people, but it was a hushed crowd. Silence blanketed everything; anyone who spoke, did so in a whisper.

More than sixty years have passed since then, and I still remember the great crowd, the oppressive silence in the theater and in our home, and my father's ashen face which looked—even though Father was of average height—as though it were floating above the assembled crowd.

Near the open casket an honor guard passed every quarter hour. Asia, her daughter Barbara, and Mikhoels's daughters Tala and Nina, his close friends, GOSET people and of course, my father—they all stood in the honor guard almost without a break.

My mother stood there for quite a bit. I also stood there several times. I remember the twinge in my heart that I was unable to free myself of in those difficult days. I mean the mixture of a sense of deep tragedy together with—I don't know what to call it—the sense of pride, of belonging to something that was both tragic and exalted. This whirlpool of emotion is unlike anything else. Only those who have had such feelings can understand what I mean, and those who have not have been fortunate.

On January 16, 1948, at noon, the official farewell ceremony took place; afterward they took Mikhoels out of the theater forever. A very large crowd also accompanied the casket from the theater to the cemetery.

Several days afterward, they organized a memorial evening at the theater. There were speeches and also artistic performances. More than anything I was stunned by the performance of Bolshoi Ballet star Galina Ulanova. Later at home, I learned that my parents were not less impressed. The dance performed by Ulanova was based on the musical work by Sen

Sans *The Dying Swan*. She danced in a circle of light that was formed on the darkened stage, directly under a huge portrait of Mikhoels toward which she repeatedly extended her arms, and upon reaching the point where her swan "died," she collapsed at the portrait's feet.

Neither at the memorial evening nor at the funeral did anyone disclose his true emotions as Ulanova had done, and not because they had not learned the art of dance but because they had learned the art of suppressing emotions that are better kept silenced.

As convention dictated, every speaker delivered his speech at the funeral service in the name of some institution, for example, one theater or another, one association or another, and so forth. The eulogy for the GOSET was delivered by Zuskin:

> Friends, the pain is great. We have been orphaned . . . You must understand how hard it is for me now, how hard for all of us . . . He was the symbol of life, and this combination, Mikhoels and death, is impossible . . . The loss is terrible; there is no way back . . . Yet we know what times we are living through in our country, we know that you, dear Solomon Mikhoels, taught us to work with passion and dedication . . . We promise you that we will work to fill, if only a little, the vacuum that was created by this meaningless death, so unnecessary, so unexpected . . . We wish you farewell.[1]

There was another thing that shook my father in those days.

On January 14, 1948, the day after Mikhoels died, the actors assembled in the rehearsal hall around the long table where they used to sit and listen to the first readings of the plays they planned to stage.

This time, among the actors gathered there was also Moyshe Goldblatt who had left the GOSET long before and later became artistic director of the Jewish theater in Kiev, the capital of the Ukrainian Republic. During World War II, this theater was sent to one of the cities in the rear lines, but at the end of the war, when it was about to return to Kiev, the authorities announced that they didn't find any room for the theater—in Kiev! In the city whose name was associated with Babi-Yar they did not find room for a Jewish theater!—and they decided it would move to Chernovits, also in the Ukraine, and it was from there Goldblatt came to Mikhoels's funeral.

Now everyone was sitting in silence. Mikhoels's absence was very pronounced, and his usual seat at the table was noticeably empty.

Bit by bit the people began to disperse. Zuskin took Goldblatt aside and told him the contents of Mikhoels's note that he had read only three days before, on January 11. Some twenty-five years later, Goldblatt would reveal in his memoirs: "According to Zuskin, Mikhoels wrote in his note that very soon something was going to happen to him, Mikhoels, and the addressee of the letter, Zuskin, would be compelled to undertake to direct the theater. The letter also held a veiled allusion to the fact that Mikhoels had been invited several times 'there' [the secret police]. Was the event in Minsk something more horrifying than a road accident? Zuskin did not expect any answer to this question."[2] Why did my father, who didn't tell anyone about this letter, not even my mother, choose to tell Goldblatt of all people? Perhaps because Goldblatt lived in a different city, a fact that naturally prevented any further discussion of the letter that was so frightening and so dangerous.

Zuskin sinks into meditation: I have to go on living. But how? What will be with the theater now, with Eda, with himself? Who will protect them? Protect? Them? Mikhoels couldn't even protect himself.

No! Zuskin doesn't dare, not even in his thoughts, guess at the real cause of Mikhoels's death. They said—a road accident. So it was a road accident, and nothing else.[3]

Zuskin remembers the moments of happiness that he experienced together with Mikhoels, and he is astonished how pouring salt on old wounds almost made him forget the real relationship between Mikhoels and himself. "Mikhoels, like all mortals, must have had his faults. I don't want to remember them and I see no reason to do so. You want the truth? I don't see them now."[4] This is what the artist Alexander Tyshler wrote immediately after Mikhoels's death.

Partner

In several places in the book I have touched upon the subject of "Mikhoels and Zuskin." I have already mentioned that in Father's attitude to Mikhoels, he addressed two personalities: he directed his bitterness at Vovsi and he delighted in his relationship with Mikhoels. I would like to add that Zuskin, despite this delight, felt a need to detach himself from the stereotype of "Mikhoels and Zuskin" and to live without reliance on that restrictive word "and."

Actually, the "and" did not always appear between their names, and this will be substantiated by the story that Zuskin told during the trial: "Now, this is interesting. Zuskin—Mikhoels. When long before the war I went to the district military committee, the district military commander looked at my military card and said, Why does it have just the name Zuskin here? Where is Mikhoels's name? These two names were so closely linked in the indictment as well . . . I kept waiting for people to mention Mikhoels and then Zuskin would follow, but no, that didn't happen."[5]

I, the daughter of Zuskin, also kept waiting for this many years, in vain. When I began to work on writing this book, I promised myself that I would succeed at the assignment that Father failed at, to separate Zuskin, not from Mikhoels, but from the axiom Zuskin-Mikhoels, or the opposite, Mikhoels-Zuskin. Now I admit that I have not succeeded in this assignment.

For those who charted the last path in Zuskin's life, this statement was a basis in spinning the web of his investigation, conducting his trial, and determining his fate. They had no interest in Zuskin's personality, his beliefs, or even the crimes attributed to him and of which he was accused. The essence of the connection "Mikhoels-Zuskin" went into effect exactly as it had been formulated absent-mindedly by the junior officer in the recruiting office years before, and it was what lay at the groundwork of their fiendish plans.

To my great regret, Father's friends, too, some very loyal to him, as well as ardent fans of his art, did not see beyond what that officer in the recruiting office saw. Even when they remember Zuskin, and even mingle their memories with love and longing, they recall him mostly as part of the axiom "Mikhoels-Zuskin." With this, my father was also worthy of being recognized as an independent personality and also remembered this way.

In 2000 a documentary film was produced in Israel about Zuskin, and the filmmakers presented Mikhoels with great respect but the focus was on Zuskin's personality, and his portrait in the film, is a living portrait with a sense of an independent self, impressive and faithful to what he was. The ones who broke that link between the two names, were, of all people, those who were born and raised in the Land of Israel, at a distance of decades and thousands of kilometers from the reality that gave rise to the axiom "Mikhoels-Zuskin."

But this book is one that I am writing. In my efforts to paint a full portrait of Zuskin, my father, I can't bypass the axiom "Mikhoels-Zuskin" both because of its being an integral part of my upbringing and my environment, and because of a need to interpret the tragic use made of it by the executioners: After all, they used it to pave the way to Zuskin's death.

And in general, the life story of each one of them detached from "Mikhoels-Zuskin" would not be a true story. "When I think of Mikhoels, I see Zuskin . . . who was an inseparable part of Mikhoels just as Mikhoels was an inseparable part of him. Together they jumped, danced, wept, and laughed . . . The destiny that embraced Mikhoels and Zuskin and led them on the path of their artistic life, this destiny, shared and tragic, did not relax its embrace until their terrible death,"[6] the artist Tyshler writes in his article entitled "I See Mikhoels."

Pavel Markov reached the conclusion that in this inseparable duo was an internal debate, in real life and on stage. "Facing Mikhoels was a man whose compliant and bashful appearance covered up his intelligence and resolve to do whatever he set out to do . . . Mikhoels's heroes knew how to struggle against a higher power or raise existential questions to the pinnacles of philosophy, Zuskin's heroes clung to their own small truth—was it really so small?—and did not intend to solve the problems of the world."[7] Actually, in the world they both inhabited, the problems were solved without them, and in the most fundamental way.

When the GOSET theater was on tour in Western Europe back in 1928, Mikhoels and Zuskin were interviewed together for a Berlin newspaper. Asked how to account for their "togetherness," Mikhoels answered jokingly: "Like a perfect creation that would be obtained if a sculptor had taken both of us as raw material and sculpted one man out of it."[8] A decade and half later, this answer given by Mikhoels was completed by Hotsmakh, Zuskin's hero in *The Wandering Stars*: "One man among so many wolves."[9]

Hunted (Beginning)

And the wolves held back. For the time being.

The days of mourning were over, and the theater opened its doors again to the public. In recent years Mikhoels had not been an actor, so there was no need to find a replacement for him and to practice. The rehearsals were held only for brushing up, and the repertory remained as it had been. And yet, it would not be right to say that life went back to normal. While the theater and the acting school returned to their routine activity, rumors flew that no one dared utter out loud.

Anyone who has never lived in the Soviet Union or another country with a totalitarian regime is incapable of understanding how rumors fly between people in silence and certainly couldn't believe it. And yet you should believe it. Rumors are indeed passed in silence. It is sufficient to give a look, a sigh, a shrug of the shoulders. You can always whisper in someone's ear, of course, but that is not really necessary. For example, regarding the reason for Mikhoels's death, everyone without exception stuck to the official traffic accident version but it is very doubtful that many of them really believed this.

Mikhoels's personality was so large and extraordinary, and death in a road accident is so banal. On the other hand, a staged death is precisely suited to a great actor, and the creator[10] that thought up such an idea extends beyond the limits of an ordinary person—in its brutality. This creator, like his subjects, needed no words; "the stenography of humphing"[11] was sufficient.

It is possible that it is the secret police that spread the rumors against the accident theory. If that was true, these insinuations were designed not to expose the truth but to intimidate and to deter. Along with the fears that the rumors connected to Mikhoels's death arouse, the air was full of more vague terrors but no less frightening: the uncertainty as to the future of the theater, the future of the Jewish Anti-Fascist Committee and anyone who was connected to these institutions.

In public Zuskin acted like everyone, pretending that everything was all right. At home it was harder to pretend.

The depressed mood that my parents sank into after Mikhoels's sudden death left its mark on our lifestyle at home. I naturally noticed that the atmosphere was gradually changing and that I was no longer the center of the family's life—for example, it seemed that no one noticed that I was walking around the house in torn house slippers. Even on the morning of my birthday there was no usual row of chairs heaped with piles of gifts. I got out of bed, and automatically, without looking, stuck my feet into slippers. My feet felt around; instead of torn lining, here was something pleasant. I looked down and on my feet were new slippers. I liked them. And yet, for a fraction of a second, I was disappointed. Was that all? And in a flash of understanding, I realized: if on my birthday, nothing was happening as in the past, it was a sign that my parents' world has collapsed, and with it, mine, too.

I feel a bit uncomfortable with my reader. Here I am speaking of events that are so momentous and I am mentioning them in a context that is seemingly less important, perhaps even trivial. Yet I will remind my reader that I am returning, and not for the first time, to the existence of the inanimate objects in our lives. This time, the slippers.

My birthday was preceded by an event that brought my father additional suffering.

Artistic Director

One day in February 1948, my parents informed me that they would be delayed at the theater after the rehearsal because there was supposed to be a general meeting. After the meeting, Father stayed for a while at the theater, and Mother came home, not alone but in the company of several actors. All of them were excited, and one of the actors updated me that at the meeting there was one topic only: who would lead the theater. The meeting was very short because the entire team voted unanimously for the proposal made by the first speaker: In Jewish families, it is customary when the father dies, that the oldest son becomes head of the family. And if the oldest son dies, then the next one takes over. In our family of actors, Zuskin was both the oldest son and the brother of Mikhoels. Whom else could we possibly follow?

It only remained to receive the okay from the authorities. However, the process probably took place in reverse: The theater administration was informed of the decision to appoint Zuskin to the job before the voting had begun. Whatever the explanation, on February 17, 1948, the Committee of Artistic Affairs published an order appointing Benjamin Zuskin, the People's Artist of the Russian and Uzbek Soviet Republics and Stalin Prize laureate, to the position of artistic director of the State Jewish Theater in Moscow.

Did this directive stir gladness in Zuskin's heart and flatter him? If so, then for a very brief moment only. After all, he used to say that official positions are not for him. In his current dejected and anxiety-ridden mood, with a sense of general uncertainty, was this the time to undertake responsibility for a theater whose future was insecure? But his alacrity or his refusal meant nothing, and determined nothing. If there was an order—orders were not debated. They were obeyed. Zuskin was aware of this, and he was also aware of something he regarded as more important. He understood that all the GOSET people were pinning their hopes on him—both because he was a leading actor and because of the general sympathy they felt for him, and because of "Mikhoels-Zuskin."

When he contemplated the fate of the GOSET, his heart ached. Now he was convinced that already in 1938 when he had considered leaving the GOSET, he had understood: the moment he leaves, the theater ceases to exist.

While filling the post of artistic director of the theater, Zuskin still continued to appear on stage as an actor. He did nevertheless give up one of the many duties he had: he stopped teaching at the acting school.

First and foremost, Zuskin was compelled to return to an occupation that he had engaged in as a youth and also as secretary of the theater: inspecting the accounting books. He discovered at once that the financial situation of the theater was extremely bad. Previously the theater had received solid government support; afterward, that was cut, and now the theater received almost no state support at all. Salvation must come from the audience. Bringing as many theatergoers as possible was supposed to fill the theater's coffers. But they had not been staging new productions recently, the current productions have been running too long, and this was not enough to cover expenses.

He arrived at the conclusion that the repertory must be dealt with. Zuskin understood that to do this, he must invest untiring efforts, but at the same time, the idea of dealing with the repertory calmed him. He was, after all, an actor, not an accountant. Zuskin was filled with energy and began to poke around in Mikhoels's working files. Here, too, he was in for a disappointment since in Mikhoels's working files he found four plays only.

In March 1948, government financial support of the GOSET theater ended completely. What to do? Zuskin decided to rework a few old plays, starting with *The Sorceress*. The play did not come off as dazzling as the one by Granovsky which was like fireworks. But today one could not think of fireworks and certainly not of Granovsky. Furthermore, Zuskin himself did not find in himself the youthful ardor or the mental energies necessary to play the Sorceress with the flight that he once had. Still it was pleasant for him and his friends to give a new lease of life to the plays that they so loved to perform in the past. After that Zuskin revived the play *Hershele Ostropoler*, which he himself had directed previously.

At the end of March 1948, they organized a gathering of the theatergoers in the theater, and in his speech, Zuskin told of the theater's plans and suggested that the people present buy subscriptions.

A few days before this gathering, on March 23, the Committee of Artistic Affairs passed a resolution to allow all theaters to sell subscriptions at a discounted price. According to the experience of the theaters where this method was already employed, it was supposed to encourage the audience to come and watch plays. At the GOSET theater, too, some of the public bought the subscriptions, but the occupancy during the performances was still only partial.

This situation created an atmosphere of dissatisfaction and unease. Zuskin himself felt it in both roles—as artistic director and as an actor. As an actor, he always built his roles with consideration for the audience's response, and now, it was hard for him to play to a half-empty hall. He found it hard to supply an explanation for this phenomenon. After all, thanks to the shift to the subscription system, the theater's financial situation began to gradually improve. Why was this happening? Zuskin wondered.

Why? Because the wolves were out for prey.

The sale of subscriptions had just started to pick up and the rumors began to fly: the secret police were following the people who visited the GOSET theater. Some of the loyal theater crowd deliberately bought subscriptions to rescue the theater from its financial straits but preferred not to actually go to the theater and remained at home. There were not many Don Quixotes, and the budget, even if improved, was still not satisfactory.

Zuskin sent a letter full of expressions of despair to one of the officials in charge of theaters for the Party Central Committee. The official promised him that the theater would not be closed down. All of the same, Zuskin continued to write letters.

To the extent that Zuskin was pinning his hopes on the promises that he received, he acted energetically to decide upon a new repertory. But when he contacted the decision makers and asked them for authorization for a play or a director he had chosen, they did not respond. Why should the decision makers bother to respond? What interest did they have in improving the budget of the GOSET theater?

Nonetheless, on May 4, 1948, the new show based on *Life is Worth Living (Kedai tsu lebn)* by the playwright Isaac Hoberman was performed. This was one of the plays kept in Mikhoels's working files. The director— Zuskin. The premiere was staged three times and the hall filled up more or less, but a short while later, the size of the audience dropped. In general, the number of theatergoers was noticeably less at all the performances.

When they staged *Life is Worth Living* ten days later, as a regular play, Zuskin noticed that there were too many empty seats in the theater. If this had been an ordinary day of the week, he wouldn't have been able to think about anything except the theater's empty box office, but the day was May 14, 1948.

May 14, 1948, is the day that the State of Israel was established. The mood of many Soviet Jews was elevated. They also felt pride that the Soviet Union immediately recognized this state, as they were proud of the Soviet Union's support for the Partition of Palestine plan voted on in the UN back in November 29, 1947. "In May 1948, with the approval of Molotov,[12] a telegram of congratulations was sent by the Jewish Anti-Fascist Committee to the first president of the State of Israel, Chaim Weizmann."[13] Its text was published in *Eynikayt*.[14] Postcards with congratulations began to arrive at the Jewish Anti-Fascist Committee and the office of the newspaper from ordinary Jews as well as from Jews in key positions, among them the congratulations signed by the artistic director of the State Jewish Theater, Benjamin Zuskin.

Zuskin's Jewish heart swelled with joy and pride. Still, he did not forget the coincidental disappearance of the recording of Mikhoels's speech at the evening dedicated to the memory of Mendele Moykher Sforim, and ominous portents overshadowed the joy.

Zuskin concealed his feelings, which normally were concealed in any case, and returned to deal with the concerns of the theater. When the answer from the powers-that-be was late in arriving, Zuskin discussed the financial plight of the theater with the administrative personnel and the accounting office. They all decided: there was no escape from firing some of the actors. This was by all means a difficult decision, but the repertory had few shows, and few of these had crowd scenes.

When my father was away from home, actresses in supporting roles used to come to our house, to speak to Mother and beg for their lives. Perhaps she could ask Father not to put their name on the list of people to be dismissed. My mother very much identified with them but she was unable to help. She knew that her husband's hands were tied, and dismissals were the solution. Solution to what?

The authorities understood that GOSET was finding it hard to surrender to the bad situation, and they tried another tack. In summer 1948, they sent the theater on tour in different cities. At first glance this was only natural, because in the past the theater had gone on such tours every summer. But it was very clear that there was a catch here. After all, the theater had just begun to work on two new productions, and they were also working on revisions of productions that were running, a necessity born by the dismissal of some of the participating actors. Furthermore, travel expenses and hotel costs in the past had been paid for by the government budget; after all, they had an interest in the propaganda aspect of the theater performances. Now the authorities were not interested in promoting Jewish culture, although they did not proclaim this officially. So, what propaganda was there to disseminate? The tour of Odessa and Leningrad guaranteed a heavy drain on the budget.

I remember the tour to Leningrad very clearly, down to the last detail. My parents took me there with them to show me this beautiful city, the magnificent museums and other fascinating sites. All of these naturally enriched my intellectual baggage, although more than all of these, what is preserved in my memory is the profound grief that encircled my father. I have already mentioned that once he hugged me and filled with sorrow, walked me back and forth in the room, and that afterward, I observed him in the role of Hotsmakh filled with this sorrow. I just didn't mention that this happened during the tour of Leningrad in that summer of 1948.

Very symbolic was the fact that he did not appear on stage in the first Leningrad performance of *Freylekhs*. He sent instead his stand-in as if he wanted to show that his theater was alive—even without him!—and that there was a young generation who would raise the banner of the theater. "From the beginning of 1948, when Zuskin became the artistic director of the theater, he was not called upon to exercise his super-sensitivity; catastrophe approached with great fanfare."[15] When the performances came to an end in Leningrad, Father felt totally spent.

Rest. Father had to rest. He did not forget the pleasant feeling that embraced the family on the two previous vacations that he had spent with my mother and me at the Baltic Sea shore. Now, too, he wanted to take his vacation there. Again we traveled to the Baltic Sea coast, but this time, the resort village was no longer on the outskirts of the city of Riga like then, but near Leningrad.

We rented a house in a lovely resort village, and my parents immediately found a social group for themselves. There, for the first time Father was pulled into a game of cards. Maybe it was his way of silencing his worries and even pushing them out of his thoughts. Father's regular partner would join him on his way home. Mother was not thrilled with this person, perhaps not only because he was a partner to the card games to which she objected, but because this man probably led her to believe that he tapped not only with his carved cane on the ground but also with his tongue—as he informed on people.

When we returned to Moscow, they called Father from the secretariat of the Jewish Anti-Fascist Committee and told him that a letter had arrived from Canada addressed to Zuskin. It turns out that the letter was from my uncle Yitshak. Yitshak told Father that their father Leybe had passed away in South Africa. This time I do not remember Father's lamentation for his father, unlike his bitter weeping when he learned of his mother's death. It is possible that because of the difficult situation in which he found himself, he did not give external expression to his pain.

Twenty years had passed since my father and my grandfather had met in 1928 in Paris. During those years, except for a short period at the beginning, my father did not correspond with his father, mother, brothers, or sisters, some living in South Africa and some in Canada, that is, in the "harmful West." He could not even correspond with his daughter, my half-sister Tamara, although she was living in "democratic" Poland.

It is interesting that Tamara did succeed in creating contacts with our grandfather. She sent him a letter from Warsaw, and Grandfather answered her: "My dear granddaughter. All is well with me. I work as the chief cutter in the largest, most fashionable clothing store in our city Johannesburg and earn a good living . . . Just one thing bothers me and that is that your father doesn't write to me for some reason. I know about his success only from the newspapers. Ask him to write to me as much as he can."[16] How could old Leybe, who lived a normal life free of fear, imagine and understand what that "for some reason" was that caused his famous son not to write to him?

Nonetheless, when I read this letter many years later, I was shocked when I noticed that it was dated January 12, 1948—the day before January 13, 1948, when Mikhoels was murdered! One day passed since that day, and Nyomke's world had collapsed completely. The twentieth century threw father and son onto distant continents, a distance that was not measured only in miles.

Immediately after he returned from his vacation, my father divided his time between directing the rehearsals and dealing with administrative matters, and in the evenings, he mounted the stage again and again, and only rarely visited the city council meetings or the Jewish Anti-Fascist Committee. At night, he could not sleep, and worries gnawed at his heart.

On the evening of September 14, 1948, Father suddenly felt sharp pains in his abdomen. Taken to a hospital, he was immediately sent to the operating room. They discovered an inflamed appendix. The operation passed successfully. Zuskin was sent to recuperate at a convalescent home near Moscow.

And so, they saved my father's life. But for what?

Zuskin recovered and gained strength. He returned to his position as artistic director of the theater. In 1999 Professor Mordechai Altshuler of the Hebrew University in Jerusalem, in his speech published at the beginning of this book, would say that this role of Zuskin was "the most difficult of his life." I agree with him. This role was indeed the most difficult. And yet—not the most frightening. The most frightening role of all still awaited Benjamin Zuskin.

After a short time the wolves' readiness to attack became apparent.

On November 20, 1948, all of the morning newspapers published the news that from now on, subscriptions and tickets to all the theaters in Moscow and the large cities would be sold through central box offices. Why did this ad, seemingly not of great importance, appear simultaneously in all of the newspapers? And if the ad was placed there, it is not clear what was the problem with selling tickets through central box offices.

In a totalitarian state, theater productions or any type of entertainment are not marginal matters. They are used to convey ideological messages. In a totalitarian state, every institution, even the smallest, is under the watchful eye of the authorities. When the central box office sells a ticket to an event at a cultural institution that is on the list requiring a report, the cashier sends the relevant reports to the relevant departments. He might also receive instructions about what to report to a certain theater. So when they informed the GOSET that the tickets had been sold out, in effect, the sale had not yet begun.

The very same day the wolves attacked.

On November 20, 1948, a decision was made by the top brass of the Communist Party and the state to disband the Jewish Anti-Fascist Committee.

Anti-Fascist (End)

CENTRAL COMMITTEE OF THE ALL-UNION COMMUNIST
(BOLSHEVIK) PARTY
NOVEMBER 20, 1948
REPORT OF THE PROCEEDINGS # 66 OF THE POLITBIURO
SESSION
[EXCERPT]

Item 81. On the Jewish Anti-Fascist Committee.

The following resolution of the Bureau of the Council of Ministers of the USSR should be approved. The Bureau of the Council of Ministers of the USSR charges the USSR Ministry of State Security with the immediate dismissal of the Jewish Anti-Fascist Committee, as the facts show that this Committee is the center of anti-Soviet propaganda that regularly delivers anti-Soviet information to organs of foreign intelligent services.

In accordance with the above, the publishing organs of this Committee should be closed and their files should be confiscated.

In the meantime nobody should be arrested.

Secretary General of the Central Committee: *J. Stalin*[17]

On November 20, 1948, I returned from school and found my parents whispering in a state of great emotion. In response to my unspoken question, they told me that a decision was made to close down the Jewish Anti-Fascist Committee. They did not add any other information. In fact, they did not know the details. Then my father went out to the corridor where a phone was hanging on the wall. He talked at length with someone. I heard the words, "You already know about Kropotkin Street?" And I understood that he was hinting at the disbanding of the Jewish Anti-Fascist Committee, which was located on that street. My mother also heard and her face was strained and went pale as though the blood were drained out. Father replaced the phone receiver and came back into the room. "Why are you talking about it on the telephone?" my mother asked in a trembling voice. Father appeared confused. "It came out by itself," he tried to justify. It is clear that he thought that Mother was right. Was Mother's concern only an expression of displeasure? It was her genuine fear speaking.

That evening Mother's sisters, Emma and Lisa, came in, their eyes frightened. Emma worked as a bookkeeper in some institute of science, and Lisa was a receptionist in a dental clinic. Could there have been any connection between these institutions and the Committee? No, but there was a reason that Moscow was called a large village where everybody knows everything. My aunts did not want to pour salt on my father's wounds, so they drew Mother aside: What would be? Mother could do nothing but shrug her shoulders helplessly.

Father recalled that he had not opened the newspaper yet. He sat down and opened the Yiddish newspaper *Eynikayt* and found an ad there: This issue, dated November 20, 1948, was the last issue of the newspaper. Beginning the next day, the newspaper would cease to appear.

The next day, November 21, 1948, at the Jewish Anti-Fascist Committee at 10 Kropotkin Street, officers of the Ministry of State Security conducted a search and seized all of its documents. That same day a search was conducted at the offices of *Eynikayt*.

On November 25, 1948, they closed the *Der Emes* Publishing House, which published books in Yiddish. The liquidation of the publishing house, which took place in the presence of its personnel, was a pogrom in every sense. In the printing department, they broke the typesetting machine and destroyed manuscripts, like barbarians attacking a peaceful village.

At the same time, they rummaged in Mikhoels's workroom, which had become a GOSET museum, and there, too, they seized everything that was connected to the Jewish Anti-Fascist Committee.

Later came the turn of the Jewish Division at the State Radio Broadcasting Authority.

Let us go back a bit and describe Zuskin as a member of the Jewish Anti-Fascist Committee.

Zuskin felt he was an extra already at the beginning of his membership in the Jewish Anti-Fascist Committee. He was not seeking honors. Yet, as a responsible person, he never refused to write an article about the theater or to attend a compulsory meeting, if he didn't have a performance that night. After Mikhoels's death, he was so busy in the theater that he kept even farther away from the Committee, and many of the Committee's activities were conducted without his knowledge and without his participation.

Thus, the Committee published statistical facts about the number of Jews who have been awarded the *Hero of the Soviet Union* title.[18] According to these figures, the percentage of the Heroes among the Soviet Jews was higher than among other Soviet nationalities. Eventually, publishing these figures would be considered a crime. After all, the Soviet Union boasts equality among all of its nationalities.

Zuskin perhaps heard something somewhere from somebody but didn't know anything for certain about gathering such data.

The Committee submitted *The Black Book*[19] to be approved by the decision makers. This is a book written in Russian by several writers, who are either members of the Jewish Anti-Fascist Committee or work for it, with a description of the Holocaust that befell Soviet Jews during World War II in Soviet territory, which was occupied by the Nazis. Publication of the book was immediately prohibited, with the same reasoning that the suffering experienced under the Nazi occupation had to be presented as experienced equally by all the nations.

Zuskin was present just at one of the meetings of the Committee presidium when they discussed *The Black Book*, but never read it.

At the end of the war and afterward, the Jewish Anti-Fascist Committee began to receive countless appeals by Jews; the Committee members tried to handle them. The appeals from ordinary Jews related to the difficulties they encountered when trying to gain admission to the universities or get a job or housing—primarily, housing. In 1944, the leadership of the Committee sent a letter to the Soviet authorities with a proposal to establish a Soviet Jewish autonomous republic in the Crimea, a peninsula on the Black Sea.

In the letter they explain that after the Holocaust, it has become clear that Soviet Jews need a territory of their own; that already in the twenties and thirties Jewish kolkhozes in the Crimea had operated successfully, while the Jewish Autonomous Oblast (region) of Birobidzhan, which was remote from the center of the country, had not enjoyed similar success.

To anyone who is versed even slightly in the Soviet reality it is clear that it was only the Soviet authorities who could plant in the heads of the Committee members the idea for such a letter.

Nevertheless, the Committee members hoped that it was possible to take care of people who had lost their homes in the terrible war. But in the minds of the Soviet executioners, the letter's content would be turned into "The Crimean Project," a project whose objective was to wrest the Crimean peninsula from the Soviet Union. "Only here [in prison] I learn that the Crimea question was an issue in January 1944,"[20] Zuskin would say during the trial.

For personal reasons Zuskin did not participate in events related to the newborn State of Israel.

On September 16, 1948, when the guest of honor, Golda Meir, the first Minister Plenipotentiary, that is, chief of the diplomatic mission of the State of Israel to the Soviet Union, accompanied by the Mission's members, appeared at the GOSET and was received with enthused applause by actors and theatergoers alike, Zuskin was recovering in the hospital since on the night between September 14 and 15 in 1948, he had undergone surgery.

Afterward Zuskin convalesced at a rest home and missed additional events: A reception where Meir was present and met a few Soviet personages in key positions and famous Soviet Jewish personalities; services in the Moscow synagogue, on October 3, 1948, the eve of Rosh Hashana, and on October 13, 1948, Yom Kippur, where some fifty thousand Jews were cheering for Meir and Israeli diplomats.

These events thrilled even my serene, quiet Aunt Emma. One fall day in 1948 Emma suggested that I join her in a walk. We had gotten far from the house and turned onto some street. "Look front and left," said Emma with an excitement I had never known her to possess. I looked; on the other side of the street, an unfamiliar flag was flying above the entrance to one of the buildings. It was the flag of the State of Israel, and this building was the home of the Israeli diplomatic mission. When we came into the entrance of my home, I heard my mother open our door on the fourth floor and I shouted with all my might, "Mama! I just saw the flag of the State of Israel!" My mother scolded her sister Emma, of course, and she demanded that I be quiet and not tell anyone what I had seen. You can understand her: the strongest emotion in those days was fear.

When, after his surgery and convalescence, Zuskin was back in the theater, he was too busy to attend most of the sessions where the Committee was discussing the State of Israel.

It bears mentioning that the Soviet Jews treated the establishment of the State of Israel in a most surprising way, perhaps surprising even themselves, and first and foremost, astounding the authorities. Thousands of Jews expressed a desire to take part in the War of Independence that broke out in the Middle East right after the proclamation of the State of Israel. These Jews contacted the Jewish Anti-Fascist Committee which for them represented the leadership of the Soviet Jewish community, but that was because they were not familiar with the official hierarchy. This is despite the fact that this leadership was not officially appointed to lead, and officially there was no Jewish community. In the letters they sent, they write: "The Jewish Anti-Fascist Committee and the editorial board of *Eynikayt* are the exclusive representatives of the Jewish population in the Soviet Union."[21] These Jews had not learned their lesson from thirty years of Soviet rule nor from the purges and persecutions. They believed in the Communist Party, in the Soviet government, and in Comrade Stalin the man. That is why they signed these letters with their full names and noted their addresses and places of work. (One should not be surprised at the disappearance of the letter writers!) Here are some excerpts from these letters: "I am proud that we, the Jews, have become a nation equal to all other nations . . . Soviet Jews should be permitted to travel to Palestine to enlist in the army there . . . How long is the Jewish Anti-Fascist Committee going to sit around doing nothing?"[22]

The Jewish Anti-Fascist Committee by dint of the role thrust upon it rejected these manifestos and emphasized at every opportunity that the only homeland of the Soviet Jews was the Soviet Union.

In fact, Zuskin was on the sidelines regarding the Committee's activities but not regarding the terrible retribution exacted because of them.

Hunted (Continuation)

"In the meantime nobody should be arrested." In this last phrase of the Politbiuro resolution the important words are "in the meantime." In the meantime, they could speak politely to Zuskin in a small, pretty house decorated with a flowering garden, where one of the branches of the Ministry of State Security had its office, although there was no sign indicating this fact, or in the empty theater in the off-hours. In the meantime, they could stalk Zuskin in the street, draw close to him and breathe down his neck, ring his telephone and cast an ominous silence, or send him a letter that was unsigned but full of threats. The fear spread by these was fiercer than the fear that the wolves that darted howling through the forest at night cast in the hearts of the lone traveler.

Zuskin was being hunted but he held his ground. When he appeared in the theater and met the agitated actors who were beset by uncertainty as to whether a rehearsal would or would not take place, everyone looked up to him: perhaps he had in his bag of tricks some magic that would restore their hope. He stood before them, as ill as he felt, exhausted from a sleepless night, but still capable of feeling what they were feeling. Zuskin knew how to sense his audience. For the first time in his life, he was not entirely sincere when he acted out the sincerity required of this role. And the actors, who were also practiced at the tricks of pretending, began to sincerely believe in his acting. "Why are you standing there like dummies? Get to work! Begin the rehearsal!" So everybody laughed and took their places. Did anyone there know what demons were threatening Zuskin, whose soul was gnawed by anguish and fear?

Eda knew. But when Zusa saw her understanding, anxious look, it seemed to him that he could assume the image of a person who believes that this too shall pass. At night he pretended to be asleep and thought in his naiveté that he could hide from Eda and conceal from her the insomnia that had plagued him ever since Mikhoels died. He didn't tell her about the polite conversations in the small pretty house or in the empty theater; he didn't share with her the experiences caused him by those who were breathing down his neck, the anonymous callers, the senders of unsigned letters. Why open another box of terrors, why cover over her fear with another fear?

Zuskin the prey wished to pour out his heart, but to whom? To friends? It was clear that there was no house where one could feel safe from eavesdroppers, but at least it might possible not to pretend, even by silence. He ran to Yekhezkel Dobrushin, his closest friend. He met there Joseph Kerler. Dobrushin and Kerler were not members of the presidium of the Jewish Anti-Fascist Committee but they were active in the Committee's institutions. The problem then applied to all of them. They sat there a whole evening. They spoke—didn't speak. They were silent more than they spoke.

From the memoirs of Joseph Kerler: "I went to accompany Zuskin to his house . . . If you only knew, Kerler, how hard it is for me! Why did Mikhoels have to go to that accursed Minsk? Oi! What did he do to us? After Mikhoels's funeral, we were facing a totally different Zuskin. There had been a great Jewish actor, blessed by fortune, beloved by all, by his theater friends, by the audience, by the critics. And now I see another Zuskin. This different Zuskin had lost his agile, elegant gait and he walked heavily, dragging his feet . . . If you only knew, Kerler . . . I am sick, very sick."[23] Kerler felt that Zuskin wanted to say something, to unburden himself, and he was silent.

Boulevard Stroller

The house where we lived was located on Tverskoi Boulevard. To make one's way from our house to the theater one would cross the boulevard breadth-wise, and to reach the School of Acting or the Moscow Actors House one walked along the boulevard in the right direction, and to reach the Jewish Anti-Fascist Committee—in the left direction.

My father also had a habit of walking to and fro when he wanted to relax, or to reach a decision. Besides, Tverskoi Boulevard was one of the places, and there weren't many like it, where Father and I felt a special intimacy between us.

After Zuskin lost Mikhoels and took his place as the head of the theater, he nearly never walked along our boulevard. Still, sometimes, in the late evening hours, in an attempt to outmaneuver his insomnia, he would walk slowly on the side lanes.

One evening when Zuskin left the theater at the end of a performance, a certain person dressed in European clothing approached him. It turned out that he was deliberately waiting for Zuskin. The man identified himself and added, I am a physician, and I live and work in Poland, in Warsaw, and I came here as part of my work. I brought you regards from Tamara; she works with me in the same hospital. With an experienced gaze, Zuskin surveyed the surroundings, didn't notice anything suspicious, was somewhat calmed, and invited the man from the foreign country to walk with him, along Tverskoi Boulevard of course. He didn't dare invite back home with him a messenger from his daughter, who had the status of a foreign resident. After all, all around his house walked messengers of the secret police.

Nor did he dare walk openly in the company of a new acquaintance. "Please, do follow me," Zuskin suggested to the guest, "then afterward, we will switch." The guest walked behind Zuskin and told him about Tamara, whom he was forbidden to even write to. "What shall I tell your daughter?" The guest quickened his steps until he was now walking ahead of Zuskin. Zuskin shifted his gaze to the length of the so-familiar boulevard, approached the guest so closely that there was no space between them, and whispered to him in Yiddish, "Tell her the ground is burning beneath my feet."

Hunted (End)

And the wolves were drawing closer to Zuskin, almost touching him. Their howling never ceased, didn't allow him to sleep at night. Their eyes gleamed in the dark.

And he continued to go to the theater, to mount the stage, conduct rehearsals, plan things. After all he had to compose the repertory. That is very essential because after the institutions that were conducted in Yiddish—the newspaper, the publishing house, the radio broadcasting division—were closed down, all that was left of the Jewish culture revolved around the GOSET . . . Until further notice.

But this great effort was not enough to repel the wolves.

The Committee of Artistic Affairs sent the GOSET on a tour in Leningrad. A tour! Again! And at a time when it was most inappropriate! In terms of the theater's budget it was truly a risky venture. Secondly, only four months had passed since the Leningrad audience watched the GOSET productions. Not only that but it was winter now, and at this time of year, the Leningrad theaters did not leave their city, and this would make it hard for the GOSET to find an available hall.

For the tour, Zuskin chose productions in which he personally would not have a part: either productions that he had no role in, or productions that another actor alternately stood in for him. Before the tour, he polished up various scenes, in particular the scenes where the stand-ins would act. He arrived in the morning to rehearsals almost unconscious, but as always in the rehearsal hall his mischievous shout reverberated, "Why are you standing there like dummies?" Even though his mood was apparent to everyone, the warmth that he radiated misled the actors into believing even for a moment and in defiance of all common sense that this was the Zuskin they had always known.

In fact, why was Zuskin investing so much in the work of his stand-in actors? Didn't he intend to mount the stage himself there? And precisely at this time when it was only his appearance on stage that offered a glimmer of hope for the theater's situation to improve?

Yet that was true: he did not plan to appear in Leningrad. Moreover, he didn't even plan to travel to Leningrad. Could that be? "I am sick, very sick . . ."

Since 1938 when my father recovered from his nervous breakdown and insomnia, he had more or less regular check-ups. As bearer of the title "People's Artist of the Russian and Uzbek Soviet Republics," he had the right to be treated at the best medical institutions in Moscow. But in 1948, no one of the illustrious physicians in these institutions had succeeded in curing the insomnia that beset my father.

Zuskin consulted with Professor Alexander Vishnievsky, the surgeon who invented a special technique for local anesthesia.

During World War II in the hospital directed by Vishnievsky, they established a department for monitoring the effect of his technique on those who had undergone surgery. After the war, the department also admitted other patients who needed treatment using various types of anesthesia, and Vishnievsky connected Zuskin with its physicians.

The doctors promised Zuskin that artificial sleep would help him, significantly, would calm him, release him from anxiety, return him to life. Even though Zuskin realized that medicine was helpless regarding the situation in which he had found himself, he still submitted to the doctors, almost unwillingly, and ultimately agreed to be hospitalized.

All of this may be understood. And still, why now of all times? And why the urgency, before such a vital tour for the theater, a tour that might determine the fate of the theater? This was not an inflamed appendix that had to be operated at once to avoid complications.

Everyone pressured him to postpone his hospital stay for at least two weeks, but he was resolute.

The GOSET executives even came to Zuskin's home to convince him to go to Leningrad. They thoroughly exhausted their entire repository of reasons, and suddenly he jumped up from his place and said, "Please excuse me, I forgot to tell Tala Mikhoels something, and she is supposed to leave." He ran down one flight of stairs, and rang Tala's doorbell. Tala would write of this surprising visit in her book: "Zuskin came in and asked us all to leave the room with the telephone. Not two minutes passed and he finished his mysterious phone call, left the room, and without saying a word to anyone, returned to his apartment. From there on fright was frozen in his eyes, which is how we learned in the days of terror to recognize those who were doomed."[24] Zuskin returned to his apartment, and the guests continued their attempts at persuasion. He cut them off with a decisive "No," and they left as they came.

There is a prevalent supposition that Father was forced to sign a document at the Ministry of State Security pledging that he would not leave Moscow and that he was forbidden to tell anyone of this pledge. Since four years later Mother and I were forced to sign such a pledge, before we were exiled from Moscow,[25] I also tend to think so. If that is true, it could be that in that telephone call, Father made a last, desperate effort to rescind the decree. Although it is highly probable that he did sign a pledge, there is no clear-cut evidence.

In the days that remained until the GOSET went on tour, Zuskin tried to behave as usual, and he almost even convinced himself that the only reason he was adamant about remaining behind was certain transient medical problems.

Unfortunately, these were not only medical problems and in no case were they transient.

Arrested

On December 15, 1948, the GOSET players, and my mother among them, left Moscow and went on tour in Leningrad. My parents found it hard to part from each other but the separation was unavoidable. Because of the dismissals in the theater, there was no stand-in for my mother's roles on stage.

On December 19, the eve before he was due to enter the hospital, my father handed a letter to one of the actors who was delayed in leaving Moscow for Leningrad.

Early in the morning on December 20, 1948, I saw my father for the last time.

I am home. From the nearby room, I hear Father packing things he will need in the hospital, and then, dressed in his coat, two bundles in his hand, he appears in the room where I am sitting. He places the bundles, the big one and the little one, on the sideboard near the door, and comes over to me. We kiss and say goodbye, and he leaves. For lack of something to do, I survey the room. What! What is this? At the edge of the sideboard I see the small bundle, probably with the slippers. Father forgot it!

I grew up in a house of actors, and actors have superstitions. For instance, if you have to come back in the middle of a trip, your trip will not be successful. Don't come back, I plead in my heart. The front door opens. He came back! I am gripped by panic. He kisses me again, takes the bundle with the slippers, and goes out.

Here again, an inanimate object, and again the slippers!

Father goes out. And he never returns. Naturally, at that moment, I could not have known that, but the panic does not leave me. I run to the window. To leave our building to get to the street, you have to cross the yard. In the dimness of the early morning, by the light of a small street lamp, I see my father floating. He is in a rush. After all, he is a courteous person, and he doesn't want to delay the cab driver.

A thought invades my mind: this is exactly how he floats above the stage in the production *Freylekhs.*

He lies in the hospital bed, between starched white sheets. He is cared for, calm, and for the first time in almost a year, a smile of happiness lights his face. He sleeps the sleep of the righteous and he dreams.

In the middle of the night between the 23rd and 24th of December 1948, in Leningrad at the home of Doctor Horatsii Shapiro, the guests continue to sit around the table. They had arrived close to midnight, after watching the show *Holiday Eve* staged by the Moscow Jewish Theater as part of its appearances in Leningrad. The guest of honor is the actress who played the leading role, none other than Eda Berkovskaya, my mother. She is not only the wife of the celebrated Zuskin but also the childhood friend of the host. Like my mother, Doctor Shapiro grew up in Minsk and studied there with Mother's brother Joseph. He became like a member of the Berkovsky family.

Eda did not want to attend this festive evening, but Dr. Shapiro's wife convinced her. It is pleasant for Eda, here in an atmosphere of attention and human warmth. Suddenly she feels fatigued. I look bad, Eda thinks, and she takes her compact out of her purse to see herself in its mirror.

And the mirror that had served her for so many years is cracked. She feels an ache in her heart. After all, Eda is an actress. And actors have superstitions. And a crack in a mirror with no reason is one of the worst kinds of news. The compact had never fallen. Eda is certain of that. She looks at the clock and tells her hosts that she must leave. They order her a cab.

In the middle of the night between the 23rd and 24th of December 1948, at the time that my mother discovers the crack in her mirror— later we compared the time—the doorbell rings in our apartment in Moscow. In my sleep I become aware of the sound of the front doorbell. What can that be? The bed of my aunt Emma, who is staying with me until Mother comes back, is empty. The doorbell rings again. From the bowels of the apartment, I hear Sonia coughing and Emma's voice in the hall, "Who is it?" "Open up!" calls a man's authoritative voice. After dressing myself hastily, I go out to the hall.

The moment Emma opens the door, three men come into the apartment. Two of them are in the uniform of the Ministry of State Security; the third is Mikhail Vashukov, the superintendent of the apartment building we live in.[26] Later we found out that they had enlisted him to be a kind of civilian witness. One of the officers, apparently the more senior of the two, holds out a piece of paper to Emma and asks her something in a lowered voice, and she answers him in almost a whisper. I can't make out the words because I don't dare come any closer to them. Only when the officer picks up the phone and says into it, "He is not here, he is in the hospital," do I understand that he is talking about my father. Silence. It is clear that the Senior Officer is listening for the answer. I come closer. "What hospital?" "The Surgical Institute of the Academy of Medical Sciences." He says something else into the receiver and then replaces it, calls the other officer and gives him an order. The second officer disappears at once. Several minutes later, another officer appears with emblems on his uniform like those of the Senior Officer. Perhaps he is also senior?

The uninvited guests begin to search the house. The First Senior takes out various objects from various places and the Second Senior sorts and makes lists. To my mind, he is more important or has special authorities. After a while the Junior Officer returns and joins the search. The three of them work methodically and efficiently. They only address us to ask, "What is this? Where is this? How do you open this?"

Although I am not allowed to speak with my aunt, I manage to get close to her without their noticing, and I ask her, "All of this because of the Jewish Anti-Fascist Committee?" The thought that all of this is connected directly to my father never occurs to me. "I don't know, I don't know anything," my aunt answers me nervously.

Silence. Suddenly I hear a shout by the Junior Officer, "Foreign currency!" The two Seniors come running. The officer who shouted is standing in the bedroom on a chair near the window and holding the end of the rod where the curtain is hung. The rod is a kind of metal pipe plugged up at both ends by wooden corks. I know that one of the plugs is too small and, to make it fit, it is wrapped in a piece of newspaper which falls into the hollow rod and gets stuck there, and to the officer it looks like bills of foreign currency. The three officers are trying to take out this paper wad, with no results. Finally they manage and understand their mistake. What a shame! They will have to wait a long time now before they are promoted.

After they empty all of the closets and all of the drawers and make a list of all the contents, they go on to sort notebooks, ledgers, letters, and other types of paper, according to a system known only to the Second Senior Officer. I slowly begin to understand the principle. Of all of the journals, for example, they pull out ads with the heading "The Jewish Anti-Fascist Committee. Informational material. For internal use only," and store it away with great care. Now comes the books' turn. The job of sorting books is most tiresome, but our distinguished guests attack the job with wondrous expertise. They organize themselves into an assembly line: the Junior Officer takes the books off the shelves in order, beginning with the top shelf, hands them to the First Senior who holds each book with its spine in the air, shakes it, pats it, and looks for handwritten dedications. Then the Second Senior glances at the author's name, and classifies the books according to a certain classification, apparently according to the level of danger that the author poses to the safety of Soviet citizenry. To the pile of books penned by the most dangerous writers, they add the books written by unidentified authors or at least unknown to our guests, as well as books with handwritten dedications or other markings.

When they move on to the books in Yiddish, they have to cross the invisible boundary separating them and us and enlist the assistance of Aunt Emma as translator.

They use Emma also to classify the furniture, the dishes, kitchen utensils, and the like. In her presence they lay on the table two sheets, two pillowcases, two towels, four handkerchiefs, my father's warm sweater, three pairs of his socks, two pieces of soap, and money, 150 rubles. In a large notebook they list everything they have placed on the table. The significance of this collecting and listing is not yet comprehensible to me; after all, I do not know yet that Father has been arrested. Later I will understand that it is the confiscation of Father's personal effects to deliver to him in prison.

The search lasts all that night and the next day, until nightfall.

My aunt Emma is forbidden to leave for work, and I am denied the right to go to school. In addition, they forbid us to answer the telephone. My other aunt, Lisa, terrified by our phone silence, decides to come to us. They allow her to enter but forbid her to go to work or to call to give notice that she will not be coming. Gradually our apartment is filling up with more and more people. The process takes place in a reversal of Agatha Christie's *Ten Little Indians*, where the characters disappeared one at a time. True, in her thriller more than a few murders are committed, but in our apartment the atmosphere is much more frightening. After Lisa comes Clara Mirkin, my piano teacher. The lesson is canceled, of course, but she is forced to remain. During those moments, the theater administration remembers that a certain document that they are seeking is with Zuskin, and assume it is at Zuskin's house. So, a member of the staff arrives, after him the deputy-director who is upset by the staff member's not coming back and by our phone silence. The caravan is rounded off with the arrival of the coordinator of the acting troupe.

The search and interrogation of all those present come to an end. The officers close the door of the large room with two wax seals and the library door on the niche in the corridor wall, with one seal. Behind the three copies of seal remains the evidence of my father as an artist and as a man. Left behind are his notes relating to the theater arts and his roles. Left behind are some one thousand five hundred books. Left behind are objects that allow a person to call his place of residence a "home." Objects like pillows, sofa, curtains, lamps.

Before those conducting the search leave, they are careful to give my aunts, Emma and Lisa, and my piano teacher, "doctor's" notes to their places of work, while I am given a similar note for school.

In the middle of the night between the 23rd and 24th of December 1948, at the entrance to the Surgical Institute of the Academy of Medical Sciences, two officers in the uniform of the Ministry of State Security appear and demand to be led to the physician on duty.

Years will pass before my mother and I learn what happened that night.

To be more precise, eight years passed. I was a student. One evening as I was about to prepare homework, I noticed that a notebook I needed was missing. I recalled a student who had sat next to me in the lecture hall, by the name of Slava Tsukerman, and I thought that he had accidentally taken my notebook. I called him. His father answered the phone. He said that Slava was not home and asked what message to give him. I told him my name and explained the matter.

The next day I came to the class late, as usual, and the lecture hall was full. Still Slava noticed my arrival and since the lecturer had not yet appeared, he ran to me and said with great emotion, "Your father, who is he? Was he an actor at the Jewish Theater?" I answered in the affirmative and Slava continued, "Do you live with your mother?" "Yes." "Well then, the both of you have to come to our house this evening. My father has something important to tell you."

That evening we visited the Tsukermans. Slava's father, a doctor by profession, told us that in 1948, he was working as a surgeon at the Surgical Institute of the Academy of Medical Sciences, and that on the night between the 23rd and 24th of December, he was the physician on duty in charge of the entire hospital. He knew about Zuskin the actor but he didn't know Zuskin the patient because Zuskin was hospitalized in a ward other than his. After Dr. Tsukerman read the arrest warrant, he said that he had been given instructions that on no account was he to disturb the sleep of the patient Zuskin. The visitors simply moved Dr. Tsukerman aside, entered the room where Zuskin was lying deep in sleep, wrapped him in a sheet, took him out of the hospital, put him into a car, and brought him to prison. And how can one fail to recall the words of Dante Alighieri:

And to a place I come where nothing shines.[27]

Those poets! Did Dante really notice that nothing shines in his "Inferno"? In an inferno where sick people were not taken out of their hospital bed straight to prison and they did not wake up to curses and blows. The contemporary writer Felix Kandel refers to Zuskin's awakening in this situation with these words: "What pig-faces surrounded him? Where is Goya to depict his sweet dreams and his rude awakening into a horrifying reality? Where is Kafka to write of the terror that beset his shocked mind?"[28]

Dante. Goya. Kafka. They are simply incorrigible dilettantes!

Alexander Solzhenitsyn, an unchallenged expert on hell—not Dante's infero—gives the arrest process this definition: "The arrest . . . is a shock that the mind does not absorb . . . It is the sharpest transition, a jump, a thrust from one situation to another . . . the arrestee is torn from the warmth of his bed, he is still weak, his mind is befogged . . . the routine arrest . . ."[29] And here I am speaking of a not-routine arrest!

Tens of thousands of people underwent the process of being arrested, but I have never heard or read testimony of any arrest of the type that befell my father.

On December 31, 1948, in the late afternoon, the theater returns from Leningrad. Lisa and I go to the train station to meet my mother. "Lisa," I tell her, "Don't tell my mother about the search. I'll tell her." But Lisa, who always gives in to my requests, persists in her refusal this time. I don't understand why she is being stubborn.

We arrive at the platform. There the families of the actors have already gathered. Most of them know Lisa and me, but to my surprise, they avoid coming over to us. The train arrives. Here is Mother. Lisa calls a porter, and he takes mother's suitcase and walks toward the cab stand, Mother and Lisa after him, and I after them. Lisa talks and talks. I don't hear her but I know what she is talking about. More correctly, it seems to me that I know what she is talking about. Mother is silent. Suddenly, all at once, she stands up. I run to her. On her face is despair, a kind of despair so terrible that nothing worse can be imagined. "Mama," I try to soothe her, "Don't get excited. It's true, there was a search. They closed off one of our rooms. But the main thing is that Papa is getting better."

At home Mother glances at the seals. Lisa urges us to go with her to her apartment, where she lives with my aunt Emma and my grandmother. Grandmother is waiting for us with a meal in honor of the new year, 1949.

The next day, at home, my mother tells me the truth.

Key Figure

In the un-real reality described in these pages, one could feel tangibly only the fears, arrests, and executions, and it was totally absurd to ask: Why?

With this, specifically regarding my father and the others who were put on trial in the same case, the answer to this question, "They were put on trial because of their membership in the Jewish Anti-Fascist Committee,"[30] seemed to be short and unequivocal.

To all appearances they were accused of something concrete: membership in an organization, which according to the definition by the investigators and the court, was engaged in anti-Soviet activity. A closer look at the heart of the issue reveals a different facet: "In the Jewish Anti-Fascist Committee . . . Jewish expressions of national pride were most publicly represented."[31] To interpret feelings of pride as hostile activity? "As long as expressions of national identity remained on stage and in Yiddish, they were rarely noticed and thus provoked little official opposition. Once these sentiments were taken off stage and into the public sphere, however, they could no longer be ignored."[32]

Mikhoels operated in areas that touched the whole Soviet public, and he did this most efficiently. Therefore, it is very noticeable that in the case of the Committee all of the conspicuous responsibility was placed on Mikhoels, even after his death. The prosecutors preferred to accept the version that Mikhoels was guilty of everything as taken for granted, and to present at the trial the relationship between him and the defendants. "Thence followed the order to arrest the two key JAC [Jewish Anti-Fascist Committee] figures, Fefer and Zuskin, Mikhoels's successors in the JAC and at the Jewish Theater . . . The MGB hoped to use . . . [them] to obtain . . . compromising materials on the deceased Mikhoels."[33]

In the Jewish Anti-Fascist Committee that actually existed, Zuskin's role was only marginal. He himself said: "I came to the Committee and was an extra,"[34] while in the fabricated case of that Committee in accordance with the fiendish plan, he was a key figure.

Paradox? Not at all.

Mikhoels, who was considered the main defendant, even though he was no longer alive, was the chairman of the Jewish Anti-Fascist Committee. One could find out about his activity from his deputy on the Committee, Fefer. For that reason, he was arrested as one of the two main arrestees. Checking with Fefer this or that fact and then distorting these facts was an ordinary matter. But it was not enough to build a case.

The case would be successfully fashioned only on condition that the main defendant's name was thoroughly blackened. Why not use for this purpose an actor who has been drugged with anesthesia? And so they arrested Zuskin the same night that they arrested Fefer.

In the eleven months and eleven days that elapsed between Mikhoels's murder and Zuskin's arrest, Zuskin underwent unimaginably severe torments. During this whole period Zuskin, although he never stopped mourning Mikhoels, was unable to eliminate from his mind the persistent thought that they were two people: one was Mikhoels, and the other was Vovsi—a thought that previously, in normal times, beset him only occasionally. In Zuskin's artistic imagination, Mikhoels was portrayed as someone crowned with a halo of shining light, with the power to restore vibrant life and the joy of creation, while Vovsi was shrouded in gloomy darkness.

When Zuskin woke up in prison, the investigators drilled him; again and again they bored into his befogged brain and they planted those four words: Mikhoels. Nationalist. Spy. Enemy. Again and again, during the three and a half years of an investigation that was the most terrible one could imagine.

Zuskin, whose function in the Committee was marginal, became a key figure also because of "Mikhoels—Zuskin." Well, what? Of the two, only the one had been murdered? Never mind. That could be fixed.

Detainee

Benjamin Zuskin was brought to detention in the internal prison of the Ministry of State Security of the Soviet Union, known to all as "Lubianka."[35]

The detainee Zuskin is wakened out of his sleep—it is better not to dwell on how he was wakened—and dragged to the office of the prison to fill out a standard questionnaire. After that, Zuskin is photographed and fingerprinted. At the end of this process, while he is still in a befuddled state, he is dragged for interrogation to Lieutenant Colonel Rassypninsky, Deputy Chief of the Investigative Unit for Especially Important Cases in the Ministry of State Security. The efficient Rassypninsky has no time to waste; he must make haste while the detainee is still confused and semi-conscious. In order to adhere to procedure, of course, he repeats some of the questions that appear on the questionnaire, and eventually comes to the main point. In fact, he does not interrogate but declares that the detainee under investigation engaged in hostile activity as part of his membership in the Jewish Anti-Fascist Committee, and the investigator demands testimony about the crimes he has committed. Zuskin denies. He does not deny the fact that he was a member of the Committee but rather the accusation that he took part in hostile activity. He never even suspected that such activity took place: "After they murdered Mikhoels, his job at the theater passed to me."[36] Therefore, he was too busy at the theater to know about something else.

There is truth in the saying: "What soberness conceals, drunkenness reveals." Isn't the dazed Zuskin like a drunken man at this point? Before his arrest—was there really ever such a time?— Zuskin would never have dared used the word "murdered." The idea was buried deep in his consciousness. Besides that, Zuskin did not intend to speak of Mikhoels's death at all. It was a slip of the tongue.

But Rassypninsky falls upon this slip with great glee. "Explain: Mikhoels was murdered?"[37] he asks and emphasizes each and every word, postponing for another time the questions he had intended to ask on other subjects.

Zuskin, muddled, mumbles that there were rumors.

I have been told once that my father almost fainted near Mikhoels's casket. In such ceremonies, as everywhere, where there is a crowd, there is no shortage of observers, including those who noticed with whom Zuskin was speaking. He was speaking with a celebrated lady: Polina Zhemchuzhina. According to the rumors, she asked him whether he thought the reason for Mikhoels's death was a car accident or something worse. This conversation, did it actually ever take place?

All of the same, some of the questions-answers from the interrogation records would be quoted during the trial.

Charged (1949)

During the investigation Zuskin gradually learns that he is guilty of betrayal of the Motherland; of anti-Soviet propaganda; of participation in a clandestine organization; and first and foremost, of bourgeois nationalism. Zuskin is termed guilty from the beginning of the investigative proceedings, although—logically—he is still a suspect and should be considered guilty only after a verdict by the court where the case is held at the end of the investigation and based on its outcome, if at all.

Logically? Didn't I warn my readers already in my Preface that logic has no place here?

Zuskin admits that he had been part of "the nationalist Jewish underground and with its head, Solomon Mikhoels."[38] That is certainly true. When he sang together with Mikhoels their song "What a Dream!" in the play *The Travels of Benjamin the Third*, and when together they sought shelter from the tempest in *King Lear*, was it not then that he had forged criminal contacts with Mikhoels?

Not once did they come back to the subject of Zhemchuzhina. Does this happen because he absent-mindedly blurted out the word "murdered," or maybe they actually planted her name in his mouth and caused him to utter it in a moment of insensibility when he found himself in transition from sleeping in the hospital to the "reality" of prison?

The interrogations are dragged on; they are devoted to the "hostile activity" of the Committee and its presidium; to the Crimean Project; to the Yiddish newspaper *Eynikayt*; to Mikhoels's and Fefer's trip to America; to receptions by Mikhoels—in the theater instead of the Committee—of Jews shouting for his help; to Zuskin—Mikhoels's relationship and Mikhoels's personality.

Zuskin, depressed by the situation and his mental state, astounded at the accusations hurled at him, utters words about Mikhoels like "a great egoist . . . loved ringing phrases and glory,"[39] that in no way reflect his essential attitude toward Mikhoels, but perhaps they lurked now and then in the depths of his heart.

The interrogations continue, and the areas in which the investigator is interested are mostly the same although from time to time they shift.

For instance—to the Jewish School of Acting. Here Rassypninsky understands instantaneously that if there is any Jewish nationalism, it must be fanned and fed to the youth. If so, then "at the Jewish School of Acting, they created the reserves to maintain and promote Jewish nationalism."[40] In truth, there was a good reason that "Rassypninsky was considered the intellectual among the Lubianka's investigators."[41] After all, he finds his way with such ease in every single subject.

Or to the "subversive ties" of Mikhoels with different people. Zuskin does not know what to say. About whom? And what about Zaltsman? The following is recorded as though Zuskin said it: "Yes, now I remember that

Mikhoels had close ties with Isaac Zaltsman, the former director-general of the plant for manufacturing tanks."[42] This statement arouses surprise: Zuskin, who will testify about himself during the trial: "My memory is poor . . . I have barely slept in four years,"[43] suddenly recalls details relating to Zaltsman who lived in another city and was known only vaguely by Zuskin. It is intriguing to know also why he was compelled to speak of Zaltsman precisely "on June 17, 1949, when only on June 24, 1949, the Central Committee of the Party decided that Zaltsman's conduct does not behoove the Party's guidelines."[44] And why does Zuskin call Zaltsman the "former director-general" when in fact, Zaltsman would be dismissed from his position as director-general only a month after this interrogation? It might be that Zuskin had a special ability to see the future, but it is more probable to assume that the investigator had a special ability to fabricate interrogation records.

The wording of Zuskin's answers seems crafted as though he were reading from a text. And perhaps he was reading from a text that was written not by him.

He was an actor, and he hurriedly learned what he was required to say in his new role: any description of Jewish activity must be supplemented with the adjective, nationalist, or, anti-Soviet. If he said that in Tsarist Russia they imposed limitations on admitting Jews to educational institutions, or that they obliterated Jewish culture, that was acceptable. But if he wanted to say that in the Soviet Union similar phenomena were taking place, he would have to add the formulaic, "These are baseless rumors," or to cast doubt on their contents by using the adverbial qualifier, 'ostensibly.' About any deed of the Committee he had to mention that it threatened the Soviet State. And so it went.

What was with my father on April 28, 1949? Did he remember that this was his fiftieth birthday? Did he think about it? How great would the excitement have been, had he been a free man! The theater would have organized a gala evening, and he, Zuskin, would have mounted the stage and acted the characters he loved to perform, and in costume, without an evening jacket and bowtie. He would present the monologue of Hotsmakh from *The Wandering Stars*; he would sing a song from *Freylekhs*, or the song of the Fool from *King Lear*. But the duet of Benjamin and Senderl, the greatest of all, the duet from *The Travels of Benjamin the Third*, he would not have performed. How do you perform a duet by yourself?

If he indeed were thinking so during an interrogation, Rassypninsky's voice would rouse him from his thoughts: "After Granovsky absconded . . ." "After Granovsky did not return . . ."[45] Zuskin has still not shaken off the cobwebs of memory from the production *The Travels of Benjamin the Third*, his best production directed by Granovsky, and he did not allow himself to use the derogatory word "absconded."

And again—under Mikhoels's influence—the accused Zuskin arrived at where he is now, and Mikhoels was a criminal. Mikhoels preferred activity on the Jewish Anti-Fascist Committee to working at the Jewish theater. Mikhoels's moods were, obviously, anti-Soviet. Again comes Zuskin's declaration that he loved Mikhoels and that he learned from him. According to the investigator's interpretation, this declaration is not innocent: If he loved him, then his connections to Mikhoels were subversive; and if he learned from him, what was it exactly that he learned?

If the record of any of these interrogations were to be published in the free world as a novella, and if a reader from the free world were to leaf through this novella, he would get the impression that two people are sitting there, an investigator in the secret police and his interlocutor, and the investigator is asking questions about a third person and receiving clear detailed answers that support the suspicion that the third person is a criminal.

But if that reader from the free world were to read that novella very carefully, he would find it to be an absolute absurdity. And truly, is it a shameful thing to be engaged in public activity at the expense of one's main job? Or is a dejected mood to be considered a crime? And what is the felony committed by someone who is an egoist or a glory seeker?

The intelligent reader in the free world, when he understands that the suspicions against the third person are based on snippets of sentences that fall from the lips of a man who has not known sleep for a long time, and that the suspect they are discussing is a dead man, the reader will demand to be compensated for the money he spent buying a novella that is devoid of sense and talent.

My father was sentenced to being the hero of a novella devoid of sense and talent for over three years.

Accused (1950)

From the beginning of 1950 on, no longer would Zuskin be interrogated by Rassypninsky but instead by Tsvetaev who was considered a person of pleasant behavior and of non-offensive language. This fact did not stop Tsvetaev from burning Zuskin's ledgers, letters, and notes, as described in the Preface to this book. Tsvetaev, whether by his own initiative or by order, introduced a new method: he documented the time the interrogation began and the time it ended.

How is it possible that the record of an interrogation that lasts four hours all fits on a page and a half, typewritten, double spaced, while the record of another interrogation also lasting four hours sprawls over close to fourteen pages of closely typed writing, single spaced and without margins?

Much later we will learn that in the interrogation, the investigator wrote single words or phrases' fragments on scraps of paper and that afterward, "Colonel Yakov Broverman, deputy chief of the MGB secretariat, embellished the testimonies so that they turned into self-accusations and confessions to criminal activities."[46] In a subsequent interrogation, the detainee being interrogated was handed a document to sign, entitled *Interrogation Record* and bearing the date of a previous one. "After weeks of torture and provocation, from the drafts of the records, from the groans and the despair, from the meaningless murmurings of the miserable interrogees, in Broverman's kitchen they concocted 'generalized records'."[47] Actually the writing of these generalized records was done by the method used by Soviet propaganda: they take a fact that is more or less true and in order to adapt it to the needs of the hour, they twist it beyond recognition, or they fabricate a fictitious "reality" around it.

During the following interrogations, Zuskin is asked about different people, but Tsvetaev has no success. Zuskin's answers are so monotonous that it is tedious to even listen to them: Yes, he knows the people mentioned. No, he had no anti-Soviet or other connections of any criminal nature with them, and not even with Golda Meir, whom he never met. Not a single detail of these interrogations shed light on the scope of Zuskin's guilt.

Nor can the great light of the universe shed light on Zuskin's solitary cell on the day of March 21. The first day of spring 1950. My mother's birthday.

Absent

How did my mother and I live without the husband and the father?

Until the theater closed down in November 1949, Mother continued to work there. She used to come to rehearsals or to performances at the last minute. That way she avoided any chance encounter or random conversation. In truth there was almost no one who sought her out or who would wish to speak to her. At best, actors, actresses, and especially the administrative staff nodded a greeting to her.

Almost nobody came to our house, and as a rule, when Mother walked down the street with me or alone, acquaintances who chanced to come upon her immediately moved to the other side of the street. Eventually my mother and I found ways to avoid this difficulty: when we walked down the street, we first looked carefully to see if any of the passersby are an acquaintance or friend, and when someone like this appeared, we immediately crossed to the other side of the street so as not to force any unease on anyone or even real danger.

On January 28, 1949, the newspaper *Pravda* (Truth) published an editorial entitled, "On the Anti-Patriotic Group of Theater Critics." In the article they accused some of the Soviet theater critics of panning Soviet playwrights while lavishing praise on Western playwrights. As a result they were termed "cosmopolitans without a homeland." The main point of the article was not to express concern for Soviet art but rather to mention the Jewish names of the theater critics. And the dam burst. The flood of defamations was accompanied by dismissals of people with those names. At best, the authorities were satisfied with firing the people. Among those defamed were theater or literary critics, journalists, impresarios, scientists—first in the fields of culture or history, then afterward in all fields. Gradually caught up in this torrent were economists, captains of industry both civilian and military, lecturers and students at the institutes of higher education, and finally, even people in the top ranks of the Communist Party and among the officers at the Ministry for State Security.

This madness lasted from the beginning of 1949 to the spring of 1953, when Stalin died. During that time, two campaigns in effect were being waged: an overt campaign against anyone who was considered a cosmopolitan and a covert campaign against nationalists, namely, members of the Jewish Anti-Fascist Committee.

More than once I have emphasized in this book that in the Soviet reality, there is no room for logic. Cosmopolitanism means "thinking and feeling beyond the nation,"[48] while nationalism declares allegiance to a nation. The conclusion: cosmopolitanism cancels out nationalism, and vice versa. And yet, the spirit of the slander suggests that both phenomena refer to the same segment of the Soviet population that is cosmopolitan and yet at the very same time nationalistic. Actually this clash between the two concepts doesn't seem to bother the authorities, because after all, this segment of the population is nothing more than the Jews.

The storm of public defamation overshadowed the tragedy of the members of the Jewish Anti-Fascist Committee, my father included.

Two months after Father was arrested, my grandmother fell ill. She had suffered a cerebral hemorrhage. She recovered almost completely but sometime later, suffered another stroke. In August 1949, my grandmother Chaya-Rokha Berkovskaya died at the age of seventy-nine. I didn't cry when I found out that my father was arrested, even though I felt fear and dread and I felt most powerfully how much I missed my father. Mother and her sisters also turned to stone and did not cry then. But when my grandmother passed away, then we all cried, Mother, Emma, Lisa, and I. It appears that facing death from disease is perceived as a legitimate, natural reason to cry, a natural expression of human emotion without it being considered a demonstration of excessive emotionality.

I would like to tell of another natural expression of human feeling. An expression that was the most courageous.

At the beginning of the summer of 1949, the union of theater actors organized a boat trip along the Volga. My mother and I decided to join this trip. The travelers were mostly actors from small towns and they did not identify my mother. Our ship reached a resort village at the Volga bank. There at a luxurious resort house, lunch awaited us. The Moscow actors, who were staying at this resort, went out to the pier to greet the newcomers; when they noticed my mother disembarking the ship, they were quick to slip away, as though they had never come. All of them.

No. Not all of them. Maria Mironova, the very popular actress-entertainer, accompanied by her small boy Andriusha, later Andrei Mironov, celebrated star of Soviet cinema, approaches my mother to welcome her. "How happy I am to see you," exults Mironova in a voice known to everyone and which could be identified from afar. My mother's acquaintance with Mironova was quite superficial, and they had never spoken together at length. Mother looks at her in panic and whispers, "Stay away from me. Don't you understand? Everyone's looking." "Let them go to hell," replies Mironova without lowering her voice.

And here we are, the four of us standing in our place, and Mironova is chatting lightly with my mother about the weather, about theatrical arts, about Andriusha's studies and about mine. Mother mentions one of Mironova's skits in which she as an "uneducated woman" complains about mathematical problems where water is being poured into one pipe and pouring out of another and concludes that children are taught just to tread water. Mironova laughs delightedly. As she takes her leave of us, she adds sadly, "Well, we have tread water a bit together, and it's been a relief." For some time after the meeting with that wonderful Russian woman, Mother could not get over her emotion.

When we returned from the trip, Mother rushed to the reception department of the State Prosecutor's Office as she had been doing once a week, week after week. There she had to stand in a long line to the counter and to hear the words said as routine, "Your husband's case is still being studied." Once in a while they accepted modest sums of money to pass on to Father.

This time they told my mother that she was allowed to bring a package with personal items: socks, towels, toiletries, perhaps a warm article of clothing, I don't remember exactly what. Mother made the rounds of the stores and bought whatever was needed. When she returned home and examined her purchases, she sighed, "I thought I bought everything.

Now I see that we are missing soap." I looked at the packages that Mother brought, and I saw several bars of excellent bath soap. "I don't understand," I said. "Here is soap." "Look," Mother replied, and turned over one bar of soap. At that time they used to sell soap without wrapping it, and I saw on the smooth part of the soap that they had stamped it with the name of the factory that manufactured it, *Svoboda* (Freedom). "Your father is very sensitive to symbols, and it will be hard for him to accept soap that is stamped with the word 'Freedom' while he is languishing between the walls of a prison." The next day we split up to canvass the cosmetics stores, and we found another type of soap.

We were not allowed to send any more packages, but during the entire period of Father's detainment, we sent money. Only after the rehabilitation did they notify us that from a certain time, they had stopped giving him the money, and in a burst of generosity, they returned the remaining sum. The powers-that-be loved order.

One evening I was sitting at home and doing my homework. Mother was learning a new song and she was singing it in an undertone so as not to disturb me. In the beginning, I ignored it but afterward, I realized that the tune sounded familiar to me. It was the song that my mother sang as she danced in the marketplace scene of *The Sorceress*, in the version that Father staged when he directed the theater. I knew by heart the words of the song, and suddenly it dawned on me that the words were different, unfamiliar. In the original, the words were:

> Throw me please some coins, some money!
> Where he is, my groom, my honey?
> Disappeared, came back no more,
> And I still am looking for . . . [49]

In the new text, there was no mention of the missing groom and the yearning bride. It had no questions and naturally no answers. I understood at once and my mother confirmed it for me. Yes, the theater management had taken the trouble to commission a new text, and they forced her to sing it instead of the original one, just to be safe, so that there would not be any unnecessary allusions.

Many people were affected emotionally by the change in text and by mother's dance, which seemed to symbolize life among the ruins. The poet Joseph Kerler gave expression to these feelings in his poem: "This dance was in Maydanek—am I wrong? / In Spain as well, during the Inquisition."[50]

Eda danced and sang a song with new words for a very short period of time. During this period, the theater was still alive and even put on two new shows. The theater was only missing an artistic director, a leading actor, a regular repertory, an audience, hope. "Only fear was there, fear, fear, fear . . . One day the fear, too, came to an end. They closed our theater,"[51] recalls Kovenskaya.

On November 14, 1949, the Committee of Artistic Affairs published an official document:

ORDER #959:

The Moscow State Jewish Theater finished the 1948 year with losses of 1,247 thousand rubles and for the ten months of 1949 has allowed losses of the sum of 815 thousand rubles. Attendance at the theater, both in years 1948 and 1949 has been at a completely unsatisfactory level, and is currently at 13.7 percent capacity . . .

THE ORDER:

The liquidation of the Moscow State Jewish Theater as of December 1, 1949, on account of its unprofitability.[52]

As though it were not they who had brutally cut all state support, as though it were not they who had terrified any potential theatergoers. "On November 16, 1949, the curtain fell for the last time on the stage of the Moscow Jewish Theater. The theater ended its life with the performance of the Jewish folk hero jester, Hershele, who joked for the last time on the boards of the stage in Moscow."[53] And so this was also Benjamin Zuskin's farewell to his audience although he was not present in the theater. After all, it was he who staged *Hershele Ostropoler* in 1937, and in 1948, he put on a new version of this show, which ended the career of the GOSET.

In that same Order #959 they declared the establishment of a Liquidation Commission.

The commission members carefully sorted everything they found, and took from the theater materials of great importance: lists of actors, minutes of discussions about the shows, and many other documents.

The reader already knows that during the search of our house, my father's personal effects were confiscated. I will add something about the photographs that were miraculously saved. Some two months after the search, a young man came to our house to return Father's photo albums to us. He was a student or a journalist just starting his career. At one time, he intended to write about Zuskin and had asked Father to lend him the albums. Father always guarded his albums with great care. Beside the photographs, there were pasted press cuttings about his roles as well as some of his articles, and inside one of them Father put the draft of his "Curriculum Vitae." What a stroke of luck that the young man had not fulfilled his pledge to return the albums as soon as possible!

After the members of the Liquidation Commission had finished the "clearing out," many items still remained in the theater.

One fine day a band of a "righteous mission" from the secret police appeared in the theater. They checked the furniture, stage props, costumes, etc. Things that they found to be in good condition, they sent to warehouses that served groups of amateur actors. The rest of the items and books they handled with an age-old method: they made a pile in the yard of the theater and set it on fire. "Alien indifferent people with a kick of their boots cast into the fire objects and souvenirs which had been precious to the hearts of the theater people. Black flakes wafted in the air, replacing the pillow feathers which typified the pogrom. Everything else was exactly like the standard, age-old pogrom."[54] Eventually the theater courtyard emptied out.

In the yard was an entrance to the living quarters of some of the actors. When evening fell, the actors began to steal out into the yard. One by one, unseen, glancing to the right and to the left, from under the black and white coating of ashes and snow, they pulled out what they could. There were very few things to salvage.

The year 1950 began with a terrifying announcement. On January 13, 1950, the media announced that the death penalty had been instituted in the Soviet Union. Not that this meant anything new for the Soviet citizen, for the death penalty had been abolished less than three years previously, but my mother was enshrouded in despair. Her reaction surprised me because I was unable to believe that there was any connection between this news item and my father's fate.

Over the course of 1950 my mother looked for work. At the beginning she tried to make use of her diploma that attested that she is a graduate of the College of Dance; perhaps she might obtain a position as a dance teacher in the youth clubs. But these clubs were defined as a part of the ideological front, and the wife of the enemy had to be prevented from teaching in them, lest she, using the medium of dance, sabotage the pure souls of the young. Then my mother gave up and began to work from home for some kind of factory that manufactured accessories for theaters as well as housewares. Our kitchen became a workshop. Mother and I made artificial flowers, or with the aid of stencils drew colorful drawings on plastic plates.

Of the former GOSET actors, only few managed to get accepted to other theaters. Most became colleagues in our work. "The GOSET theater troupe, almost in its entirety, suffers punishment throughout its lifetime. Stupefying work, minimum pay. Life rudely interrupted. Toxic fumes emitted from the paints make breathing difficult. Strength ebbs, talents fade, helplessness plows furrows on a face devoid of makeup."[55]

Gradually Mother brought our beautiful pieces made of china and silver to a second-hand store. And the store manager, an admirer of Zuskin and friend of one of the GOSET actors, sighed bitterly and pasted on stickers showing a price higher than the item's value.

Mother went to the Prosecutors Office to ask the same questions and receive the same answers, devoid of reason and meaning. My mother's morale and mine was low because of our concern for Father. Our thoughts oppressed us relentlessly. What was happening with him? During the time of the Rosenbergs and Slansky trials, our mood became even more gloomy.

Julius and Ethel Rosenberg, American scientists who worked in the field of atomic energy, were condemned to death in the electric chair for handing over secrets about the atom to the Soviet Union. In the Soviet Union, the verdict, rendered in spring 1951, was received with sanctimoniously stormy protests, even though the Rosenbergs had indeed betrayed their country. Yet they were never beaten in prison or starved. They were certainly not deprived of sleep. Espionage in nuclear energy was not a top priority for Mother and me, but the scene in the play about the Rosenberg affair that the Polish theater brought to Moscow shocked us. In this scene, the Jewish couple the Rosenbergs were waiting in prison for their execution.

By the end of 1951, in Czechoslovakia, fourteen top-ranking members of the Government and the Communist Party in this country were arrested and in 1952 executed, among them Rudolf Slansky, the Party's secretary-general. They were accused of spying for the West. Out of fourteen, eleven, Slansky included, were Jews. If in the case of the Rosenbergs my mother and I had associations and premonitions, then here, where "the hand of Moscow" was obviously involved, we no longer had any doubt that the problem in Czechoslovakia was also our personal problem.

Forgotten

"On March 1950, the first stage in the JAC case ended. During the years of investigation the conception of the trial had changed. Initially the broader-scale trial had been planned . . . This broader trial never took place. The reasons for its cancellation call for further study. It is known, however, that in 1950 several principal participants—Solomon Lozovsky, Joseph Yuzefovich, and Benjamin Zuskin—retracted confessions that had been obtained through threats, blackmail, and torture."[56] How did Father endure the first investigation stage? And how did he endure the year and a half, from March 1950 to September 1951, when there were no interrogations? Who knows what they were doing to him during this period of time? What was his physical and mental condition?

After all, Father's condition could not be measured by human criteria. "Insomnia is the greatest means of torture which leaves no marks on the body," says Solzhenitsyn, and I wonder: Were Father's torturers satisfied with depriving him of sleep or did they use additional means that do indeed leave marks on the body? "Insomnia," continues Solzhenitsyn, "clouds the brain, breaking the will. A person loses his 'self'."[57] So, one day follows the next, and one sleepless night follows the other, night after night, day after day.

He feels that he has been forgotten. What is going on?

True, there were retracted confessions, and even without this alteration, the Ministry of State Security had no security that it would be possible to conduct a trial because even if there were charges that were not denied, these were still not enough for an open trial in the setting that Stalin demanded.

For "giving up the idea" there were other circumstances, as well. "The interest [of the MGB] . . . in the arrested JAC leaders diminished considerably . . . At that time all the forces . . . were directed toward creating a new anti-Semitic hoax, namely, the 'branch' case about the 'espionage activities' of Myriam Ayzenshtadt, Nakhum Levin and Samuel Persov [Committee members executed in 1950] and . . . preparing the legal punishment for the . . . so-called Leningrad group . . . This state of affairs continued through mid-1951, when a drastic cleansing took place within the MGB."[58]

Ultimately the Minister of State Security Victor Abakumov was arrested, and his former subordinate, Mikhail Riumin, was promoted by Stalin personally, through a series of ranks and positions until he became Deputy-Minister of State Security. The interrogations of JAC members resumed with renewed vigor, and with a total disregard for the retractions of previous admissions of guilt.

Convicted (1951–1952)

In the new round of the investigation, the content of the interrogations was not different from the ones that preceded them— meaningless questions and answers about various people. Despite this there was something that arouses our attention.

First of all, Zuskin, as other detainees, was asked not just about various people but primarily about their ties—with him and others. One may suppose that these interrogations were conducted to obtain testimony that would supply support for representing the Jewish Anti-Fascist Committee as the center of an extended espionage ring.

Second, instead of using the expression "anti-Soviet activities," as had been the practice previously, they used the expression "anti-Soviet criminal connections." Riumin, who "obtained questions that had been prepared by Stalin himself,"[59] demanded much more clear-cut phrasing.

Third, part of the questions revolved around the physicians. It is precisely at that time that in the Ministry of State Security, they began to prepare the infamous "Doctors' Plot."

Zuskin's investigator also was replaced. Now it was Major Pogrebnoi who provided the detainee with a resolution where the reason for the investigation's renewal was stipulated: "For looking for new testimonies of Zuskin's espionage activities, and for a better exposure of the crimes of Zuskin and his cohorts."[60] That same day the investigators of all of Zuskin's "cohorts" signed identical resolutions.

For three straight years Zuskin had been waiting for the opportunity to be asked about his life's work. But the investigator was positive: Theater was nothing but a guise for hostile activity. Wait a minute, the theater "was"? Yes, Pogrebnoi announced to Zuskin, the theater has been closed for some time. And Zuskin said unhesitatingly: "This was the right thing to do."[61] He would repeat this sentence in his final word in court, too, and explain: "I ended up in the Moscow Jewish Theater completely by chance, and that then became my life's tragedy."[62] When I read for the first time these words spoken by Father, I couldn't believe what I was seeing. How did Father dare pronounce them? Father? The Zuskin who was the flesh and blood of the Jewish theater?

But first, the theater after the murder of Mikhoels and after Zuskin's arrest, with no public and no money, was not worthy of existing. Second, even if we assume that Father was born to the Jewish theater, he was in fact accepted specifically to GOSET by total coincidence, and here it is appropriate to recall the story of the typewriter. Third, in 1938 he did consider the possibility of leaving GOSET, but it was not because of any willingness to give up Jewish art; it was rather because of his profoundly heartfelt attitude to Jewish art, which his theater had started to move away from.

Defining his career at the GOSET using the phrase "became my life's tragedy" needs no interpretation, for Zuskin included it in his final words in court on July 11, 1952, exactly one week before the court pronounced its verdict condemning him to death, and one month and one day before he was executed.

Zuskin was called upon to express his opinion about the conclusions of the expertisa. Expertisa? What is that? "Attempts were made to obtain . . . some evidence of espionage activities . . . The task didn't appear difficult to the MGB . . . Nonetheless . . . the case was falling apart . . . To substantiate the fabricated conclusions reached in the investigation, a group of experts was set up . . . But despite all the subtlety, trickery, embellishments, outright inventions, and crudely overt pressure on the expert witnesses, the MGB was not able to obtain convincing documents testifying either to espionage or nationalistic activities."[63]

And the interrogations continued. It may be said that Zuskin's crimes can be summarized as three activities: sold, infiltrated, smuggled. Sold— his soul to the espionage rings. Infiltrated—the Jewish Anti-Fascist Committee. Smuggled—nationalist ideas into the Jewish theater.

The interrogations came to an end, and March 7, 1952, Zuskin was informed that the list of the charges would be resubmitted to him.

After the resubmitting of charges to all the detainees in the case, the investigators retreated into their workrooms. There, in the peaceful and quiet atmosphere, the investigators filled out the "Statements of Conclusion of Investigation"[64] one statement for each detainee. The forms had not changed since March 23, 1950, when the first investigation stage came to an end, but still there was "very hard" work to do on them, by hand: to extend the defendants' declarations and to modify some numbers.

The conversion of the Roman numeral I to the Roman numeral II reflects a situation where the organizers of the case were left with no choice. In the Criminal Code of the Russian Republic, the Roman numerals are used to mark the sub-clause giving the details of the crime defined in the clause. Thus, the crime defined in clause 58-10 is "Anti-Soviet Propaganda" and in sub-clause I, one of the particulars is given: "by calling for Subversion against the Soviet Authorities," while in sub-clause II, the particular is: "by taking advantage of nationalist superstitions in certain segments of the population." Since no evidence was found of calls for subversion of the Soviet authorities, it was decided to use the sub-clause, which was easier to prove legally. If, for example, in the Jewish theater the audience applauded in honor of Zuskin when he portrayed a Jewish character of any kind, did they not demonstrate fidelity to national superstitions by doing so? And if so, was this not a demonstration of anti-Soviet propaganda by Zuskin?

Furthermore, the number of the Criminal Case had to be changed in the Statement, and this patently reflected the new attitude toward the handling of the case. The aim was to present the future case not as a collection of individual crimes but as a wide-ranging and well-organized enterprise, both anti-Soviet and pro-American, and Zionist, too. And for that purpose, out of a slew of files of persons related to the Jewish Anti-Fascist Committee, they selected fifteen cases, and these were united into one case.

The decision to create the unified case was made on March 5, 1952, exactly one year before the death of Stalin, who was the inspiration for the "Jewish Anti-Fascist Committee Case." Zuskin's personal file number 2020 was included, under the definition "Volume 23," in Case Number 2354, the file shared by fifteen men and women.

And this time, the trial was going to take place.

Preparing for Trial

The trial was an event and had to be prepared for.

In this there was actually nothing new for Zuskin who had always been scrupulous about preparing for whatever role he played. Except that now, the role that awaited him was not an individual role determined by Case File no. 2020 but rather a role where he was part of a crowd scene as described in Case Number 2354, which was shared by fifteen defendants.

The organizers of the trial were also preparing for it. And they were not lacking in experience. Already during the 1920s, State Prosecutor Nikolai Krylenko contended that to succeed in a trial "one must take pains not to err in selecting the defendants . . . Only he who survives the selection and winnowing process—heal him, feed him, and stand him on trial."[65]

The process of "healing" is documented: "The medical department of Lefortovo Prison hereby confirms that the detainee Benjamin Zuskin was found to be suffering from cardiac atherosclerosis and moderate hypertension."[66] The truth is that no one intended to give my father any medical treatment.

As to the outdated directive "feed him," it is possible that the executioners kept pace with progress and decided to supplement it, if not to totally replace it, with a new order: "torture." As far as I know, at the Lefortovo Prison they treated the prisoners much worse than they did at the Lubianka.

I am writing about my father and I would like to focus all of my attention on him alone and his path of suffering all the way to the gallows. But I cannot ignore the fact that in the last act of his life, he was decreed to walk this path with others. I thus feel an obligation to the others as well, and therefore I will bring here a full list of the defendants who were put on trial together with my father:

Bergelson, David, *Yiddish writer and playwright.*

Bregman, Solomon, *Deputy Minister of State Control in the Russian Republic.*

Fefer, Isaac (Yitsik), *Yiddish poet, deputy head of the Jewish Anti-Fascist Committee.*

Hofshteyn, David, *Yiddish poet.*

Kvitko, Leyb, *Yiddish poet, particularly poetry for children, which was translated into the languages of all of the nationalities in the Soviet Union.*

Lozovsky, Solomon, *Director of Soviet Information Bureau (Sovinformburo), and head of the Chair of International Relations at the Higher Party School; 1939–1946: Deputy Minister of Foreign Affairs.*

Markish, Perets, *Yiddish poet and playwright.*

Shimelyovich, Boris, *physician. Medical Director of the prestigious Botkin Clinical Hospital, Moscow.*

Shtern, Lina, *Director-General of the Institute of Physiology at the Academy of Medical Science of the Soviet Union and member of this academy. Head of the Chair of Physiology at the Moscow Medical School.*

Talmi, Leon, *translator and journalist.*

Teumin, Emilia, *Deputy-editor of the diplomatic dictionaries.*

Vatenberg, Ilia, *Editor-in-chief at a state publishing house of books translated from foreign languages.*

Vatenberg-Ostrovskaya, Chaika, *wife of Ilia Vatenberg, translator at the Jewish Anti-Fascist Committee and at the publishing houses.*

Yuzefovich, Joseph, *researcher at the Institute of History, Soviet Academy of Sciences.*

Zuskin, Benjamin, *actor, Artistic Director of the Moscow State Jewish Theater.*

Of the fifteen, six were prominent personages in Jewish culture in the Soviet Union: Poets David Hofshteyn, Perets Markish, Isaac (Yitsik) Fefer, and Leyb Kvitko, the writer David Bergelson, and the actor Benjamin Zuskin. "By the time Zuskin was interrogated, he had learned that his prosecutors had little interest in the aesthetic or ideology of the Jewish theater."[67] They had interest in nothing actually characterizing any of the accused. They had in advance determined their own criteria upon which the job of classifying and selecting the group of fifteen was performed.

And while preparing the documents for the trial, the cooks in Broverman's kitchen were never overly particular about the fine points of aesthetics nor about the handwritten scribbles by the investigators. At times they simply rolled one sentence or another, regular or aesthetic, from one generalized record to another, or even between investigation "protocols" and court documents. Whatever expressions were written, the defendants were forced to find their way among them. "The defendants had eight days to read through forty-two massive volumes."[68]

Case File Number 2354 consists of forty-two volumes, and they had to be studied in eight days (from March 15 to March 22, 1952), an average of eight hours a day, in other words, in 64 hours.

Each of the forty-two volumes consists of close to 400 pages. This means: all told, they had to read 42 x 400 pages, or 16,800 pages, which is an average of 262 pages per hour, or 4.25 pages per minute. "It is hard to imagine how these tormented people could read forty-two volumes in eight days. But they did it."[69] Zuskin pondered how to record it all in his memory, because the defendants were not allowed to record anything with pencil on paper, and his unique memory was worn down under such conditions. And yet, Zuskin remembered. They all did.

The sophisticated torture summoned up for Zuskin had begun as early as January 13, 1948, the day that Mikhoels was murdered, and had not stopped since that time. After the 1,523 days and nights of torments beyond what the mind can grasp, they threw him some wretched eight "working days," like a bone to a dog. It seemed to him that his life, which was hanging in the balance, would be saved if he only could respond to every single word that filled the four and a quarter pages that he had to read every minute. But the authors of the plot were indifferent. They stuck to their plan. They knew that the noose tied around the neck of the victim would tighten all by itself, regardless of the number of pages or minutes.

While the accused studied the investigation records in the volumes containing the collective criminal case, the top ranks of the Ministry of State Security were already sending a draft of the Indictment to the Party's Central Committee and to its head, Stalin.

On April 3, 1952, the Party's Central Committee approved the Indictment draft and instructed the Military Collegium to hand down a death sentence to fourteen of the group of fifteen defendants, and Lina Shtern to be exiled to some remote wilderness. (Today's historians suppose that in exile, under severe living conditions, she was to continue her research focused on prolonging human life expectancy. Could it be that Stalin had intended to elude the way of all flesh?)

And all of this took place exactly one month and a half before the trial opened.

Ultimately, thirteen men and women were executed: In mid-June of 1952, Solomon Bregman lost consciousness. In consequence he was deemed unfit to stand trial, and was hospitalized in the prison hospital, where he was to die in January 1953.

"On May 8, 1952, the judicial farce began."[70] "From the start the Court had to make every effort to conceal the groundlessness of the accusations . . . The trial was a fiction, a mere formal action directed by the Ministry of State Security on Stalin's orders."[71]

Actor. Jew.

Even before Case Number 2354 was sent on to the Military Collegium, "a group of investigators suggested removing Benjamin Zuskin, Emilia Teumin and Chaika Vatenberg-Ostrovskaya from among the accused because . . . the accusations against them were weak. Riumin categorically turned down the suggestion out of fear that the case would collapse altogether."[72] He continued to persuade Stalin of the validity of the charges against the entire group, but he knew that they were groundless.

The Chairman of the Military Collegium, Alexander Cheptsov, also knew that. A few days before the end of the trial, he even contacted the Party Central Committee and asked for permission for a recess so that he could restudy Case Number 2354. His request was denied. With this, if between the date of pronouncing the death penalty on July 18, 1952, and the day the sentence was carried out on August 12, 1952, nearly a month passed—what kind of month was it for the condemned?!—then perhaps the case would indeed have been cast into doubt.

Yes, the "common case" was dubious, and the common indictment, absurd. In the indictment, the name of each one of the fifteen indicted is accompanied by a paragraph mentioning his "crimes." Just how dubious and absurd this common indictment was is illustrated most tangibly in the paragraph that concerns my father. Following is the excerpt: "The defendant Zuskin . . . produced plays at the theater . . . arousing nationalistic feelings among their Jewish viewers."[73]

Once I had thought that my father was charged with these non-crimes because when they fabricated the charges against his fellow-defendants, they did not leave any charges for Father, not even a fabricated one, not even the faintest shadow of a charge.

Today I realize that I was wrong. This was the charge: Arousing nationalistic—and more precisely, national—feelings. This was the most likely and the most serious of the other charges, and it was true for all of them.

As Zuskin was busy preparing for the trial and concentrating on reading the volumes that make up Criminal Case 2354, he understood clearly how false everything written there was. During the trial, he would tell the truth.

Now he understood that the investigators had forced him to learn a role with monologues about the Jewish theater as a "center of Jewish nationalism." Yes, there was no one like these investigators for cunning and skill. They were confident, because they had overcome other people, stronger than Zuskin. Wait a minute, other people? Yes, that is certain. But not people like him. He would learn the role that he had to play so that he could declare during the trial:

I am an actor.

"I thought much about the tragic fate that befell them both, and it is only now that I see that Mikhoels and Zuskin were murdered to a large extent because they were actors. They threatened the Stalinist regime, because as a result of the intuition and meta-senses which are built into actors, they deciphered the essence of this absolute dictatorship,"[74] an historian of the theatrical art was to say years afterward.

The art historian relates to something intangible, while the investigators wanted to grab onto actual deeds, to decipher them. Nonsense! Were the people on trial truly being tried for anything they actually did? Forty-two thick volumes documenting the preliminary investigation, and eight more volumes, no less thick, documenting the course of the trial, are nothing more than fifty volumes of mutterings that the secret police edited or distorted as served their needs.

Zuskin more than once "withdrew within himself but he never gave in, no matter what,"[75] because he was governed by an "unusual harmony,"[76] far outweighing fifty volumes devoid of any harmony, even though in all these volumes to Zuskin, one of the fifteen accused, only one fortieth portion relates.

Apparently there is justice in the words of the above theater historian, but I would add: they were not just actors; they were Jewish actors.

It is true that Zuskin never expressed this feeling aloud. He himself said this: "I don't know how to make speeches. I can only play a role; I can read what is already written."[77] Nonetheless, he was imbued with a strong sense of his people, and it is that spirit that drove him to act as he did, and ultimately led to his death.

HIS DEATH AS A JEW.

The executioners who turned his flesh to ash were not aware of what is written in the Book of books of the Jewish people: "There is no man who has power over the spirit to imprison the spirit" (Ecclesiastes 8:8).

11

Epilogue

MAY 8–JULY 18, 1952
TRIAL

Court record of the Military Collegium of USSR Supreme Court
    Court consisting of:
    Presiding officer: Chairman of the Military Collegium, Lieutenant
General of Justice Alexander Cheptsov.
    Members: Major General of Justice Yakov Dmitriev.
    Major General of Justice Ivan Zarianov.
    Secretary: Senior Lieutenant Mikhail Afanasiev.
    Conducted without a government prosecution or defense team
participating.

MAY 8, 1952; NOON

CHAIRMAN. I declare this session of the Military Collegium of the
    USSR Supreme Court open. The Case to be heard involves
    accusations of treason against . . . [1]
        The secretary reported that the accused . . . were brought to
        the court session under guard. The defendants . . . gave testimony
        about themselves . . .
ZUSKIN. I, Benjamin Zuskin, was born in 1899. I am originally from
    Lithuania, from the city of Panievezhys, Lithuanian Soviet
    Socialist Republic. My father was a tailor. I first studied in the
    Academy of Mining . . . I was awarded the Order of the Red Ban-
    ner, received the medal for Valiant Labor during the great patri-
    otic war, 1941–1945, and I am a laureate of the Stalin Prize, second

degree. I have never been a Party member. I am a People's Artist of the Russian Soviet Federal Socialist and the Uzbek Soviet Socialist Republics. Before my arrest I was the artistic director of the Moscow State Jewish Theater. I was arrested on December 24, 1948. I received a copy of the indictment on May 3, 1952.[2]

CHAIRMAN. Defendant Zuskin, do you understand your rights?

ZUSKIN. I understand my rights.

CHAIRMAN. What petition do you have for the court?

ZUSKIN. I have some petitions. The indictment states that I sent a number of articles to the American press about the state of art in the Soviet Union. I have already said that I wrote about the work of the Moscow State Jewish Theater. I wrote no more than four or five articles about the artists. I ask that these materials be appended in the Case materials so that the court has an idea what was in these articles of mine . . .

CHAIRMAN. The Military Collegium of the USSR Supreme Court, having heard the defendants' petitions and conducted immediate deliberation, has determined that the petitions will be decided upon the course of the Trial . . .

Defendant Zuskin, do you understand the Indictment?

ZUSKIN. Yes, I understand it.

CHAIRMAN. Do you plead guilty?

ZUSKIN. In part . . . [3]

JUNE 11, 1952; 20:40
TESTIMONY BY ZUSKIN

CHAIRMAN. Defendant Zuskin, to what do you plead guilty?

ZUSKIN. As a member of the Jewish Anti-Fascist Committee, I bear responsibility for its activity . . . The degree of my guilt will be determined by the court.

CHAIRMAN. Tell us about your activity.

ZUSKIN. I would like to read a statement about my testimony.

CHAIRMAN. You may convey your statement to the court through the secretary.[4]

JUNE 12, 1952; 14:45

The continued interrogation of Zuskin. Zuskin answers the questions of other defendants.

FEFER. You testified that instead of engaging in propaganda, the Jewish Anti-Fascist Committee sent out classified information. Did you learn of it from the forty-two volumes [of the Case]?

ZUSKIN. All that I had to say about that was unknown to me prior to my arrest.

With this, Zuskin's testimony is concluded.[5]

JULY 2, 1952
DETERMINATION REGARDING THE DEFENDANTS' PETITIONS

The Military Collegium of the USSR Supreme Court

Having studied the appeals filed during the court proceedings by the defendants, as follows: . . . and Zuskin—to include in the Case materials literary works written by them (poetry, stories, and articles) that would present them in a positive light . . .

Taking into consideration the fact that the literary works referred to in the appeal are not directly related to the accusations . . .

Seeing no basis for granting the abovementioned appeals,

Has decided: to dismiss the appeals . . . [6]

JULY 11, 1952; 12:45
THE DEFENDANTS' FINAL STATEMENTS

From the Final Statement by the Defendant Zuskin

Citizen Judges of the Military Collegium!

In my final statement I would like to say a bit about my life. I was eighteen when the Great October Revolution took place . . . After the Revolution I became a full and equal citizen of the USSR . . . I ended up in the State Jewish Theater . . . and that became my life's tragedy . . . In conclusion I want to say to the court that I feel that my conscience is clear . . . I have done nothing hostile or malicious . . . [7]

At 5:50 PM the court withdrew to the deliberation room for sentencing. On July 18, 1952 . . . at 1:05 PM, the court session was closed.[8]

In the Name of the Union of Soviet Socialist Republics the Military Collegium of the Supreme Court of the USSR . . . in a closed deliberation in Moscow, from July 11 to July 18, 1952, has studied the Case of the accused:

> . . .

> 9. Zuskin, Benjamin L'vovich, born in 1899 . . . [9]

The preliminary investigation and the court proceedings have established that to mobilize the Jewish population abroad in the struggle against fascism and to publicize the achievements of the USSR in the foreign press, the Jewish Anti-Fascist Committee was founded in April 1942 under the aegis of the Soviet Information Bureau.

Defendant Lozovsky . . . as the deputy director [and afterward the director] of the Sovinformbureau . . . used the Jewish Anti-Fascist Committee to unite Jewish nationalists to struggle against . . . the Soviet state . . . to arouse nationalistic and Zionist sentiments among the Jewish population and spread slanderous rumors that anti-Semitism was supposedly flourishing in the USSR . . . All of these criminal activities . . . attest to the fact that the Jewish Anti-Fascist Committee was transformed into a center of nationalistic activity and espionage . . . [10]

Afterward there is a detailed enumeration of the "hostile activity" of each of the defendants in the Case, including an enumeration of the charges attributed to Zuskin.

Defendant Zuskin . . . as a member of the presidium of the Jewish Anti-Fascist Committee and at the same time a leading actor at the Moscow Jewish Theater, which, as established by the Case materials, was one of the nationalistic propaganda branches of the Jewish Anti-Fascist Committee, together with Mikhoels, produced plays at the theater that extolled ancient Jewish ways, small town traditions and daily life and presented the Jewish people as tragic and doomed, thereby arousing nationalistic feelings among their Jewish viewers. He also sent a number of nationalistic articles to America about the state of the arts in the USSR . . . [11]

On the basis of the aforementioned, the Military Collegium of the Supreme Court of the USSR finds . . . , Zuskin, . . . guilty of committing the crimes referred to in articles 58-Ia; 58-10 part II; and 58-11 of the Criminal Code of the Russian Federation. Guided by articles 319 and 320 of the Code of Criminal Procedure of the Russian Federation, the Military Collegium of the Supreme Court of the USSR has sentenced:

. . .

Zuskin Benjamin . . .

on the basis of article 58-Ia of the Criminal Code of the Russian Federation to the severest measure of punishment for the crimes committed jointly:

execution by firing squad

with all of their properties to be confiscated.[12]

The sentence is final and not subject to appeal.[13]

August 13, 1952
The sentence . . . was carried out on August 12, 1952.

March 2, 1953
Fifteen cards were received to be entered into the central card file.

April 4, 1953
The cards were marked with the archive numbers.[14]

Darkness.

It is only from here, from the distance of sixty years, that I am capable of contemplating this darkness.

I see my father. He is standing in the middle of the room facing the judges. Although during the daytime, the room is lit by the sunlight and at night by electric lights, my father is still placed in the darkness.

I see my father in a cellar without windows. Even the flicker of fire that flashes from the rifle cannot pierce the darkness.

But what is this?

Darkness.

Darkness on stage. From a distance the shots of a dying battle are heard. The sounds of battle become dimmer and are replaced by a mournful tune.

Against the dark background candles appear. The candles are held by Badkhen's assistants but due to the darkness, the spectator cannot see them, and it appears that the candles are floating in the air.

In Moscow, in the State Jewish Theater, the premiere of *Freylekhs* opens.

In my mind I move back in time and see myself in my distant childhood, in a darkened auditorium, I see how in front of my eyes, an enchanted fairytale is woven, and out of the darkness a figure begins to emerge. It is the figure of Reb Yekl. This is the First Badkhen, this is the spirit of joy, and a small part of him is the spirit of sadness. This is Benjamin Zuskin, my father.

He floats from one end of the stage to the other. He looks at the candles flickering with an opaque light. In the sky, which is the ceiling above the stage, a single star shines.

A wave of the handkerchief held by Reb Yekl, and my father extinguishes the star and the candles, one by one. With every candle that is extinguished, the auditorium and stage are gradually illuminated, until a radiant light envelopes everything. The dim sounds of music grow louder and above them, the ringing triumphant voice of Reb Yekl grows stronger, the voice of Zuskin, a modest man, quiet, decent, far from being a fighter.

I hear him. Because neither time nor all of the evil in the world can vanquish his joyful call:

Blow out the candles!
Blot out the sorrow!

PART TWO

12

Benjamin Zuskin in His Own Words

Curriculum Vitae

My Path in Life and on Stage

I was born on April 28, 1899, in Ponievezh, a small town in Lithuania.

My father completed six years at the reali school. After the death of my father's only brother, my stubborn grandfather insisted that he stop his preoccupation with science, which was his greatest ambition, and enter the tailoring business in order to carry on the family tradition. My father went to Dresden, where he graduated from the Fashion Academy and returned to Ponievezh. He was never satisfied with tailoring as his main occupation; he studied medicine by himself, and very effective medications were prepared according to his prescriptions. He was interested in diverse fields of knowledge and had a special aptitude for public activity. Thus, in his town whose population was largely Jewish, he organized a society for helping needy and sick Jews, and he was one of its directors.

My father's house was always teeming with people: customers who went to the sewing workshop, poor people who were helped by the society he set up, family members who lived on the outskirts of Ponievezh, or even strangers who came to seek help or advice. Our home was open, and every day, dozens if not hundreds of people passed through.

My childhood was spent in this atmosphere, the childhood of a sensitive and high-strung youngster. In my childhood I underwent the experiences of the poor Jews in my town more than I underwent my own experiences. I learned to love the people who had been crowded into the Pale of Settlement.

Later, these impressions from my childhood served me and helped me in my work as an actor.

Opposite our house was a performance hall, the only one in town. It was the "Illusion" movie theater. Itinerant theater troupes also gave performances on its small stage. During the times that they were appearing in our town, our noisy house became even noisier. Actors and troupe directors knew that the Zuskin home was always open to them. They enjoyed themselves in our house. My parents were welcoming hosts and the actors ate and drank, had a good time and laughed, and after the performances, they would sit with us into the night. All of the members of my family, even my old grandmother, were theater buffs.

When I was six, I saw a show for the first time. It made a tremendous impression on me. Ever since, my favorite diversion was to put on performances in the shed in our yard. In these shows, I was the only actor. Cotton, which was plentiful in my father's sewing shop, was used to make me a beard, and coal from the kitchen was makeup. When the theater troupes came to our town, I used to be absent from school for days. I helped the actors find lodgings and stage props; I fulfilled their requests most willingly, and in return, they let me watch the performances.

Sometimes I was allowed to enter the inner sanctum, behind the scenes. With my own eyes I saw how actors live. At that time pupils were not allowed to sit in the audience, so I watched the performances from behind the curtains, and that brought me great delight.

At the age of five, I began to attend the heder. I was lucky: my teacher had an obvious talent for acting.

At a very early age I was noted to possess a proclivity to observe the people around me, to take in their body language, facial expressions, manner of speech, and to imitate it all. My teacher would encourage me to imitate people. For example, the mother of one of the pupils would come to the heder and ask to talk about her son's behavior. My teacher would wink at me and hint that I should follow the conversation. When the time was ripe, I was supposed to reproduce the conversation, and my teacher would comment.

I was always imitating someone. There was a ragman in town nicknamed "Ginger." I imitated him so well that his nickname stuck to me.

Occasionally I would imitate someone in the presence of my family or friends, and the onlookers would immediately identify the victim.

I loved all kinds of performances. When the circus came to town, I felt an obligation to go and see it.

I remember my first appearance and my failure. I was about ten and supposed to appear in an amateur theater, in the play *With the Stream* (*Mitn shtrom*) by Sholem Asch, in the role of an eight-year-old boy. I was excited, I learned the role, but just before the play was to open, I panicked and ran home. The role was played by another boy. I suffered greatly over that.

Later I would put on entire plays in our shed. The plays were in Russian or Yiddish. We wrote plays based on the works of Tolstoi and Turgenev. I was about thirteen at the time and I attended the reali school, even though it was hard to get accepted there because of the limitations imposed on Jews.

When it was boring at school, I would draw in the notebook that I always kept open in front of me. I drew portraits mainly, and I did them in pencil so that I could erase later or add a moustache, or some item of makeup or alter the features.

We had a teacher of language and literature, a hunchback with unforgettable eyes, filled with sorrow. He also had an instinct for acting. He loved to hear his pupils recite with feeling, and I was his favorite.

June 3, 1915. The Grand Duke Nikolai Nikolaevich, the commander-in-chief of the Russian army, published an edict ordering all Jews to leave the province along the border with Prussia. Almost the entire population of Ponievezh was forced to leave. They gave us only a few hours to collect our belongings and after that, we spent several days at the train station, under the open sky, in the rain and hail. Under these conditions babies were born, old people died.

Finally we arrived in the city of Penza. There I continued studying at the reali school. In Penza there was a good theater and I visited it frequently. It was a Russian theater. I saw all the performances and I related to them with the utmost seriousness. There were consummate Russian actors, and for me, they were like teachers.

September 1916—that is the period that marks the beginning of my career as an amateur actor. In Penza, theatrical groups operated as part of

the Committee to Aid Refugees. I wanted to join. For the audition, I prepared the story *Back from the Draft* (*Funem Prizev*) by Sholem Aleichem.
My performance impressed the testers greatly. From then on I became an
amateur actor whose name was well known.

At the reali school, I was a director in the acting club. Stepan Ivanov-
ich Stepanov, the teacher of Russian language, encouraged me in this
job. I directed different vaudevilles, for instance, *It's a Family Affair, We'll
Settle It Ourselves* (*Svoi liudi-sochtemsia*) by Alexander Ostrovsky. I did
not act in the club's plays because these were in Russian and I didn't feel
that I could sound credible in Russian. When I had a chance to appear
in Yiddish, I acted under the influence of the rather good Jewish actor
from Vilna, Shriftzetser, who perished in the Vilna Ghetto during World
War II.

Everyone who knew me realized that I had a passion to act. Already in
Ponievezh the Jewish actor Sokolov said of me: "From this boy there will
yet grow a great Jewish actor." Eighteen years later when he saw me acting
in Paris, he was delighted that his prophecy had been fulfilled.

I took part as an amateur in various plays and performances. They
wrote in the newspaper about one of these performances: "Several actors
appeared and one of them [they meant me] has a glowing career as an
actor in store for him, on condition that he doesn't get side-tracked into
slapstick." This was a collection of skits called *An Evening of Sholem
Aleichem.*

In 1919 my parents went back to Lithuania. I remained alone. I worked
for the Prison Service and at night, I studied.

In Penza, one of very good actors who heard me recite took me by the
hand and said, "You have to be an actor; go to the Moscow Art Theater."

I tried not to miss a single show in Penza, especially when actors from
the capital appeared there. My work at the time was also connected with
the theater: I was an instructor [in the field of culture] in the political
department of the Ural Mountains District's Military Headquarters. All
of these affected my decision to become an actor. In 1920 I transferred
from Yekaterinburg, where I had been studying at the College of Mine
Engineering, to Moscow where I continued my studies at the Academy
of Mine Engineering. During that time, the State Jewish Theater with its

School of Acting had just moved to Moscow from Petrograd. In 1921, I was accepted to the School of Acting and I left the Academy of Mine Engineering. Three months later I was accepted to the theater and became a regular actor. On September 24, 1921, in the theater auditorium decorated with the works of Chagall, I gave my first performance in the role of the First Jew in the play *It's a Lie!* based on Sholem Aleichem.

The show, which was my first real milestone, was *The Sorceress*, a manifesto of the young theater. I played the leading role. The role was very difficult, technically as well. In the course of my work on the role I practiced day and night, and I reached the capability of performing fifty somersaults in a row, and more.

The second milestone for me was the role of Senderl in the play *The Travels of Benjamin the Third*. Then, for the first time, I was given the opportunity to portray before an audience the lyrical element that I so admire in man. Despite his grotesque outer appearance, Senderl is very human.

Another milestone was the play *The Wandering Stars*. Thanks to it, I gained a deeper understanding of the meaning of life. I interpreted Hotsmakh's character as someone who detects in the boy the qualities of a great actor and not someone who is exploiting him. In this play my hero says just before he dies, "The doctors say that I need rest, air, and the sea . . . For what do I need rest, air, and the sea without the theater?" And to me, that sentence became the central motif of the role.

In all of my protagonists, I try to find a dream, the hope of a better life. That is a very national trait: in the past when the Jewish people lived under difficult conditions, of persecution, hunger, poverty, it drew its strength from optimism, from its faith in justice.

Among the roles that were milestones in my career is also the role of the Fool in *King Lear*, which for me symbolized the tragedy in helplessness. The clever Fool, who is wise at reading people's hearts and understanding human nature, is unable to help the King, not even a little bit. This situation is one of the most difficult in my own life.

I relate to all of my heroes on stage with emotion mixed with something of an infatuation. However, the most sublime place is reserved for Senderl in *The Travels of Benjamin the Third*, based on the work by

Mendele Moykher Sforim, the grandfather of Yiddish literature. Senderl is a little man with a great soul, a man who is treated with contempt, perhaps even ugly.

I usually start to look for the distinctive traits of the character I must portray from its external appearance as I imagine it. When my thoughts about the image blend with this appearance, one can say that the ground-work for the role has been prepared. I have a very good visual sense, and in my memory I keep an entire gallery of people whom I have met in my lifetime.

In looking for how to build Senderl's external image, the difficulty was that Solomon Mikhoels is shorter than me, and in the role of Senderl, I was supposed to be shorter than him, because Don Quixote took counsel with the stars whereas Sancho Panza is an earthy creature.

In general, when I am pregnant with a role, it hounds me and I am unable to free myself from it. So, as I was working on Senderl, I once saw a wagon driver with bowlegs like someone who suffered from rickets. I almost let out a shout. I realized that I needed just those legs. They imme-diately reduced my height.

The role of Senderl was my most beloved role.

The stage is dear to me because of the world of characters I portray, because of the possibility of speaking to my audience about some of these people. At the same time, and I am speaking in all sincerity, what interests me today is not the cheers of the theatergoers but the ability to show the audience the richness of the human soul. Each role is a chapter in my own life story. The more varied the chapter, the more it interests me.

My favorite roles are those that pique my curiosity—complex charac-ters full of internal contradictions. For example, the Fool in *King Lear*, Senderl in *The Travels of Benjamin the Third*.

My heart is captivated particularly by the image of the person who is derided and humiliated, but who loves life, even though he encounters obstacles placed before him through no fault of his own. Hotsmakh, the hero of *The Wandering Stars*, is one such character.

I appeared on stage in this production many times. Nonetheless, it never happens on the day before an evening performance that I don't work on the monologue where Hotsmakh relates how he became a comedian.

In my roles I try to find features that are close to my heart, like, for example, in the play *The Wandering Stars*, in the role of Hotsmakh. Although the point of departure for working on this role is a given character, I leave my own imprint on it from my personal life.

How do I start to work on the character of Hotsmakh? By portraying a man who is full of joy of life, a bold young man. Afterward he changes. I try to highlight the change in Hotsmakh's life by the use of makeup. During the course of the show, I also switch my wig: in the first act, his hair is thick and curly, and when he becomes the theater director, his hair is smooth and slick.

I love small roles very much. I love to be silent on the stage. I hate words that are empty of meaning. I think there has to be some serious significance to silence on the stage. That is one of the reasons that I love to play the role of the Fool in *King Lear*: he is silent for the entire Act One, and only at the very end, he sings his song.

You cannot ignore the spoken text, but the theater by nature is a play, a game.

Over my lifetime, I have passed up several roles. That is what I did in the period when I began to work in the theater, when they would offer me roles that seemed outside my capabilities or my aspirations. I was quite young then. Now I would not pass up these roles, because I think that the actor's mission is to overcome the difficulties.

What I am playing in *The Capricious Bride* reminds me of some of my previous works. It is not interesting. My present ambition is to make the roles that seem foreign to me, more familiar.

A few words about the literature in my life. Sholem Aleichem is the writer who most thrills my soul. Who else? I love to read Dostoyevsky. What I love in his writing is the profound analysis of human behavior and feeling. I have reread his works many times, and each time, I found something new. My favorite is *Crime and Punishment* (*Prestuplenie i nakazanie*). Other writers have also had an impact on my development as a human being and an artist, such as: Yitshak Leybush Peretz, Lev Tolstoi, Dickens, Balzac. I keep returning to them in the course of my life. Chekhov is my favorite playwright. I admire Chekhov's style of writing: his text is full of meaning and at the same time, very spare.

I draw a bit. I began already in childhood. Now I use drawing when I need it in my work as an actor.

Music, especially folk music, has greatly influenced my development as an actor. Y. L. Peretz has an expression: Music is more sublime than the word. I love to insert music in my work. Singing a song is much more powerful than delivering a monologue.

My vocation in the theatrical arts includes, to a large extent, the work of teaching. Already in the academic year of 1932–1933 I began teaching at the Jewish School of Acting, and beginning in 1936, I am giving a regular course.

Several cycles of students have graduated their studies with me. My purpose is to bring each and every one of my students to speak in the language that characterizes him exclusively. In my work here, I combine theory with exercises.

I strive to educate my students in the spirit of love for the theater, love of the actor's work, in a spirit that does not contain self-indulgence. Only an educated person, a person with the highest ideals, can be a good actor. Well-formulated ethical principles is what I try to instill in my students from the beginning of their studies and throughout the four years. As to the second-year students, I require them to go back to passages they prepared in the first year; my third-year students—to the passages of the second year; that is how they can see what a distance they have come.

Teaching does not interfere with my work as an actor; on the contrary, it enriches me.

Along with the theater, I also worked as a film actor.

In 1935–1936, I began to work as a director. I directed the productions *Hershele Ostropoler, The Enchanted Tailor, Freylekhs,* and *The Family* (together with Pavel Markov); recently I directed an evening of miniatures—short variety skits. I do quite a bit in the field of entertainment and one-man shows. Entertainment attracts me because it requires the actor to reach the pinnacle of his expressive ability. In addition to that, I directed several final productions at the School of Acting. My approach to directing is like that of an actor, and here I do not reinvent the wheel. In the productions that I staged, I loved more than anything to work with the actors.

The work in collaboration with the composer or the artist also interests me as a director. I am entranced by the possibility of examining how characters are created, how they are given meaning, filled with life. A mise-en-scene for me is speaking between the lines, and I strive to reveal meaning through the mise-en-scene. As a director, I carefully follow the development of one character or another, but I see the entire production only hazily. In general, on stage, it is the actor first and foremost who excites me.

There were shows where I was both actor and director (*The Enchanted Tailor, Freylekhs*). That was very difficult. When you, as director, are also on the stage as actor, more than once you find yourself moving away from the character you are portraying and looking at the performance of other actors. I think that in such cases I was saved by my ability to marshal all of my skills as an actor.

I believe that in an actor who devotes part of his time to teaching or to directing, his work as an actor becomes more important.

My Work on a Role

Every literary work that I read—be it play, story, novel, or even newspaper article—I read as an actor. I cannot read something just to know what is happening. I become interested in the people being told of, I try to imagine them, to surround them with an atmosphere, try to enter their inner world, to discover the essence of their personality.

When I read a play where I have to portray one of the roles, first of all it is the play as a whole that is important for me. I do not see only myself in the show. First and foremost I take in the entire play, imagine to myself how the life of my hero develops in the world of the play, endeavor to understand what he is thinking about, what are his ideas, what is his worldview. Only after that, I relate to the language and other important aspects.

I read the speaking parts of my role several times, and with great attention, delve into them, connect them in my mind with a given mise-en-scene. In the first days I go everywhere with a notebook and afterward, the text becomes part of me.

When I think of the role, I begin with the depiction of the character's movement, his psychological rather than physical movement. Afterward, I try to define the importance of the role in relation to the production or the act or the scene. After I formulate my perception of the role, and the director shapes his perception of the production, then I begin to visualize the look of the character from my childhood memories. For that purpose I draw upon recollections from the world around me. These external impressions are mined either from literature or childhood memories, and gradually before my eyes the type which I am seeking as an artist begins to take shape.

In the work on my role, I copy over the speaking parts and I do that more than once. It is important for me. In my notes on the recopied text, I decide what is the meaning between the lines in certain of these passages.

I invented for myself a kind of ruler for notes, and in my verbal textual analysis of the role I mark on it pauses or emphases. When I return to working on my role, I read these annotations like a musician reads musical notes. If I have properly understood the character and its development, I will perform the role with a sense of integrity.

There was a period when I used to repeat the text endlessly, now I don't think of the words. More than that: I reached the conclusion that there is no need to learn the role word for word. In this way I feel freer. Of course this does not apply to rhymed text. Apparently I have become confident enough of my work to understand: it is not the word that I utter which is so important. What is important is what I want to express by means of that word.

In our theater, the period of reading a play aloud around the table is fairly long, and I like that. From my standpoint, preparing an outline of the role is the most interesting and the most tormenting job. On the other hand, finding the right tone for the words or sentences uttered by my hero is something I can do only after I learn in practice the space in which my protagonist lives. Intonation is born together with movement.

How I start to work on the text? I find a passage, for example, that is highly important for the roots and essence of the character, and then I ponder the manner of speech: is it loud or soft, fast or slow.

As I think about a role, I have a need to imagine the life situation of my hero. I try to delve as deeply as possible in order to understand him. This is absolutely essential for me in order to know the character.

In the production *Four Days*, I play the role of a Polish print shop worker. I re-read the books by a few revolutionaries. This helped me very much. I not only envisioned this man's past but I also tried to imagine what his future would have been, had he survived. I tried to understand the internal psychic structure of my hero and his thoughts, aspirations, and wishes.

Another example: Rabbi Akiva in *Bar Kokhba*. When I was preparing this role, I read a great deal. I thought a great lot—out of a desire to create a bridge between the distant era of Akiva, the second century, and our times, so that the character would be convincing.

For the role of Kabtsenson, I also needed the protagonist's life history, although the play itself was a vaudeville, and in productions of this kind, the approach is completely different. For example, there is a scene like this: I am hiding from the old man, and he immediately discovers me. The performance is full of similar situations, lacking all logic, and all must be justified.

I work a lot and as though I am under a tremendous crushing pressure. During the period when I am working on a role, I have a habit of wandering the streets, peering eagerly into the faces of passersby. Sometimes, a movement or intonation that I picked up in a chance encounter contributes something. It is from there that the impressions emerge, but until I can cry triumphantly: That's it! time is required.

My procedure for working on a role is composed of three stages. The first stage is the preparatory stage, or more precisely, the analysis. After that comes the second stage, which is synthesis. The third stage is presenting it to an audience. Until I see the production in its entirety, I do not decide upon final intonations, even though I take great pains to arrive at them. When I see a character that suits my ambitions, I am already able to find the appropriate intonations.

In most of my roles, the monologues and dialogues are not rhymed, but I have also played roles that were: Rabbi Akiva, the Fool. I prefer that the text be in the original language and not translated. The best translation in comparison with the source does not convey the range of feeling and sound.

When we worked on the play *The Millionaire, the Dentist and the Pauper* by Labiche, directed by the French director Léon Moussinac, I asked Moussinac to say a sentence here and there in French so that I could get the "scent" of the language. In the production *Four Days* I portrayed a Polish workman, and I made sure that the Polish nuance would be heard only in several of the words. Just to emphasize speech is not interesting. One studs the character's speech with a word of a national tone even if it is barely understood. That gives characterization; it is very important. And most important is to do this in good taste and in proportion.

In this sense, I was highly impressed by the acting of Michail Chekhov in the role of Frazer in *The Flood* (*Potop*). Throughout the production he pronounces only twice and each time only one word with the characteristic national accent, but it was sufficient to produce the effect of conveying Frazer's nationality.

I think the manner of speaking on stage must be somewhat elevated, even if the subject of the play is day-to-day reality. Words have tremendous power, and the word must be concise, distilling the message it contains.

A Jewish actor must be alert to an additional problem. In appearing on stage, he is not certain that all of the theatergoers understand what he is saying because many of them don't understand Yiddish or are not proficient in it. I am aware of this, and so I add to my message other dramatic elements, or use music and pass up the verbal script. On the other side, living words as uttered on the stage are quite important for the development of the Yiddish language, and its enrichment and purity. In our theater, we work hard on vocabulary, on pronunciation, on the musical aspect of the language.

We had a production called *Boytre the Bandit*. When I sought material for constructing the image of Boytre, I was reminded of an event that happened in my childhood. We had a distant relative who was never spoken of in the presence of children. One day a tall man with a long red beard and sad eyes appeared in our house. Our relatives were having a wedding, and now there appeared this man, leaning against a tree and standing there by himself. I see a tear rolling down his beard, and he says,

"It could have been that way for me, too." It turns out that on the basis of malicious and false informing, he was sentenced to imprisonment; when he came back, people avoided meeting him. I tried to present Boytre as a little man, an ordinary person who because of circumstances is forced to do extraordinary things. The point of departure for me was not his heroic outward appearance but rather his human soul.

In the show *Two Hundred Thousand*, I was a shadkhen who appears on stage by parachuting in with an umbrella. In order to convince others, one has to be convinced oneself. I went down a rocky road in seeking impressions that would lead to a model on which I could fashion the character. And again my childhood memories came to the rescue. I recalled a small shop where every one of its products was sold for twenty kopecks. The shop owner, when he handed something to a customer, would actually skip-dance as he moved from one to the next. I transferred those patterns of behavior to my Shadkhen. The effect was a prancing, dancing character. I also took from the shop owner his unique way of speaking.

When as a child I went to the heder, two peddler women sat opposite the heder. One spoke in a bass voice, the other in a thin, high-pitched voice. Both served as inspiration to me for the character of the Sorceress. When I appeared in the production *The Sorceress*, I portrayed a magical character but the source of my approach to it was rooted in totally genuine people. Once a childhood friend watched the show *The Sorceress*, and he said to me in wonder: "That's them, those two women!"

I will not say that my hero on stage is entirely fashioned according to one person. Frequently I take from one type several personality traits and from another, external features: I take this or that detail from different people I know. The purpose is to load the character with the main traits of these people, to present individual characteristics or details that, as a whole, will create the outline of the persona as fully as possible.

The character of the luckless agent in *Luftmentsch* was created using a different method. Solomon Mikhoels played the part of Menakhem Mendel, the Luftmentsch, an agent brimming with ideas and energy, a lively person who seemed to spout a million words a minute. The production director suggested that I play the role of a person who accompanies the Luftmentsch, as a kind of shadow.

Particularly because in the written version of the play, there is no such character, and I created the other luftmentsch by myself, the one who follows Menakhem Mendel, I decided to create a character who is the opposite of Menakhem Mendel. If Menakhem Mendel is a chatterer, my hero must be taciturn. I decided to achieve this effect by using the language of opposites, but I wasn't able to get a handle on this character until I remembered the man whom I actually knew in real life.

Not long ago, in *The Capricious Bride*, I had a role portraying a kind of a simpleton typical for an operetta, a vaudeville. I finished preparing the role only after I met an actor at a rest home who was appearing at one of the provincial theaters, a typical comic actor. His face, his bald spot—these showed me how the character I was working on should look.

When I work on a role, I draw upon everything from my environment that I consider fitting for the given role. If the material is familiar, that makes it easier; but if I don't feel comfortable with the material that I have, it is harder. For example, fashioning the persona in the French play *The Millionaire, the Dentist and the Pauper* demanded from me the kind of exertion that I had not known in working on Jewish characters, despite the fact that I had been in Paris and I saw people of the kind I needed for the role, and I am very familiar with French literature such as: Balzac, Maupassant, Flaubert, and Hugo.

In the production *The Measure of Strictness*, based on the play by Bergelson, which deals with the first years of the civil war, I portrayed a doctor who never stops muttering, "I'm on the sidelines," "Politics does not interest me," but at the same time, he causes damage to the Revolution with his actions. After I was given the role and I read the play and heard the director's stage directions, I started to think about this man, I started to search for such characters in Russian literature, I remembered my school mathematics teacher.

When I work on a role, I have to make sketches of the portrait, costume, makeup.

Can I form a character only on the basis of his external appearance? No. First of all, one must properly understand the essence of the character.

Am I satisfied by the movements that I make spontaneously, or intonations that are created as though by themselves as I work on a role? No.

I must continue to develop them. This is really essential. Among all of the possibilities, I must choose only one. Likewise, I do not aspire to any gesture that is any kind of external stunt. The gesture in acting is like the subtext in a speech or dialogue, and therefore the gesture is of great importance. That said, I prefer not to fashion the gesture completely, and I leave a lot for room for the gesture that is born naturally.

When preparing a role, I do not use a mirror; I think that the custom of using one is detrimental.

Theater art is a synthetic art, in the most profound and genuine sense of the word. This art is comprised of diverse tools. I have no preference for one component over the others; I treat each of them equally.

What value do I attribute to the first encounter with the lighting or stage props? First of all, it is annoying, afterward, you get used to it. In essence, it is annoying until you get used to it. That is the way with the costumes also. At rehearsals I learn to accept my protagonists when I am wearing my regular clothes, and each new item in fashioning the character arouses a different response. So I try to get myself used to the props I have to appear with in the show in advance. For example, if I am supposed to appear with a pipe, I will choose to walk around with a pipe in my personal life, too. It helps.

The sense that the character is indeed "born" awakens in me when my preparatory work is approaching the end. Sometimes a detail in the makeup or in the costume can create the feeling that the role has become absolutely highlighted.

According to my approach, the costume is not merely the outward expression of the character. If I clothe myself in an item of apparel from the character's costume, I perform, without fully realizing it, the positions and movements that are related to the costume.

My expectations of the lighting are also high. If a stage is illuminated in bright colors, that is one thing, and if in dark colors that is another. The lighting has a very strong impact. Therefore, until the full dress rehearsal, I am always moving around on the edges, not really confronting the character face to face.

The greater the actor opposite whom you act, the greater is his contribution to the way that you act. I was fortunate: fate brought Solomon

Mikhoels to be my partner on stage. When I mount the stage to act along-side Mikhoels, my spirit is uplifted, celebratory.

What do I expect of my partner? The more sophisticated my partner is, the more profound, brilliant, interesting he is, the more he enriches the character that I am playing as well.

My work on a role continues even after the premier opening. As much as I work in conditions of peace and quiet in the rehearsal hall, ulti-mately everything depends on my encounter with the audience. Today I work more quickly on the role. In the past I had a feeling that in the production I am walking along the edge of an abyss, and because of that I wanted to prolong the stages of preliminary work. Now after having accumulated a certain amount of experience, I prefer to accelerate the pace of my work.

There is a rule to which I adhere: it seems to me that it is not good for an actor to keep improving his role during the rehearsals in order to arrive at the final crystallization of it. You must leave something for spontane-ous performance during the show, something fresh, not polished. In most cases I carefully keep to the outline, I don't change the mise-en-scene—it can stay unchanged for the five hundred times that the play is staged, but in every performance I try to refresh my acting in some way.

I believe that the actor must feel free on stage, not in the sense that he is appearing "in his underwear" but in the sense that the feeling of free-dom must be such that when something unexpected happens on stage, he will not be confused.

Work on a role lasts years. Impressions accumulate, new nuances are added. When the production is already running, I often catch myself say-ing: why didn't I add this detail before?

The role crystallizes into a definite shape in a show that is being put on for the twentieth or thirtieth or fiftieth time. Only then can it be prop-erly evaluated. Does that mean that afterward I stop working on the role? No, it's not that way. I appeared in *King Lear* approximately five hun-dred times, and I never got tired of it, although there are other roles that became lifeless for me.

In the play *King Lear* I feel that I am walking on the blade of a knife. There is a great scene in it where I don't utter a single word. Once during this scene I heard laughing in the audience at a moment that was not intended for laughter. I tormented myself over it for a long while and wondered: Why is the audience responding that way? I caught on that I was performing a certain move more abruptly than required. From the aspect of the actor's ego, that is pleasant—after all, the audience is responding—but in terms of the entire production, it is intolerable.

On the day before a production, I like to stroll the streets. I choose a long route so that I have time to think. I choose for myself passages from the role and mull them over: maybe it can be changed here, or perhaps find new intonations there. And if I find something new, I incorporate it into the role during the show and then I continue to search.

The actor's private life is closely connected to his artistic work. The link between life and creation is so strong that they can't be separated. So over the years you relate differently to the same role.

Characters become deeper over time. Let us take, for example, *The Travels of Benjamin the Third*, the best thing that I was ever able to do. The more I thought about my role in this production, the more the depth of it was revealed to me. I started to assess it differently, to enrich it with the mature life experience of my own life.

How do I feel on the day of a show and during the performance itself?

On my way to the theater, where I must appear in a show, I try to think only of the role that awaits me, of the important points in it.

On stage I listen to my own intonations and evaluate myself. I have not turned this rule into a "law," although it happens very frequently. I try to look at myself through the eyes of the spectator, keeping track of myself. In the intermission, I can speak about matters that are not related to my role on stage, and it doesn't interfere with me.

A stage appearance is not only acting; it is also labor. Take me, for example: my work in the production of *The Capricious Bride* earned me the label "a rubber doll, a man without any bones." Everything seems to have been achieved with ease, but the result is actually achieved with great pains. The spectator does not see this. He sees only the result.

On stage, do I share my protagonist's feelings? It is possible but not in every role. I love the old men and women, and when I was young, I portrayed their characters many times; the wisdom of the old is dearly loved by me. The roles of Rabbi Akiva in *Bar Kokhba* and of the old teacher in *Arn Friedman* are very dear to me.

How does my mood affect the way I act? When I am in a bad mood, I try to grasp onto the role in order to forget my pain. That can happen in both drama and comedy. You cannot always tell the spectator about yourself using the role. It depends on the role. There are circumstances where something is eating at me from within, and it merges with the role I am playing, like, for example, in the play *The Wandering Stars*. After all, the aim of art is to present life, but to present it using artistic means.

I am an apprehensive person and when I receive a new role, it seems to me that I will never master it. In my creative work, every beginning is difficult for me. I do not like to participate in an artistic event and hardly ever do. And if I do, then I prefer to appear not "in white tie and tails," but in the makeup and costume of the character, which creates a theatrical atmosphere.

I love to act in an atmosphere of intimacy, close to the audience. The best thing for me is acting in my own theater hall. I have become accustomed to it.

There was a period when I would go to the theater to take part in a production, for example, *The Sorceress*, like a man who is being brought to the gallows, even though I had dizzying success. And the more that I acted, the more that I succeeded, the greater were my anxieties, my sense of responsibility, my feeling that I would not deliver what was required of me.

The moments of complete satisfaction with my work are few. And as an actor matures, as he rises in his profession, he is correspondingly less satisfied with himself. A person's maturation leads him to increase his demands of himself. It is precisely because I have matured, I have accrued twenty-five years of experience on stage, that I prefer professional, useful criticism which truly does help, over empty comments of the type: Great, excellent!

The actor grows together with his age.[1]

My Sholem Aleichem

Sholem Aleichem. These are the words a Jew uses to greet whomever he chances to meet. It is no coincidence that at the beginning of his creative career, the great classical Jewish writer adopted for himself this simple and unexpected expression as a brilliant pen name. By choosing this name, the author aspired to emphasize his closeness to his reader, to maintain intimate contact with his people, to speak to each and every one of his readers as though he were an old acquaintance, to talk with him face to face about the most emotional subjects . . .

In my mind's eye I see how Sholem Aleichem, pen and notebook in hands, walks through the Pale of Settlement—down the winding streets teeming with humanity, in the small towns and shtetls where poor Jews scurry about, scorned and hungry. He examines the atmosphere with careful attention, listening with full concern to every single one. He does not abandon his heroes during the mass migration after the horrific pogroms of 1905. Together with them he travels to America, in order to see how his heroes live under new conditions. Everything that Sholem Aleichem saw and heard and turned over in his brilliant mind and felt in his generous heart—all of these he gave back to his people in the form of his wonderful creations that reflect the pulsing of the life of the people.

He became a part of the fabric of the life of the people and was integrated within them. Sholem Aleichem opened my eyes to see them, but not only that—also to love them.

Many times it happened that I heard the people who came to our house would finish their tale of woes like the heroes of Sholem Aleichem: "May God grant us length of days—sorrows we already have plenty of." Or "What I'm telling you is a story for Sholem Aleichem . . ."

Hey, Menakhem Mendel, how goes it? How are your children? This is how we greeted one of the regular visitors to our house when he arrived. His real name was Meir Levit, but in our town they called him Menakhem Mendel, after the character created by Sholem Aleichem. Like Sholem Aleichem's famous protagonist, Meir Levit was a shlemazl, an unlucky person . . .

I remember Heykel the sickly bookseller. He is like Mikhoels-Reb-Alter in our production *Mazel Tov!* We borrowed from him thin books from the series *The Family Library.*

Anshel the tailor, a great expert in making patches, a poor man and always joking, was taken straight out of Sholem Aleichem's storybook

Poor and Happy (*Areme un freylekhe*). He used to say to Heykel the book-seller, "What you are giving me? I don't want literature. I want Sholem Aleichem . . ."

The poetic characters of Sholem Aleichem have enriched my life ever since my childhood. The heroes—lyrical, moving, warmhearted—of his stories for children became my friends; I didn't stop thinking about them. It was then that my boundless love for the great Sholem Aleichem was born, and his works have accompanied me all of my life . . .

Of course, not everyone read Sholem Aleichem in depth, not every-one understood him and accepted him.

Many "intellectuals" saw Sholem Aleichem as primarily a clowning humorist, a writer of clever stories, filled with witticisms or jokes. In their narrow vision they did not understand the essence of Sholem Aleichem's work, the absolutely right, profoundly critical thinking that underlay every work of his. They did not discover his humane attitude and his adherence to it . . .

I learned to read Sholem Aleichem and to understand him properly at the Moscow State Jewish Theater. Thanks to the productions of our the-ater based on Sholem Aleichem's works in which I had participated as an actor—I began to re-evaluate Sholem Aleichem. Our theater had the privi-lege of being the first to uncover the social roots in Sholem Aleichem's creations, of presenting a genuine Sholem Aleichem. The eminent author could certainly have credited the theater with all this. In light of the work in the theater on Sholem Aleichem's plays, the nature of the writer's oeu-vre became clear to me . . .

In truth, Sholem Aleichem's laughter is laughter born in sorrow. He shows the tragedy by means of humor and laughter, and he does it bril-liantly and simply. Comic and tragic, laughter and tears, these two oppo-sites are woven together and they cannot be separated.[2]

What I Learned from the Cinema

In the film industry, as in the theater, the actor must set himself one sin-gle goal. Using the artistic means he has, he must create an authentic character, full of life and vibrancy, the portrait of a person, with all of his colorfulness and contradictions.

The actor's art is a radically individualistic art. In everyday work on himself, painstakingly and systematically, in accumulating experience, in passing from one character to another, the actor elaborates his personal approach toward internalizing an image and then representing it.

The uniqueness of the actor is in his being both the object of his own creation as well as the creator.

The actor is the author of the character. The director must disappear within the actor, writes Nemirovich-Danchenko. And I think that the actor must process the play or the script using his artistic tools so that the literary work bears the personal stamp of the actor.

The work of the theater actor and the film actor has much in common, although there are also many differences.

The first stage of the actor's work is preparation, or more correctly, accumulation. At this stage I believe there is no difference between the film actor and the theater actor. During the stage of rehearsals, I do find differences: in the theater, rehearsals are held from beginning to end, in order, systematically; in film, the role seems to be composed of patches, you can be filmed first in a segment from the end of the film, and three months later—in the opening segments. I think that a film actor should rehearse only the segments that are important in fashioning the role and leave room for spontaneous, natural performance in front of the camera.

As a theater actor, I do not agree with the approach that the work on a role ends when the stage of rehearsals ends. The character continues to take shape during the appearance before an audience. The audience is an integral part of the theater actor's work. In the cinema, the actor is naturally prevented from evaluating himself based on the audience response.

The theater actor who works in film must abandon the working methods he has adopted in the theater. In cinema, it is essential that the actor maintain maximum contact with the camera lens. The camera lens not only catches every detail but intensifies it (in close-up). Thus the film actor's job is harder than that of the theater actor: standing in front of the camera, he must marshal all of his talents.

In film more than in the theater, the director is the supreme authority for the actor. It seems to me that during a film shoot, the director has to act as a surrogate for the audience.

A film actor must be sincere, authentic, perfectly natural. An actor who has a certain role in a film performs it once in a lifetime. In theater, if it ever happens that I act poorly once, I can comfort myself by thinking that whatever didn't succeed today will be successful tomorrow. In cinema, that is impossible.

What must the film actor do to bring about the full utilization of his expressive talent? He will not achieve this unless he fully feels the character he is portraying. His methods of expression must be precise, concentrated, fully calculated.

An especially important point is the actor's self-control. At every moment, the actor must be alert to what he is doing, he must be vigilant, have a developed sense of proportion, good taste, modesty. And the most important point—he must not think about the camera.

The actor must know the technology of the filming process. What mediates between the actor and the audience is the microphone. You must take into account its characteristics; you must practice the physical side of speaking. When the director is involved in editing the film, you must trust him and his taste. The director is interested in the film's success and therefore he will not insult the actor; the segments where the actor is at his best will always be left in the film.

You must look at the segments that have already been shot. That is obligatory. The actor will learn from them how to look at his work critically and to strive for higher achievements.

These are my conclusions in general, and in particular based on the experience I gained in the field of cinema.

Has my work in cinema contributed anything to my work in the theater? Yes, a great deal. Especially by virtue of the differences, the actor emerges at an advantage. A theater actor does not remain indifferent when he works in film. That said, in the theater, I would ascend the stage and feel the breathing of the audience. It is exhilarating. But in film where the actor acts before an imaginary audience, his imagination must be more developed than that of the theater actor.[3]

King Lear's Fool

The Fool in *King Lear* is not like other characters of fools in Shakespeare. Here, the Fool denies authority, he is a nihilist, occasionally a fortune-teller, but the King's tragic fate does not spare him. Shakespeare, who is faithful to reality and concrete detail, gives expression to the tragedy of the Fool through a description of his behavior and actions.

King Lear's Fool is not a jester in the narrow definition of the profession, that is: a comedian, entertainer, sharp-tongued author of satiric verse. He is not merely amusing his master, telling jokes, making witty comments, singing, laughing at society, or entertaining it. While carrying on professional acts of mischief, King Lear's Fool is revealed as someone whose intelligence is developed, whose heart is sensitive. He shows himself to be a creature with above-average abilities and well-educated by the criteria of his time. The Fool uses the privilege he is given by the definition of his job to fire barbs and shafts of sarcasm. With great talent and an acerbic tongue, he aims precisely at the false-hearted environment of the King's court, without favor or mercy. He hurls the truth at the King even if it is cruel and unpleasant. During the many years the Fool has served the King, he manages to get to know him and his milieu. A close emotional connection is created between the King and the Fool. It emerges that the Fool's intimate connection with Lear is as essential for the King as the King's close friendship with the Fool. Lear ponders philosophical thoughts; he confronts his subjective worldview with the objective course of historical events. The Fool is the personification of mundane concrete wisdom, of real life. So in their way of thinking and in their nature, they are polar opposites. And yet at the same time, they complete each other.

Lear publicly announces his plan to divide his kingdom. The Fool regards himself as included in all components of the King's personality and accustomed to his whims, but he is taken by surprise by the King's declaration. The King's declaration leads to the following results: Lear curses his daughter Cordelia, beloved by him, and the Fool; he banishes his devoted subject the Earl of Kent; transfers full control over his kingdom to his greedy, power-seeking daughters Regan and Goneril, and to their husbands—the hardhearted Duke of Cornwall and the ineffectual Duke of Albany. Immediately afterward the King begins to act most strangely. All of the goings-on astonish the Fool. For the first time in his life, the Fool hides away from the King for two full days.

The Fool understands the King's fateful error. Lear, who was at the height of his dominion and enjoyed unlimited power and self-confidence, erred in thinking that if everyone flattered him and bowed down to him that they genuinely admired him for who he was, for his intelligence and resolution. It never occurred to him that they were acting that way because they had to submit to his kingly authority. The Fool understands well that Goneril and Regan, who were awarded the power to rule, would do everything to continue to maintain control, and that the ambition for power and dominion would come to replace the daughters' respect for their father. Yes, the elderly King Lear, advanced in years, powerful and wise, is making a disastrous error.

King Lear commits an act of foolery and is forced to pay a terrible price for it. The Fool must prove to King Lear that he has made a mistake and the mistake is irrevocable; that he is causing harm to both himself and his kingdom.

The Fool, as was his wont, clothes his expressions of sorrow and suffering in buffoonery; he mocks the King whenever he is in the King's presence. His mocking ditties combine sarcastic wit with unbounded warm-heartedness, love, and devotion to the King along with anger at him. These verses reflect the Fool's deep pain and trepidation for Lear and for the fate of the kingdom. Using jests, the Fool is either flattering the King or verbally flogging him. Lear understands that the Fool's comments are justified, and they reflect the truth. The Fool practices a plan of double meanings: the joke, which reflects the height of common sense, when uttered by him becomes a device which may be understood as either consolation or as censure. This tool is used to reveal the truth. Lear undergoes a process of coming to his senses, of understanding what has been done, of the most profound mental suffering; during this process, in the tempest scene, he becomes mentally unhinged. The Fool senses advantage over the King, but he does not abandon him, even seeking to amuse him in order to heal his wounds. The Fool tries to reduce the weight of the burden that this unfortunate old man is carrying.

The King has divested himself of his values, and according to the unshakeable laws of history, he is condemned to die. And he does die. The Fool suffers intense, poignant torment. It could not be otherwise for a human being who is helpless to prevent the death throes and the death of his cherished friend whom he had served with great loyalty all the years of his life.

The description that I have sketched served as the basis for my work on the personality of the Fool. The production director Sergei Radlov, an eminent expert in the field of theater in general and particularly Shake-spearean theater, directed me such that I am grateful to him, and he built for me mise-en-scenes which brought me to a deeper understanding and to as perfect as possible exposure to this complex character. The director constantly emphasized the reciprocal relations between the King and the Fool. I try to reveal the Fool's inner world, full of contradictions, using the external activities typical of a circus clown: eccentric movements, a disjointed manner of speaking rich in vulgarisms, sudden jumps from mild mockery to cruel derision and from there to melancholy and tender lyricism.

This is the most difficult artistic task that I have ever faced.

For the first time in my life, as an actor, I am touching a Shakespearean character. My great joy is understandable as well as my great excitement.[4]

13

Letters

Benjamin Zuskin to Eda Berkovskaya

December 19, 1948

Eda my dear one,

You can very well imagine what I felt (and still feel) after you went away. I cannot describe it in words. I have been eating myself up all of these days, but I am in such a state that, believe me, I couldn't do otherwise. I do not want to add to what has already been said. After all, you are the only one who has seen the pain of my torment. I have no more strength to suffer, it is beyond mortal ability.

Tomorrow, December 20 at 8:00 A.M. my cure will begin at Vishnievsky's hospital. I will be there for approximately ten days. Today Dr. Tarasov came to visit me. We spoke at length. He is a kindhearted and amazingly sensitive person. He shows so much interest in what is happening to me, he so wants to support me that I feel like crying.

Everything is ready at the hospital for my treatment. I believe with all my heart that I will finally pull out of the condition that has tortured me these last long months. I want, I must be healthy, at all costs! I owe it to the theater, to our family. That is as clear as day to me. Very soon I will be back to my work, I will be full of vigor and energy and will give the theater everything I have, as it always was.

Eda, my dearest, don't worry about me. I am admitting myself to the hospital because I am convinced that in the shortest time I will regain my strength, and I promise you and all our friends that *far dem tsor vet mir nokh hobn nakhes.*

I will write to you from the hospital if I can, because after all, I am supposed to be asleep, in a deep sleep. (If I could only achieve that!) In any event, I will ask someone from the staff to call our house regularly and to give information about my condition, so that you will stay on top of things. Please tell Grigorii Borisovich and Lev Mikhaylovich whom I have caused so much trouble, that I will do everything that I can so that I can get back to work as soon as possible, and together with them, lead our theater.

Warmest regards to all of our friends.

I believe, yes, I do really believe that in the nearest future we will be together again and that there will be the end of my sufferings.

I kiss you hard my long-suffering, my beloved Eda

Yours, Zus.[1]

Eda Berkovskaya to Tamara Platt

July 15, 1956

My dearest Tamara,

Finally I have a chance to send you a modest package and a detailed letter.

I came back from vacation a few days ago. I spent my vacation around the Riga region, on the Baltic Sea coast. I was invited by old friends of ours who have a summer home there. I rested well, but I was sad the whole time. When a person is on vacation, when life is calm, without concerns or running around, without working, that is when melancholy, sadness, a sense of loneliness arise. In addition to that, I miss my daughter Ala. This summer, Ala is working and so she can't join me. She was accepted to two institutions of academic education: day studies in civil engineering and night studies in foreign languages. It's a shame that there were previously obstacles in her way to acquiring an education.

You know, Tamara, now that I can tell you about everything in detail, I don't know where to start, and it seems to me that my story would be pale on paper and that I am unable to tell it as I feel it. Clearly when we meet I can explain more thoroughly. I will be able to pour my heart out.

I will just tell you one thing: the storm that passed over our heads tore everything out by the roots, destroyed everything, and liquidated it all completely. Today I see what moral strength we needed to safeguard ourselves and to keep our heads high. We did go about with our heads held high because we were confident of our purity and our sincerity.

When they took Father from us, it was like a bolt out the blue. It was incomprehensible to the point of senseless. Why???

For almost a year our theater was in the process of dying. They tortured me, mocked me. The theater director and many friends pretended not to know me. I was forced to continue under these conditions, in addition to our private tragedy. And at the same time, I understood nothing, I knew nothing about what was happening to Father. I have been told nothing about his fate.

Materially, our situation was very bad. The whole year, until the theater closed, we received no salary. I had to sell many of our possessions. After they closed the theater, they paid us the cumulative salary that hadn't been paid for several months, and we had a bit of relief, but all doors were closed to us, and everyone pretended that they didn't know me.

I found a pitiful job and I earned pennies. I used to bring money for them to give to Father; by then I already knew where he was.

We lived that way for four years. Obviously I am telling you all of this briefly, without going into depth. It is hard to describe the sleepless nights, the torturous suffering, the tremendous pain which we both feel today, too, to speak of what is eating at us from inside, without let-up.

In the beginning of 1953, they exiled us from Moscow. We went out to the unknown. We were impoverished, devastated by grief. We were in dread of the future. We were afraid that everything had been destroyed irreparably.

And on top of all of this, Father's life. What is happening to him? Why did they do this to him? Fear pervaded us and we were afraid to live.

A year and a half later we returned from exile. There were strangers living in our house. For ten months we lived with Lisa and Emma. Finally they gave us back only one room in our former apartment. There were no furniture or books of ours left in it; all we had were just miserable remnants of possessions that we had taken with us into exile. We had to begin life from the very beginning.

I received monetary compensation for the furniture and books that we had left, and also Father's salary for the last two months of his work in the theater. After some time I began to receive the special pension that is paid to me as the widow of a man who had an elevated status and who was wrongfully executed. We bought some things here and there—for the years that Father had not been with us, and I didn't have a regular job, our situation had completely deteriorated and we sold whatever we could. I ordered winter coats for Ala and me. We bought a few items of furniture, quite modest. Now it is a little less difficult for us.

I am suffering now from not working in the theater, to which I had devoted my entire life.

Nonetheless, all this time we have tried not to show outwardly our emotional state. We never parted from our sense of humor, we tried to notice the good in life, not to focus on the sense of our own tragedy. We have had a strong friendship with Tala and her family and her sister Nina [the Mikhoels family]. The shared sorrow has brought us together. Even now we are able to sit together, laugh, tell jokes, chat about whatever, but the conversation always rolls around to that thing: what we have been through, what happened to the heads of our families.

My dear Tamara, we all want you to come. We will speak about everything, and you will understand it all.

Yours, Eda.

P.S. Sorry I wrote so disjointedly, it's because I am too excited.[2]

Eda Berkovskaya to Tamara Platt

August 19, 1956

My dearest Tamara,

After our phone talk, I feel that I have nothing more to write. You will be coming to us very soon. We are all happy that you are coming. By then, Tala with her family and Ala, too, will be back after their vacancies.

On August 12, the memorial day for Father, friends gathered at our house. We exchanged memories of him. Earlier, in the morning, I went to the cemetery and I sat near the graves of my mother and of Mikhoels. It is especially sad near Mikhoels's grave. I recalled the artistic career of Mikhoels and Father. What a wonderful duo of actors they were! A duo by God's grace. How passionate they were about the theater. They lived the theater, its art. How they loved the word, the singing, the music, the movements of our people. And what great significance they had for the people.

What an awful and tragic fate! Can it be that all of this will be forgotten?

All the best to you. Soon we will see each other.

Kisses, Eda.

P.S. I didn't write to you that people who visited our house on August 12 remember all of the important dates in Father's life, they live the characters he played, his songs and jokes. There were lots of flowers and we decorated Father's portrait with them.[3]

Zuskin's Friends and Pupils to His Wife and Daughters

September 24, 1956

Our dear Eda, Tamara, and Ala,

Today, September 24, 1956, marks thirty-five years to the beginning of our beloved Benjamin Zuskin's artistic career.

Allow us, the friends and pupils of Benjamin Zuskin on the memorial day to his most rich stage activity, to share our sorrow with you and express our pride that it was our destiny to know him.

His remarkable personality and brilliant performances as an actor, the characters he fashioned with artistic perfection, none of these will ever be erased from our memories and hearts. Thanks to his profound understanding of life, his talent as a teacher, his modesty, and his caring attitude to his friends and pupils, generations have been trained and have grown up to be artists who deserve the exalted title of actor–human being.

We will keep forever the radiant memory of your husband and father. He will be a shining example of the most high-minded human traits for us and our children.

Our dearly beloved! May your heartfelt pride in this brilliant life overcome your grief.[4]

Notes

Bibliography

Index

Notes

Epigraph

Eda Berkovskaya, letter to Tamara Platt, August 19, 1956. See the full letter in this book, 280. Author's possession. Eda Berkovskaya is the second wife of Benjamin Zuskin. Dr. Tamara Platt is Zuskin's daughter from his first marriage.

Foreword: Zuskin in My Mind's Eye

1. Words delivered on the evening marking the 100th birthday of Benjamin Zuskin at the Jerusalem Cinamathèque, April 28, 1999. Reproduced with the permission of Mordechai Altshuler.

Preface

1. Osip Mandelstam, "Chetvertaya proza" (Fourth Prose) in *Sobranie Sochinenii* (New York: Inter-Language Literary Associates, 1971), 2:177. Osip Mandelstam (1891–1938) was a Russian poet of Jewish origin, one of the premier Russian literary figures of the twentieth century.

2. Alexander Borshchagovsky, *Obviniaetsa krov* (Blood on Trial) (Moscow: Progress, 1994), 165.

3. Vladimir Koliazin, ed., *Vernite mnie svobodu: Deyateli literatury I iskusstva Rossii I Germanii—zhertvy stalinskogo terrora* (Give Me Back My Freedom: Literature and Culture Figures, Russians and Germans—Victims of Stalin's Terror) (Moscow: Medium, 1997), 347. Polkovnik: Russian equivalent for the military rank of colonel.

4. Benjamin Zuskin, "Curriculum Vitae," typewritten manuscript (in Russian), 1946. See full text, 251–68, in this book, quote on page 260. Author's possession.

Part One
1. Prologue

1. *Badkhen*: traditional Jewish entertainer at weddings and other festive events.

2. According to Solomon Mikhoels, "Concept for *Freylekhs*," typewritten manuscript (in Russian), 1945. Courtesy of Natalia Vovsi-Mikhoels and Nina Mikhoels. Description of the play *Freylekhs* including poetry fragments—here, in sub-chapter *Reb Yekl* in Act Four, and in the Epilogue—is based upon the above-mentioned source.

3. Anna Akhmatova, "Poema bez Geroya" (Poem Without a Hero), in *Sochinenia* (New York: Inter-Language Literary Associates, 1968), 2:118. Anna Akhmatova (1889–1966): a great Russian poetess.

4. Koliazin, *Vernite mnie svobodu*, 358. Military Collegium: Unit in the Supreme Court to try high military and political personnel in the Army, and counter-revolutionary activists.

5. Joshua Rubenstein and Vladimir Naumov, *Stalin's Secret Pogrom: The Postwar Inquisition of the Jewish Anti-Fascist Committee*, trans. Laura Esther Wolfson (New Haven: Yale University Press, 2001), 389. Permission for reproduction by publisher.

6. Koliazin, *Vernite mnie svobodu*, 335.

7. Rubenstein and Naumov, *Stalin's Secret Pogrom*, 387–87.

8. Ibid., 395.

9. Vladimir Naumov, ed., *Nepravedny Sud: Poslednii stalinskii rasstrel* (An Unjust Trial: Stalin's Last Execution) (Moscow: Nauka, 1994), 331.

10. Ibid., 305. Beginning in 1917, Ponievezh was called Panievezhys in Lithuanian, but the Jews continued to call it Ponievezh, and it appears by this name throughout the book, except for quotations from official Soviet documents.

2. Act One (1899–1920)

1. Antoine de Saint-Exupéry, *Courrier Sud*. I quote this from memory.

2. Solomon Mikhoels, "Moya rabota nad 'Korolem Lirom' Shekspira" (My Work on *King Lear* by Shakespeare), in *Mikhoels: statii, besedy, rechi*, (Mikhoels: Articles, Talks, Speeches), ed. Konstantin Rudnitsky (Moscow: Iskusstvo, 1965), 122.

3. The *heder* is the traditional religious school where young children are taught to read the Torah and other texts in Hebrew.

4. 1905: beginning of the First Russian Revolution: On January 9, 1905, the Tsar's soldiers shot into a crowd of unarmed demonstrators.

5. Joseph Brodsky, "Natiurmort" (Still Nature), in *Kholmy* (St. Petersburg: Kinot-senter, 1991), 218.

6. Mikhoels, "Moya rabota," in *Mikhoels*, 124.

7. Sholem Aleichem, "Dos messerl" (Penknife), in *Oysgeveylte verk*, (Moscow: Emes, 1948), 44.

8. Benjamin Zuskin, "Chemu nauchilo menia kino" (What I Learned from the Cinema), *Iskusstvo kino*, no. 3 (March 1938): 44. See full text, 270–72, in this book, quote on page 272. Reproduced with permission by Israel Goor Theater Archives and Museum, Jerusalem.

9. Minna Magid to granddaughter Nakhama, typewritten letter, 1970. *Shabbosim*: Yiddish for the Sabbaths, celebrated from Friday evening to Saturday night.

10. The Beilis Affair: A trial that was held in Tsarist Russia, 1911–1913, following a blood libel. A Jewish clerk, Menakhem Mendel Beilis, was accused of murdering a Christian boy, who was found dead in a suburb of Kiev before Passover. The false testimony was refuted and, in 1913, a jury acquitted Beilis.

11. St. Petersburg: a Russian city near the Gulf of Finland on the Baltic Sea. Built in 1703 by Tsar Peter the Great and named for him. Between 1712–1918 it was the capital of Russia. In 1918–1924 its name was changed to Petrograd; between 1924–1991 it was called Leningrad. Beginning in 1991, it was again called St. Petersburg.

12. The February Revolution: A revolution that broke out in Tsarist Russia in February 1917. It brought about the end of the tsarist regime and was followed by a democratic form of government; among others, it put an end to the Jewish pale of settlement. The provisional government that was established afterward was overthrown in October 1917.

13. Magid, Letter.

14. Ibid.

15. Actually, Zuskin was close to being received in the Hebrew studio, which soon afterward became the Habima (Stage – HE) theater. In Moscow, it gave its performances in Hebrew from 1918 to 1926, when it left Soviet Russia. After a few years of wandering it established in Palestine; in 1958 it was called "The Habima – Israel's National Theater."

3. First Interlude

1. Naumov, *Nepravedny Sud*, 307.
2. Koliazin, *Vernite mnie svobodu*, 338.
3. Naumov, *Nepravedny Sud*, 297.
4. Koliazin, *Vernite mnie svobodu*, 344.
5. Naumov, *Nepravedny Sud*, 305.
6. Ibid., 308.
7. Ibid., 307.

4. Act Two (1921–1928)

1. Trials, both held in Moscow, in which groups of engineers were accused of deliberately causing damage to Soviet industry and setting up anti-Soviet undergrounds. The accused were sentenced, upon fabricated charges, either to death or to various terms of imprisonment.

2. Eduard Bagritsky, "Proiskhozhdenie" (Origin), in *Stikhi i poemy* (Moscow: Khudozhestvennaya literatura, 1956), 119.

3. Yevsektsia: The Jewish Section of the Russian Communist-Bolshevik Party.

4. People's Commissariats, or, for short, Commissariats: The title of the Soviet government ministries between 1917–1946.

5. GOSEKT: Abbreviation of Gosudarstvenny Yevreyski Kamerny Teatr (Russian): The State Jewish Chamber Theater.

6. Benjamin Zuskin, "Dvadtsat' let Moskovskogo yevreyskogo teatra" (Twentieth Anniversary of the Moscow Jewish Theater), *Kul'tura i zhizn'*, no. 12 (December 1939): 3.

7. *Kratkaya yevreyskaya entsiklopedia na russkom yazyke* (The Shorter Encyclopaedia Judaica in Russian) (Jerusalem: Keter, 1982), 2:466.

8. Alexei Granovsky, "Matroteynu vetafkideynu" (Our Aims and Tasks), in *Chagall: Dreams and Drama: Early Russian Works and Murals for the Jewish Theatre*, (English/Hebrew), ed. Ruth After-Gabriel (Jerusalem: The Israel Museum, 1991), Hebrew Part, 37.

9. Osip Mandelstam, "Mikhoels," in *Sobranie sochinenii* (New York: Inter-Language Literary Associates, 1969), 3:107.

10. Alexander Deutsch, *Maski yevreyskogo teatra* (Jewish Theater's Masks), (Moscow: Iskusstvo, 1927), 12.

11. Alexandra Azarkh-Granovskaya, *Vospominania. Besedy s Duvakinym* (Memoirs Recorded by Duvakin) (Jerusalem, Moscow: Mosty kultury–Gesharim, 2001), 101.

12. Ibid., 136.

13. Deutsch, *Maski yevreyskogo teatra*, 15.

14. Ibid., 16.

15. *Kratkaya yevreyskaya encyclopedia*, 2:210.

16. Azarkh-Granovskaya, *Vospominania*, 114.

17. Pavel Markov, *Teatral'nyie portrety* (Portraits of Theater Figures) (Moscow: Iskusstvo, 1974), 455.

18. Zuskin, "Dvadtsat' let."

19. Ziva Amishai-Maisels, "Chagall's Murals for the State Jewish Chamber Theater," in *Chagall: Dreams and Drama*, English Part, 28.

20. Boris Zingerman, *Parizhskaya shkola* (Paris School): *Picasso, Modigliani, Chagall, Soutine* (Moscow: Soyuzteater, 1982), 240.

21. Amishai-Maisels, "Chagall's Murals," in *Chagall: Dreams and Drama*, English Part, 28.

22. Mandelstam, "Mikhoels," 107.

23. Mikhoels, "Moya rabota," in *Mikhoels*, 121.

24. Yekhezkel Dobrushin, *Zuskin* (Moscow: Der Emes, 1939), 5.

25. Ibid., 9.

26. Azarkh-Granovskaya, *Vospominania*, 133.

27. Abram Efros, "Nachalo" (Beginning), in *Mikhoels*, 393.

28. Ibid., 391.

29. Joshua Liubomirsky, *Af di lebensvegn* (On the Ways of Life) (Moscow: Sovetsky pisatel', 1976), 197.

30. Moyshe Goldblatt, "A vort vegn Zuskinen" (A Word about Zuskin), *Sovetish heimland*, no. 1 (January 1970): 122.

31. Deutsch, *Maski yevreyskogo teatra*, 15.

32. Markov, *Teatral'nyie portrety*, 459.

33. *Tefillin* (Hebrew): Two small black boxes containing Biblical texts with black straps attached to them, which Jewish men attach to head and arm during weekday morning prayers and considered a fundamental of religious faith.

34. Scene of seduction Mirele. Tracks #1, *I am Buba Yakhna*, and #2, *Come with me!* Recordings on CD, *Cubo-Futurist Klezmer (1922–1938)* (in Yiddish). Courtesy of Prof. Mel Gordon, Berkeley University, the only copyright holder, 2005, of these recordings.

" . . . *kum tsu mir, tokhter meine* . . ." (Yiddish): Come with me my daughter.

35. Liubomirsky, *Af di lebensvegn*, 201.

36. Efros, "Nachalo," in *Mikhoels*, 392.

37. Ibid.

38. Azarkh-Granovskaya, *Vospominania*, 133.

39. Alexander Gurshteyn, "Iskusstvo Zuskina" (Zuskin's Art), *Teatr i dramaturgia*, no. 4 (April 1935): 33.

40. Azarkh-Granovskaya, *Vospominania*, 134.

41. "Three raisins" is the English translation of *drai pintelech* in Yiddish.

A *pintele* may be translated either as "small point"—in the meaning of "get to the point" or "hit the nail"; or as "small raisin"—in the meaning of "zest." Here both meanings are relevant. In addition, "Jewish raisins" is an allusion to "something special," given that the best Passover wines are made with raisins.

42. Deutsch, *Maski yevreyskogo teatra*, 33.

43. Simha Raz, *A Very Narrow Bridge: Sayings of Rabbi Nakhmen of Breslov* (Jerusalem: Keter, 1999), 255.

44. GOSET: Abbreviation of Gosudarstvenny yevreysky teatr (Russian): The State Jewish Theater.

45. Khone Shmeruk, "By Night at the Old Marketplace by I.L. Peretz at the Moscow Jewish Theater," in *The Jewish Theater in the Soviet Union: Studies—Essays—Documents*, ed. Mordechai Altshuler (Jerusalem: Hebrew University, 1996), 240.

46. Alfred Kerr, "Das Moskauer Juedische Akademische Theater," *Berliner Tageblatt*, October 10, 1928.

47. Zuskin, "Curriculum Vitae," 267.

48. Mendele has written two versions of *The Travels of Benjamin the Third*: in Hebrew and in Yiddish.

49. "Tuneyadevke" means "Parasiteville," or "Droneville" from *tuneyadets* (Russian)—parasite, drone.

50. Liubomirsky, *Af di lebensvegn*, 217.

51. Zuskin, "Curriculum Vitae," 256.

52. Dobrushin, *Zuskin*, 24.

53. Scene in the Inn. Track #8, *Banket dream*. Recordings on CD, *Cubo-Futurist Klezmer (1922–1938)* (in Yiddish). Courtesy of Prof. Mel Gordon, Berkeley University.

54. Redheaded, or Red, Jews: a legendary nation related to lost tribes of Israel. Rahab the Whore: Biblical personage.

55. Zalmen Lev, "Fun Yarden biz Volga," *Yiddish*, no. 8/9 (August/ September 1928): 5.

56. Scene in the Inn, continuation. Track #8, *Banket dream*. Recordings on CD, *Cubo-Futurist Klezmer.* Song lyrics: trans. Mark Levinson.

57. Efros, "Nachalo," in *Mikhoels*, 404.

58. Zuskin, "Curriculum Vitae," 268.

59. Speech by Solomon Mikhoels (in Russian), 1947, as preserved in my memory.

60. Zuskin, "Curriculum Vitae," 264.

61. Dobrushin, *Zuskin*, 28.

62. Song, as preserved in my memory.

63. Joseph Roth, "Mit dem rechter Fuss" (On the Right Foot), *Leipziger Volkszeitung*, November 23, 1928, 6.

64. Franz Servaes, "Das Moskau Juedische Akademische Theater," *Berliner Localanzeiger*, May 10, 1928.

65. Hans Taschemka, "Beschpechung mit zwei Schauspielern. Was haben Michoels und Zuskin derzehlen" (Interview with Two Actors: What Have Mikhoels and Zuskin Told), *Welt-am-Abend*, November 20, 1928.

66. Ibid.

67. Vladislav Ivanov, *GOSET: politika i iskusstvo 1919–1928* (GOSET: Politics and Art) (Moscow: GITIS, 2007), 376.

68. Ibid., 377.

69. Magid, Letter. See also in Act One in this book, 21.

70. Ivanov, *GOSET*, 378.

71. Ibid., 378.

72. Mikhail Chekhov (1891–1955). Son of Alexander Chekhov, brother of the writer Anton Chekhov, and of a Jewish mother. One of the most impressive of the Russian actors. Also worked as a director, acting teacher, and theoretician of theatrical art. In 1926 emigrated from Soviet Russia. His later career which was unknown to Zuskin: Finally moved to the U.S. Along with being an actor and authoring the book *On the Technique of Acting*, a best-seller for the cinema and theater actors and directors, he became famous as a director-teacher who shaped actors such as Marilyn Monroe, Clint Eastwood, Yul Brynner, and others.

73. Nathan Volkovysky, "Pis'mo iz Berlina" (Letter from Berlin), *Poslednie novosti*, August 11, 1928.

74. Ivanov, *GOSET*, 250.

75. Alfons Goldschmidt, "Das Juedische Theater in Moskau," in *Das Moskauer Juedische Akademische Theater* (Berlin: Die Schmiede, 1928), 21.

76. Alfred Kerr, "Das Moskauer Juedische Theater," *Berliner Tageblatt*, October 12, 1928.

77. La Parisiènne, "Théâtre Juif de Moscou," *L'Umanité*, July 9, 1928.

78. Saul Koster, "Théâtre Académique Juif de Moscou," *Le Journal de Rotterdam*, October 15, 1928.

79. Marcel Cohen, "Théâtre Académique Juif de Moscou," *De Tribune*, November 2, 1928.

80. Bernard Dean, "The Moscow Jewish Academic Theater," *The Times*, London, August 28, 1928.

81. Nathan Falk, "Das Moskau Juedische Akademische Theater," *B.Z.am Mittag*, October 19, 1928.

82. Alfred Kerr, "Das Moskauer Judische Theater," *Berliner Tageblatt*, October 14, 1928.

83. *Dybbuk*, from Hebrew *davak* (glue): in Jewish mythology, a malicious possessing spirit believed to be the soul dislocated from a dead person and that clings inside the body of a living one. Here it is also a kind of a hidden allusion to the play *The Dybbuk* by S. Ansky produced in Habima theater (see note 1 in Act One) and presented in Europe a little bit before GOSET.

Cholent: traditional festive meal of East-European Jews.

Tisha B'av (ninth day in the month Av): an annual fast day in commemoration of the destruction of the First and Second Temples in Jerusalem and the subsequent exile of the Jews from their land.

84. Lev, "Fun Yarden biz Volga," 7.

85. Ibid.

86. Fabian Engel, "Theater fun Moscow," *Berliner Tageblatt*, November 11, 1928.

87. Nakhmen Mayzel, "Alexei Granovsky," *Literarische Bleter*, no. 19, 1937.

5. Second Interlude

1. Koliazin, *Vernite mnie svobodu*, 348.

2. Naumov, *Nepravedny sud*, 310.

3. Koliazin, *Vernite mnie svobodu*, 352.

4. Naumov, *Nepravedny sud*, 310.

5. Rubenstein and Naumov, *Stalin's Secret Pogrom*, 386. Mikhoels is the pseudonym; Vovsi—family name of this same person.

6. Koliazin, *Vernite mnie svobodu*, 344.

7. Rubenstein and Naumov, *Stalin's Secret Pogrom*, 388.

8. Naumov, *Nepravedny sud*, 299.

9. Ibid., 308.

10. Ibid., 301.

6. Act Three (1929–1938)

1. Nikolai Nekrasov, "Umru ya skoro" (I Will Die Soon), *Polnoye sobranie sochinenii* (Leningrad: Nauka, 1982), 3:120.

Nikolai Nekrasov: Russian poet (1821–1878), classic of Russian literature.

2. Ilia Ilf and Yevgeni Petrov, trans. Anne O. Fisher, *The Little Golden Calf* (Burlington: Russian Life Books, 2009), 411.

3. Boris Zingerman, *Parizhskaya shkola*, 294.

4. Jeffrey Veidlinger, *The Moscow State Yiddish Theater* (Bloomington: Indiana University Press, 2000), 115.

5. In the mid-1920s, Jewish kolkhozes were established in the Crimean peninsula. *Kolkhos* (Russian "*kollektivnoye + khoziaystvo*" = collective + farming) was a form of collective farms in the Soviet Union, 1918–1991, including Jewish kolkhozes in the Crimean peninsula, 1923–1941.

6. Zuskin, "Curriculum Vitae," 262.

7. Name of the city St. Petersburg during the years 1924–1991.

8. In French: *Le Millionaire, le Dentiste et le Pauvre.*

9. Jean-Richard Bloch, "Si Labiche était à Moscou!" *L'Umanité*, December 26, 1934.

10. Ibid.

11. Mikhoels, "Moya Rabota," in *Mikhoels*, 125.

12. Leonid Leonidov, *Vospominania, statii, besedy, perepiska, zapisnyie knizhki* (Memoirs, Articles, Talks, Ledgers) (Moscow: Iskusstvo, 1960), 408–09.

13. Yoseph Ben-Dov, *Kria beklafim* (Reading Cards) (Jerusalem: Keter, 1999), 163.

14. Sofia Nels, "Korol' Lir v postanovke GOSETa" ("King Lear" as staged in GOSET), *Teatr*, no. 5 (May 1935): 128.

15. Rachel Pollack, *Salvador Dali's Tarot* (London: Rainbird, 1985), 10.

16. Zuskin, "Curriculum Vitae," 266.

17. Andrew Cecil Bradley, "Shakespearean Tragedy," Commentaries in *The King Lear* by William Shakespeare, ed. Russell Fraser (New York: St Martin Press, 1920), 131.

18. Georgio Strehler, "Il Re Lear di Shakespeare," *Per un Teatro Umano* (Verona: Feltrinelli, 1973), 280–81.

19. Georg Wilhelm Friedrich Hegel, *Estetika* (Moscow: Nauka, 1975), 111.

20. Azarkh-Granovskaya, *Vospominania*, 134.

21. Vagram Papazian, "Korol' i shut" (The King and the Fool), in *Zhizn' artista* (Moscow–Leningrad: Iskusstvo, 1960), 410.

22. Sofia Nels, "Tri razgovora c Gordonom Kregom" (Three Interviews with Gordon Craig), *Sovietskoye iskusstvo*, March 5, 1935.

23. Inna Vishnievskaya, "Zvezdy nie padayut, zvezdy bluzhdayut" (Stars Are Not Falling, Stars Are Wondering), *Kultura*, no. 2 (1966): 12.

24. Felix Kandel, "Zakoldovanny teatr" (The Bewitched Theater), in *Vrata iskhoda nashego* (Tel-Aviv: Biblioteka Aliya, 1980), 36–37.

25. Fool's song. The song does not exist in the Shakespearean play but in the GOSET production. The quoted song's excerpt: Track #12, *I am a jester*. Recordings on CD, *Cubo-Futurist Klezmer (1922–1938)* (in Yiddish). Courtesy of Prof. Mel Gordon, Berkeley University.

26. *Shleykes* (Yiddish): suspenders.

27. Leonid Trauberg, "Vozvrashchenie Veniamina" (Return of Benjamin), *Sovetsky ekran*, no. 2 (1988): 30–31.

28. Alexander Griboyedov, *Woe from Wit*, trans. Andrei Vagapov, (Moscow: VGBIL, 2001), 68. Alexander Griboyedov (1795–1829): renowned Russian poet and politician.

29. Zuskin, "Curriculum Vitae," 262.

30. Recruit: in Tsarist Russia between 1705–1874, a man who was drafted into the army and served for an extended period of time (up to 25 years). Certain segments of the population, such as peasants, the lower-middle class, and Jews, were required to supply a regular quota of manpower to this service.

31. Zuskin, "Curriculum Vitae," 263.

32. Sergei Yutkevich, "Istoria zagublennogo filma" (A Tale of a Ruined Film), in *Sobraniye sochinienii* (Moscow: Iskusstvo, 1991), 2:183–84.

33. Veidlinger, *The Moscow Yiddish Theater*, 159.

34. Raz, *A Very Narrow Bridge*, 269.

35. Isaac Babel, "Rebbe," *Konarmia* (Red Cavalry) (Moscow: Izdatelstvo khudozhest-vennoy literatury, 1957), 46.

36. Mandelstam, "Mikhoels," 107. See in Act Two in this book.

37. Mikhoels, "Lozh' religii" (Lie of Religion), in *Mikhoels*, 178.

38. *Mikhoels*, "Rol' i mesto rezhissera v sovetskom teatre" (Task and Place of a Director in the Soviet theater), in *Mikhoels*, 202.

39. Ibid., 211–12.

40. Veidlinger, *The Moscow Yiddish Theater*, 188.

41. Natalia Vovsi-Mikhoels, *Moi otets Solomon Mikhoels* (My Father Solomon Mikhoels) (Moscow: Vozvrashchenie, 1996), 101.

42. Dobrushin, *Zuskin*, 60.

43. Shmuel Halkin, "Bar Kokhba," *Stikhi, ballady, dramy* (Moscow: Sovetsky pisatel', 1958), 24.

44. Dobrushin, *Zuskin*, 58.

45. DetFilm: Studio for movies for children and youth.

46. Zinovy Fridliand, "Teatr tragicheskikh komediantov" (Teater of Tragic Comediants), *Literaturnaya gazeta*, March 6, 1935.

47. Zuskin, "Curriculum Vitae," 265–66.

48. Lea Avrutina, "Yitsuv hadmut beamanuto shel Shlomo Mikhoels: yikaron hakontrapunkt vemaarekhet haleshonit harav-revedit" (The Image Creation in the Art of Solomon Mikhoels: Contrapunkt Principle and Multi-Layer Language System), in *The Jewish Theater*, ed. Altshuler, 287.

7. Third Interlude

1. Koliazin, *Vernite mnie svobodu*, 350.
2. Naumov, *Nepravedny sud*, 312.
3. Koliazin, *Vernite mnie svobodu*, 337.
4. Rubenstein and Naumov, *Stalin's Secret Pogrom*, 388.
5. Koliazin, *Vernite mnie svobodu*, 345.
6. Rubenstein and Naumov, *Stalin's Secret Pogrom*, 385.
7. Naumov, *Nepravedny sud*, 308.
8. Rubenstein and Naumov, *Stalin's Secret Pogrom*, 391–92.

8. Act Four (1939–1947)

1. Leonid Finkel, "Videnia o zhizni I sud'be Eteli Kovenskoi" (A Sketch of Life and Destiny of Ethel Kovenskaya), *Mishpokha*, no. 19 (April 2005): 22.
2. Israel Rubinchik, "Mayn rebe Binyomin Zuskin" (My teacher Benjamin Zuskin), *Yerushalmer almanakh*, no. 20 (1990): 52.
3. Docent in an educational institution in Soviet Union was more or less parallel to associate professor in the U.S.
4. Rubinchik, "Mayn rebe," 53.
5. Ibid.
6. Giorgio Vasari, *Le vite dei piu eccelenti pittori, scultori e architettori* (The Lives of the Most Excellent Painters, Sculptors, and Architects) (Firenze: G. Milanesi, 1881), 301.
7. Liubomirsky, *Af di lebensvegn*, 214.
8. Ibid., 216.
9. Rubenstein and Naumov, eds., *Stalin's Secret Pogrom*, 386.
10. Victor Levashov, *Ubiystvo Mikhoelsa* (Murder of Mikhoels) (Moscow: Olymp, 1990), 336.
11. Markov, *Teatral'nyie portrety*, 458–59.
12. Liubomirsky, *Af di lebensvegn*, 217.
13. Leyb Kvitko, "Solomon Maimon," *Komsomolskaya Pravda*, December 26, 1940.
14. Inna Vishnievskaya, "Den'gi dla kul'tury?" (Money for Culture?) *Teatr*, no. 2 (February 1993): 13.
15. Zuskin, "Curriculum Vitae," 257.
16. Vishnievskaya, "Den'gi dla kul'tury?" 14.

17. Sholem Aleichem, *Bluzhdayushchie zvezdy* (Wandering Stars)(Moscow: Text, 1999), 56.

18. Vishnievskaya, "Den'gi dla kul'tury?" 14.

19. Zuskin, "Curriculum Vitae," 255.

20. Vishnievskaya, "Den'gi dla kul'tury?" 14.

21. Ibid.

22. Sholem Aleichem, *Bluzhdayushchie zvezdy*, 301.

23. Borshchagovsky, *Obviniaetsa krov*, 165.

24. Shimon Redlikh, *Yevreysky antifashistsky komitet v SSSR* (Jewish Anti-Fascist Committee in Soviet Union) (Moscow: Mezhdunarodnyie otnoshenia, 1996), 47.

25. Vishnievskaya, "Zvezdy nie padayut," 12.

26. Rubenstein and Naumov, *Stalin's Secret Pogrom*, 394.

27. Gennadi Kostyrchenko, *Out of the Red Shadow: Anti-Semitism in Stalin's Russia*, trans. from Russian (Amherst: Prometheus Books, 1995), 33.

28. David Bergelson's play *Prince Reuveni*, is essentially based on the works of Max Brod, Josef Opatoshu, and David Pinsky, writings which all bear the same title. All three works are based on Reuveni's dairy, which was adapted by his contemporary, Yosef Hacohen.

29. Veidlinger, *The Moscow Yiddish Theater*, 244.

30. Anastasia Pototskaya-Mikhoels, "O Mikhoelse bogatom i starshem" (About Mikhoels the Rich and the Older), in *Mikhoels*, ed. Rudnitsky, 525.

31. Azarkh-Granovskaya, *Vospominania*, 133.

32. Veidlinger, *The Moscow Yiddish Theater*, 243.

33. Finkel, "Videnia," 23.

34. Zuskin, "Curriculum Vitae," 267.

35. Goldblatt, "A vort vegn Zuskinen," 122.

36. Zuskin, "Curriculum Vitae," 257.

37. Kaddish is the prayer recited by Jews in memory of the dead.

38. *Makhzor l'am Israel: Tefilot Yom Kippur* (Prayer Book for Jewish People: *Yom Kippur* Prayers) (Tel Aviv: Sinai, 1971), 55.

39. Yekl, Ber. Names common among Ashkenazic Jewry in songs and jokes. Used as a nickname for *klezmerim* (Jewish musicians): Yekl-Fiddle ("fiddle" in Yiddish means "violin"); Berl-Bass (Berl is the diminutive form of Ber; "bass" means "contrabass).

40. *Kapote* is a man's long coat worn by Hassidic Jews of Eastern Europe. *Tsitsit* are the fringes worn on garments by Jewish men according to Jewish law.

41. Vishnievskaya, "Zvezdy nie padayut," 13.

42. Vladimir Pimenov, "Dve sud'by," *Teatr*, no. 6 (June 1990): 128.

43. Vishnievskaya, "Zvezdy nie padayut," 13.

44. Tamara Avetisian, *Nezabyvayemoye* (Kiev: Slovo, 1998), 125.

45. Deutsch, *Maski yeveyskogo teatra*, 15.

46. Mark Donskoi, "Nepokorennyie" (Unvanquished), *Pravda Ukrainy*, January 1, 1944.

47. Vovsi-Mikhoels, *Moi otsets*, 101.

48. Veidlinger, *The Moscow Yiddish Theater*, 264.

49. *Esther Rabah*, chapter 7, §10, Soncino translation.

50. Sergei Yutkevich, "Istoria zagublennogo filma," 193.

51. *Nakhama* in Hebrew means "comfort."

52. Joseph Kerler, 12 oygust 1952 (Jerusalem: Eygns, 1978), 115.

53. Vishnievskaya, "Zvezdy nie padayut," 12.

54. Vladimir Lidin, "Zuskin," *Teatr*, no. 1 (January, 1960): 87.

55. Ibid., 88.

56. Ibid.

57. Benjamin Zuskin, Words delivered at the farewell ceremony for Solomon Mikhoels (in Russian), January 16, 1948. Twelve-page typewritten record, 4. *Mikhoels* collection, Israel Goor Theater Archives and Museum, Jerusalem. Reproduced by the permission of the Archives.

58. Vishnievskaya, "Zvezdy nie padayut," 13.

59. Zuskin, "Curriculum Vitae," 267.

60. Rubenstein and Naumov, eds., *Stalin's Secret Pogrom*, 396.

9. Fourth Interlude

1. Koliazin, *Vernite mnie svobodu*, 335.

2. Rubenstein and Naumov, *Stalin's Secret Pogrom*, 396–97.

3. Koliazin, ed., *Vernite mnie svobodu*, 352.

4. Rubenstein and Naumov, *Stalin's Secret Pogrom*, 384.

5. Ibid., 387–88.

6. Ibid., 389.

7. Koliazin, ed., *Vernite mnie svobodu*, 350.

8. Rubenstein and Naumov, *Stalin's Secret Pogrom*, 383.

9. Ibid., 394.

10. Ibid., 393.

11. Ibid., 395.

12. Naumov, *Nepravedny sud*, 305.

13. Ibid., 308.

10. Act Five (1948–1952)

1. Benjamin Zuskin, Words delivered at the farewell ceremony for Mikhoels, 5–6. In the statement, "Yet we know what times we are living through in our country," Zuskin

meant that life in post-war conditions is not easy and despite this, one must hold out. Someone quoted this statement from memory in a distorted form, and it sounded as if Zuskin is hinting to the cruelty of the state. It is simply wrong to attribute to Zuskin political intentions.

2. Goldblatt, "A vort vegn Zuskinen," 127.

3. Nearly fifty years after the tragic event, more information came to light. Due to the complex merge between the political maneuverings and anti-Semitism, of Stalin and his "King's men," it was decided to liquidate Mikhoels. Mikhoels was brutally murdered. His body was thrown onto a deserted side road, and a heavy truck ran over it so that it would seem like a road accident.

4. Alexander Tyshler "Ya vizhu Mikhoelsa" (I see Mikhoels), in Rudnitsky, ed., *Mikhoels*, 498.

5. Rubenstein and Naumov, *Stalin's Secret Pogrom*, 386.

6. Tyshler "Ya vizhu Mikhoelsa," in *Mikhoels*, ed. Rudnitsky, 501.

7. Markov, *Teatral'nyie portrety*, 458.

8. Taschemka, "Beschpechung mit zwei Schauspielern."

9. Sholem Aleichem, *Bluzhdayushchie zvezdy*, 300.

10. A hint to Stalin.

11. See in this book, 174.

12. The USSR Foreign Minister and the First Deputy Premier to Stalin.

13. Redlikh, *Yevreysky antifashistsky komitet*, 272.

14. *Eynikayt* (Yiddish): Unity. The Soviet Yiddish-language newspaper.

15. Borshchagovsky, *Obviniaetsa krov*, 166.

16. Leybe Zuskin to his granddaughter Tamara, handwritten letter (in Russian), 1948. Author's possession.

17. Kostyrchenko, *Out of the Red Shadow*, 112–13. Politbiuro (Russian)—Politic Bureau: the supreme policy-making body of the Communist Party of the Soviet Union in the period of 1917–1952.

18. Hero of the Soviet Union: In the years 1934–1989, this was the highest honorary title awarded for an act of extraordinary valor. The title was accompanied by awarding the decoration of the Order of Lenin, the Gold Star medal, and a special certificate.

19. *The Black Book*: A book that documents the brutal murder of the Jews in parts of the Soviet Union that were temporarily occupied by the Nazi Germans during the war years, 1941–1945. Collecting the relevant information and preparing *The Black Book* for publication was carried out by the Jewish Anti-Fascist Committee. Heading this project were two writers, Ilia Ehrenburg and Vasilii Grossman. Dates and events which were part of the book's publication history:

1944: First publication of the book in France (French edition); ban on publishing it in Russian in the Soviet Union.

1945: Publication in Moscow, in two parts and with deletions (in Yiddish).

1946: Publication in Romania of the first part of the book (in Romanian); publication in the U.S. (in English).

1948: Smashing of the typeset composition in Russian of *The Black Book*, which was ready for print.

1980: Publication in Jerusalem (in Russian).

1993: Publication in Vilna (in Russian). This edition includes an afterword where the story of the preparation of the book by the Jewish Anti-Fascist Committee was told for the first time; of the wrecking of the typeset composition at *Der Emes* publishing house; of the fate of the members of the Jewish Anti-Fascist Committee (those who were executed and those who were sentenced to prison or the gulag). This edition has been translated into many languages in countries around the world.

20. Rubenstein and Naumov, *Stalin's Secret Pogrom*, 389.

21. Redlikh, *Yevreysky antifashistsky komitet*, 284.

22. Ibid., 290–93.

23. Kerler, *12 oygust 1952*, 60.

24. Vovsi-Mikhoels, "Moi otets," 11.

25. The authorities used to make people whom they intended to arrest or exile sign a pledge not to leave their place of residence (thus making them available as needed). My mother and I were forced to sign such a pledge approximately one month before we were exiled from Moscow. See also page 301, note 3 (Letters).

26. Building superintendent: This job includes responsibility for maintaining the apartment building; the job also includes ensuring that residence is only to people who are entitled to live in the building. In the Soviet Union in the period described in the book, any change of address was contingent upon receiving approval from the relevant authority, to which the building superintendent was connected.

27. Dante Alighieri, "Inferno," canto 4, line 151, *La Commedia Divina*, trans. H. W. Longfellow (New York: Modern Library, 2003), 39.

28. Kandel, "Zakoldovanny teatr," 36.

29. Alexander Solzhenitsyn, *Arkhipelag GULAG* (Milano: Antibolshevic Block of Nations, Part I, 1973), 18.

30. Joshua Rubenstein, words delivered in Jerusalem, 2001. Courtesy of Joshua Rubenstein.

31. Veidlinger, The Moscow Yiddish Theater, 274.

32. Ibid.

33. Kostyrchenko, *Out of the Red Shadow*, 112–14.

34. Rubenstein and Naumov, *Stalin's Secret Pogrom*, 394.

35. Lubianka: a prison. This is where Zuskin was held during almost the entirety of the period of his being under arrest. The official name of the place is the Internal Prison of the Ministry of State Security, and it is located in the building of Ministry's offices

in central Moscow. The name of the square where the building is situated, between 1926–1991 was: Dzerzhinsky, after the first head of the Soviet Secret police; up to 1926 it was, and from 1991 till now is: Lubianskaya. With this, the nickname, *Lubianka*, stuck to the square and the prison.

36. Koliazin, ed., *Vernite mnie svobodu*, 340.

37. Ibid.

38. Ibid., 341.

39. Rubenstein and Naumov, eds., *Stalin's Secret Pogrom*, 386.

40. Borshchagovsky, *Obviniaetsa krov*, 228.

41. Ibid., 229.

42. Kostyrchenko, *Out of the Red Shadow*, 223.

43. Rubenstein and Naumov, *Stalin's Secret Pogrom*, 394.

44. Kostyrchenko, *Out of the Red Shadow*, 224.

45. Koliazin, ed., *Vernite mnie svobodu*, 342

46. Naumov, *Nepravedny sud*, 8.

47. Borshchagovsky, *Obviniaetsa krov*, 95.

48. Pheng Cheah and Bob Robbins, eds., *Thinking and Feeling Beyond the Nation* (Ann Arbor: University of Michigan Press, 1988). The book investigates the phenomenon of cosmopolitanism.

49. Song's lyrics, quoted from memory.

50. Joseph Kerler, *12 oygust 1952*, 112.

51. Finkel, "Videnia," 24.

52. Veidlinger, *The Moscow Yiddish Theater*, 270–71.

53. Mordechai Altshuler, "Teatron Yiddish ve hatsibur be Israel" (Yiddish Theater and the Israeli Public), in *The Jewish Theater*, ed. Altshuler, 52.

54. Kandel, "Zakoldovany teatr," 43.

55. Ibid.

56. Naumov, *Nepravedny sud*, 9.

57. Solzhenitsyn, *Arkhipelag GULAG*, 129.

58. Kostyrchenko, *Out of the Red Shadow*, 124.

The Leningrad Affair: In 1949–1953 Communist Party activists and key figures who were connected in one way or another to the local government in Leningrad and the surrounding area were arrested or liquidated at the initiative of Stalin. They were accused of crimes against the state. In actuality, Stalin who was more than seventy years old considered them as potential rivals.

59. Naumov, *Nepravedny sud*, 9–10.

60. Koliazin, *Vernite mnie svobodu*, 350–51.

61. Rubenstein and Naumov, *Stalin's Secret Pogrom*, 480. See the Epilogue in this book, 323.

62. Ibid.

63. Naumov, *Nepravedny sud*, 10.

64. Koliazin, *Vernite mnie svobodu*, 351.

65. Alexander Solzhenitsyn, *Arkhipelag GULAG*, 398.

66. Koliazin, *Vernite mnie svobodu*, 353.

Lefortovo prison: Located in Moscow in an area where at the beginning of the eighteenth century a royal palace and the first military hospital in Russia once stood. Named for Admiral Lefort, a Swiss national who served in Russia under Tsar Peter the Great.

67. Veidlinger, *The Moscow Yiddish Theater*, 272.

68. Naumov, *Nepravedny sud*, 11.

69. Ibid.

70. Ibid.

71. Kostyrchenko, *Out of the Red Shadow*, 129–30.

72. Naumov, *Nepravedny sud*, 10.

73. Rubenstein and Naumov, *Stalin's Secret Pogrom*, 490. See the Epilogue in this book, 245.

74. Pimenov, "Dve sud'by," 129.

75. Markov, *Teatral'nyie portrety*, 459.

76. Azarkh-Granovskaya, *Vospominanya*, 134.

77. Rubenstein and Naumov, *Stalin's Secret Pogrom*, 388.

11. Epilogue

1. Rubenstein and Naumov, *Stalin's Secret Pogrom*, 65. From here on, in the text of the *Trial*, the names of, and the paragraphs concerned with, all the defendants but Zuskin, are omitted.

2. Ibid., 68.

3. Ibid., 74–77.

4. Ibid., 383–84.

5. Ibid., 400.

6. Ibid., 428.

7. Ibid., 480.

8. Ibid., 480.

9. Ibid., 482.

10. Ibid., 484–88.

11. Ibid., 490.

12. Ibid., 491–92.

13. Koliazin, *Vernite mnie svobodu*, 358.

14. Ibid., 360.

Part Two
12. Benjamin Zuskin in His Own Words

1. Benjamin Zuskin, "Curriculum Vitae." See also note 4 in Preface.

2. Benjamin Zuskin, "Moi Sholem Aleichem," in *Sholem Aleichem—pisatel' i chelovek* (Sholem Aleichem—a writer and a man), ed., Moyshe Belenky (Moscow: Sovetsky pisatel', 1984), 260–64.

3. Benjamin Zuskin, "Chemu nauchilo menia kino," 43–44. See also note 8 in Act One.

4. Benjamin Zuskin, "Shut Korolia Lira," *Sovetskoye iskusstvo*, February 11, 1935. Reproduced with permission by Israel Goor Theater Archives and Museum, Jerusalem.

13. Letters

1. Benjamin Zuskin to Eda Berkovskaya, handwritten letter (in Russian), December 19, 1948. Author's possession. The phrase *far dem tsor vet mir nokh hobn nakhes* (for undergoing these troubles, we will yet have joy) is written in Yiddish. Grigirii Borisovich: Fishman, administrative director of GOSET. Lev Mikhaylovich: Pulver, GOSET's in-house conductor.

2. Eda Berkovskaya to Tamara Platt, handwritten letter (in Russian), July 15, 1956. Author's possession.

3. Ibid., August 19, 1956. The both letters were sent from Moscow to Warsaw. "We were exiled from Moscow"—in January 1953, my mother and I were sent to exile in the city of Kokchetav in the Kazakh Republic, in its northeastern area that borders on Siberia; we were brought there in railroad cars designed for prisoners, with barred windows. The journey included stops at transit prisons in a number of cities along the route. The exile was supposed to last ten years but after Stalin's death in 1953, we were returned to Moscow in the summer of 1954. When exiled, we did not know that Father was no longer alive. We were informed of my father's execution only at the end of 1955.

4. Zuskin's friends and pupils to his wife and daughters, typewritten letter (in Russian), September 24, 1956. Author's possession.

Bibliography

I list here the books, book chapters, and journal articles that have been of use, either completely or partially, in the making of this book, as well as in the creation of its general concept. I also consider these sources as suitable for those wishing to pursue the study of the materials dealt with in my book. Newspaper articles, personal correspondence, and verbal communication reports are not listed here since their references in the book are specific and localized, and they are accompanied with detailed endnotes.

After-Gabriel, Ruth, ed. *Chagall: Dreams and Drama: Early Russian Works and Murals for the Jewish Theatre* [English/Hebrew]. Jerusalem: The Israel Museum, 1993.

Aleichem, Sholem. *Bluzhdayushchie zvezdy* (Wandering Stars). Moscow: Text, 1999.

————. *Oysgeveylte verk* (Works). Moscow: Emes, 1948.

Altshuler, Mordechai, ed. *The Jewish Theater in the Soviet Union* [Hebrew]. Jerusalem: The Hebrew University, 1996.

Avetisian, Tamara. *Nezabyvayemoye* (The Unforgettable). Kiev: Slovo, 1998.

Azarkh-Granovskaya, Alexandra. *Vospominania. Besedy s Duvakinym* (A. V. Azarkh-Granovskaya's Memoirs Recorded by V. D. Duvakin). Jerusalem–Moscow: Gesharim-Mosty kultury, 2001.

Bagritsky, Eduard. "Proiskhozhdenie" (Origin). In *Stikhi i poemy* (Verses and Poems), 119–21. Moscow: Khudozhestvennaya literatura, 1956.

Ben-Dov, Yoseph. *Kria beklafim* (Reading Cards). Jerusalem: Keter, 1999.

Borshchagovsky, Alexander. *Obviniaetsa krov* (Blood on Trial). Moscow: Progress, 1994.

Bradley, Andrew Cecil. "Shakespearean Tragedy." In *King Lear* by William Shakespeare, edited by Russell Fraser, 225–42. New York: St. Martin Press, 1920.

Cheah, Pheng, and Bob Robbins, eds. *Thinking and Feeling Beyond the Nation*. Ann Arbor: University of Michigan Press, 1988.

Deutsch, Alexander. *Maski yevreyskogo teatra* (Jewish Theater's Masks). Moscow: Iskusstvo, 1927.

Dobrushin, Yekhezkel. *Zuskin*. Moscow: Der Emes, 1939.

Ehrenburg, Ilya and Vasilii Grossman, eds. *Chornaya kniga* (The Black Book). Jerusalem: Tarbut Publishers, 1980. Translated by David Pattersen as *The Complete Black Book of Russian Jewry*. Broonswick, NJ: Transaction Publishers, 2002.

Goldblatt, Moyshe. "A vort vegn Zuskinen" (A Word about Zuskin). *Sovetish heimland*, no. 1 (January 1970): 120–27.

Gurshteyn, Alexander. "Iskusstvo Zuskina" (Zuskin's Art). *Teatr i dramaturgia*, no. 4 (April 1935): 30–42.

Halkin, Shmuel. "Bar Kokhba." In *Stikhi, ballady, dramy* (Verses, Ballads, Dramas), 20–62. Moscow: Sovetsky pisatel', 1958.

Hegel, Georg Wilhelm Friedrich. *Estetika* (Aesthetics). Moscow: Nauka, 1975.

Ilf, Ilya, and Yevgenii Petrov. *The Little Golden Calf*. Translated by Anne O. Fisher. Burlington: Russian Life Books, 2009.

Ivanov, Vladislav. *GOSET: politika i iskusstvo 1919–1928* (GOSET: Politics and Art 1919–1928). Moscow: GITIS, 2007.

Kandel, Felix. "Zakoldovanny teatr" (The Bewitched Theater). In *Vrata iskhoda nashego* (The Gates of our Exodus), 30–54. Tel-Aviv: Biblioteka Aliya, 1980.

Kerler, Joseph. "12 oygust 1952" (August 12, 1952). Jerusalem: Eygns, 1978.

Koliazin, Vladimir, ed. *Vernite mnie svobodu: Deyateli literatury i iskusstva Rossii i Germanii—zhertvy stalinskogo terrora* (Give Me Back My Freedom: Literature and Culture Figures, Russians and Germans—Victims of Stalin's Terror). Moscow: Medium, 1997.

Kostyrchenko, Gennadi. *Out of the Red Shadow: Anti-Semitism in Stalin's Russia*. Translation from Russian. Amherst: Prometheus Books, 1995.

Leonidov, Leonid. *Vospominania, statii, besedy, perepiska, zapisnyie knizhki* (Memoirs, Articles, Talks, Correspondence, Ledgers). Moscow: Iskusstvo, 1960.

Lev, Zalmen. "Fun Yarden biz Volga" (From Jordan to Volga). *Yiddish*, no. 8/9 (August/September 1928): 4–8.

Levashov, Victor. *Ubiystvo Mikhoelsa* (Murder of Mikhoels). Moscow: Olymp, 1990.

Lidin, Vladimir. "Zuskin" [Russian]. *Teatr*, no. 1 (January, 1960): 79–88.

Liubomirsky, Joshua. *Af di lebensvegn* (On the Ways of Life). Moscow: Sovetsky pisatel', 1976.

Mandelstam, Osip. "Mikhoels." In *Sobranie Sochinenii*, 2:106–10. New York: Inter-Language Literary Associates, 1971.

Markov, Pavel. *Teatral'nyie portrety* (Portraits of Theater Figures). Moscow: Iskusstvo, 1974.

Mayzel, Nakhmen, "Alexei Granovsky." *Literarische Bleter*, no. 19 (1937): 3–4.

Naumov, Vladimir, ed. *Nepravedny Sud: Posledny Stalinsky Rasstrel* (An Unjust Trial: Stalin's Last Execution). Moscow: Nauka, 1994.

Nels, Sofia. "Korol' Lir v postanovke GOSETa" (*King Lear* as staged in GOSET). *Teatr*, no. 5 (May 1935): 125–29.

Papazian, Vagram. "Korol' i shut" (The King and the Fool). In *Zhizn' artista* (The Life of an Actor), 405–19. Moscow–Leningrad: Iskusstvo, 1960.

Pimenov, Vladimir. "Dve sud'by" (Two destinies). *Teatr*, no. 6 (June 1990): 126–29.

Raz, Simha. *A Very Narrow Bridge: Sayings of Rabbi Nakhmen of Breslov* [Hebrew]. Jerusalem: Keter, 1999.

Redlikh, Shimon. *Yevreysky antifashistsky komitet v SSSR* (Jewish Anti-Fascist Committee in USSR). Moscow: Mezhdunarodnyie otnoshenia, 1996.

Rubenstein, Joshua, and Vladimir Naumov, eds. *Stalin's Secret Pogrom: The Postwar Inquisition of the Jewish Anti-Fascist Committee*. Translated by Laura Esther Wolfson. Introduction and Comments by Joshua Rubenstein. Preface by Vladimir Naumov. New Haven: Yale University Press, 2001.

Rubinchik, Israel. "Mayn rebe Binyomin Zuskin" (My Teacher Benjamin Zuskin). *Yerushalmer almanakh*, no. 20 (1990): 40–48.

Rudnitsky, Konstantin, ed. *Mikhoels: statii, besedy, rechi* (Mikhoels: Articles, Talks, Speeches). Moscow: Iskusstvo, 1965.

Solzhenitsyn, Alexander. *Arkhipelag GULAG*. Milano: Antibolshevic Block of Nations, 1973.

Strehler, Georgio. "Il Re Lear di Shakespeare" (King Lear by Shakespeare). In *Per un Teatro Umano* (Theater for a Human), 270–301. Verona: Feltrinelli, 1973.

Toller, Ernst, Joseph Roth, and Alfons Goldschmidt. *Das Moskauer Juedische Akademische Theater*. Berlin: Die Schmiede, 1928.

Veidlinger, Jeffrey. *The Moscow State Yiddish Theater: Jewish Culture on the Soviet Stage*. Bloomington: Indiana University Press, 2000.

Vishnievskaya, Inna. "Den'gi dla kul'tury?" (Money for Culture?). *Teatr*, no. 2 (February 1993): 11–15.

———. "Zvezdy nie padayut, zvezdy bluzhdayut" (Stars are not Falling, Starts are Wandering). *Kultura*, no. 2 (1966): 10–13.

Vovsi-Mikhoels, Natalia. *Moi otets Solomon Mikhoels* (My Father Solomon Mikhoels). Moscow: Vozvrashchenie, 1996.

Yutkevich, Sergei. "Istoria zagublennogo filma" (A Tale of a Ruined Film). In *Sobranie sochinienii* (Works), 2:173–84. Moscow: Iskusstvo, 1991.

Zuskin, Benjamin. "Chemu nauchilo menia kino" (What I learned from the cinema). Iskusstvo kino, no. 4 (April 1938): 42–45.

———. "Curriculum Vitae," typed manuscript. Moscow, 1946.

———. "Dvadtsat' let Moskovskogo yevreyskogo teatra." *Kul'tura i zhizn'*, no. 12 (December 1939): 2–3.

———. "Moi Sholem Aleichem" (My Sholem Aleichem). In Belenky, Moyshe, ed. *Sholem Aleichem—pisatel' i chelovek* (Sholem Aleichem as a Writer and a Man), 260–67. Moscow: Sovetsky pisatel', 1984.

Index

Italic page number denotes illustration.